Clip Studio Paint by Example

Understand how to use CSP in a faster and more productive way for concept art, illustrations, and comics

Ludovico Serra

BIRMINGHAM—MUMBAI

Clip Studio Paint by Example

Associate Group Product Manager: Pavan Ramchandani
Publishing Product Manager: Aaron Tanna
Senior Editor: Sofi Rogers
Content Development Editor: Rakhi Patel
Technical Editor: Shubham Sharma
Copy Editor: Safis Editing
Language Support Editor: Sofi Rogers
Project Coordinator: Manthan Patel
Proofreader: Safis Editing
Indexer: Vinayak Purushotham
Production Designer: Shankar Kalbhor

First published: June 2021

Production reference: 1280621

Published by Packt Publishing Ltd.
Livery Place
35 Livery Street
Birmingham
B3 2PB, UK.

ISBN 978-1-80020-272-6

www.packt.com

This book is dedicated to the community of Clip Studio Paint that helped me when I started learning about this software in 2013. Without them, this book would not exist.

- Ludovico Serra / Lennybunny

Contributors

About the author

Ludovico Serra, whose pen name is Lennybunny, has a bachelor's degree in painting and a master's degree in illustration from the Academy of Fine Arts of Rome. He has twice won the MVP award in Clip Studio Ask and is also a Clip Studio Paint Evangelist.

About the reviewer

Elizabeth Staley is a visual artist and blogger who loves horses, animation, comics, and true crime. She began her digital art journey using Adobe Photoshop, but in recent years, has started using Clip Studio Paint. She is the author of *Mastering Manga Studio 5*, *Manga Studio EX5 Cookbook*, and *Learn Clip Studio Paint*. When she isn't creating art, she can be found at the barn with her horse. She currently lives in Pennsylvania, USA, with her husband.

Table of Contents

3

Creating 3D Backgrounds in CSP

4

Using Your 3D Props to Create a Scene

5

Implementing 3D Characters in CSP

6

Importing 3D Characters in CSP

7

Making Your Own Illustration

8

Creating Your Own Comic

9
Building Your Own Concept Art

10
Creating Your Own Portfolio

11
CSP Vocabulary

Other Books You May Enjoy

Index

Preface

Clip Studio Paint (**CSP**) is powerful art software that can help you create artwork with its in-built material organizer, 3D integration, and group work features. It also provides other features that can speed up the workflow of illustrators, concept artists, and comic artists. *Clip Studio Paint by Example* covers tools and workflows relating to concept art, illustrations, and comics in detail. You'll learn everything from creating a brush and setting up a canvas to using the powerful tools and techniques you need to create a professional art portfolio.

Who this book is for

This Clip Studio Paint book goes beyond the technical stuff that helps beginner-level as well as intermediate artists who are new to working in a digital environment and need a more streamlined and seamless workflow relating to illustrations, concept art, and comics in Clip Studio Paint. No prior knowledge of Clip Studio Paint is required to get started with this book.

What this book covers

Chapter 1, Up and Running with CSP, provides a brief introduction to CSP with its pros and cons, analyzing the software in relation to others on the market and teaching you some common stuff, such as creating a brush, setting up a canvas, and creating an auto-action. Plus, you will find a small glossary of the functions relating to illustration, concept art, and comics that you can use to find a topic easily.

Chapter 2, Adding Brushes to CSP, talks about how to create brushes in CSP, how the brush engine works, and how to create a basic multipurpose brush and a seamless random texture brush.

Chapter 3, Creating 3D Backgrounds in CSP, talks about how to use 3D in CSP. With the addition of **Clip Studio Modeler** (**CSM**) bundled with the purchase of CSP, it is essential to talk about it, because with this you can import and rig characters easily (less easy is creating a character from scratch) and create reusable and editable scenes and props with just one click.

Chapter 4, Using Your 3D Props to Create a Scene, talks about how you can use previously created 3D props to create reusable changeable scenes.

Chapter 5, Implementing 3D Characters in CSP, explains how to create a 3D human character in Blender. This chapter will give you some basic skills on modeling, retopo, and UV mapping for creating 3D human models in Blender. Bear in mind that this isn't a guide to make a game-development-standard 3D model but a guide in which we will use those basic concepts to create 3D assets to use in CSP.

Chapter 6, Importing 3D Characters in CSP, explains how to import a character in CSM. This chapter will give you some basic knowledge on texturing human characters and rigging skills. Plus, you will get a pretty advanced understanding of how to use CSM to create posable characters to use in CSP.

Chapter 7, Making Your Own Illustration, teaches you about illustrations and how to set up your workspace and use the CSP tools to make cartoon and realistic illustrations with some tricks that will speed you up. Plus, we will look at creating brushes that you can use as workhorses to give you a realistic feeling.

Chapter 8, Creating Your Own Comic, shows how to set up your workspace, creating brushes fitted for the job and using the tools of CSP to go through the phases of creating a comic, from storyboarding, using the story editor and material folder, to the printing phase, using CSP and other software.

Chapter 9, Building Your Own Concept Art, shows how to integrate the 3D functions in CSP, materials, auto-actions, and everything at your disposal to speed up your concept art. We will see how to create props (from tile sets and weapons to a small house/cabin), an environment (a basic natural environment, a city environment, and a fantasy environment), and character concept art (sci-fi, fantasy, and normal).

Chapter 10, Creating Your Own Portfolio, presents a practical use of your skills. We will create together three portfolios for each of the sections (illustration, comics, and concept art). I will explain how you will need to construct them based on the subject and where to publish your artwork and portfolio.

Chapter 11, CSP Vocabulary, provides a glossary with a brief explanation of all the main CSP functions with a reference to the page on which it is talked about extensively in the book.

To get the most out of this book

You will need the most recent CSP version; as of the time of writing, this is the May 2021 update. To best experience this book, it's preferable that you use the EX version of CSP. The chapters related to Blender were done with Blender version 2.90.

Software/hardware covered in the book	OS requirements
Clip Studio Paint	Windows, macOS, Android, or iPadOS
Clip Studio Modeler	Windows or macOS
Blender	Windows, macOS, or Linux

This book doesn't require any prerequisite knowledge; it was made with beginners in mind. So, sit down, relax, and enjoy reading.

Download the color images

We also provide a PDF file that has color images of the screenshots/diagrams used in this book. You can download it here: `https://static.packt-cdn.com/downloads/9781800202726_ColorImages.pdf`.

Conventions used

There are a number of text conventions used throughout this book.

`Code in text`: Indicates code words in text, database table names, folder names, filenames, file extensions, pathnames, dummy URLs, user input, and Twitter handles. Here is an example: "Now we just need to create a layer folder called `storyboard` inside every frame folder."

Bold: Indicates a new term, an important word, or words that you see onscreen. For example, words in menus or dialog boxes appear in the text like this. Here is an example: "To activate it, you just need to open a page and go to **View | On-screen area (webtoon)**."

> **Tips or important notes**
> Appear like this.

Get in touch

Feedback from our readers is always welcome.

General feedback: If you have questions about any aspect of this book, mention the book title in the subject of your message and email us at customercare@packtpub.com.

Errata: Although we have taken every care to ensure the accuracy of our content, mistakes do happen. If you have found a mistake in this book, we would be grateful if you would report this to us. Please visit www.packtpub.com/support/errata, selecting your book, clicking on the Errata Submission Form link, and entering the details.

Piracy: If you come across any illegal copies of our works in any form on the Internet, we would be grateful if you would provide us with the location address or website name. Please contact us at copyright@packt.com with a link to the material.

If you are interested in becoming an author: If there is a topic that you have expertise in and you are interested in either writing or contributing to a book, please visit authors.packtpub.com.

Share Your Thoughts

Once you've read *Clip Studio Paint by Example*, we'd love to hear your thoughts! Scan the QR code below to go straight to the Amazon review page for this book and share your feedback.

https://packt.link/r/1800202725

Your review is important to us and the tech community and will help us make sure we're delivering excellent quality content.

1
Up and Running with CSP

Hi, I'm Ludovico Serra (otherwise known as Lennybunny), *Clip Studio Evangelist* and two-time winner of the *MVP award*. Please note that this will not be a classic manual in which I explain all the functions of **Clip Studio Paint** (**CSP**) or how to do all of the technical stuff, such as creating a canvas or creating a simple brush (we will create brushes, but it will be a little bit different than the classic "add a texture to this brush"). If you need information about the technical stuff, there are other books you should read, such as *Learn Clip Studio Paint Third Edition by Inko Ai Takita* (At the time of writing, this book wasn't published. It will be published in August 2021), and *Clip Studio Tips* by *Liz Staley*.

This book will be more of a workflow example, in which I will show you how to use CSP in a faster and more advanced way, even if you are a beginner with the software. Also, this book will be completely and utterly based on my own experience with digital software and my own artistic view, so feel free to adapt everything I tell you to your experience and needs. In addition, this first chapter is for an absolute beginner or someone who is coming from other software, just so that I know for sure that we are on the same page regarding basic knowledge. So, if you're not an absolute beginner, go to *Chapter 2, Adding Brushes to CSP*, where you will find the fun stuff!

I will cover the basic functions of CSP later in the *General CSP functions* section, but for now, I will concentrate on some fundamentals.

This chapter will cover the following topics:

- Comparative anatomy – an introduction to CSP

- Setting up your workspace and mapping your shortcuts

- General CSP functions

Comparative anatomy – an introduction to CSP

In my experience, with *Clip Studio Ask*, you can encounter a lot of early frustration if you are coming from other software and try to apply your previous habits to CSP. One of the first frustrations is opening the software and expecting everything to be ready from the get-go. CSP is not like this, for good reason, but let's compare CSP with two other programs: Photoshop (2020) and Krita (4.2.9). I will compare it with a vanilla opening, so it means I will not modify anything after a clean installation.

The Photoshop interface

Photoshop doesn't really require that much of an introduction; it started as photo-manipulation software and, thanks to its versatility, you can now use it for drawing. There are a ton of tutorials on how to use it. Let's see the vanilla interface:

Figure 1.1 – Adobe Photoshop interface

Looking at the vanilla interface, we can see something rather intriguing, which is that the windows are more oriented for photo editing. On the right side, we have a series of panels dedicated to colors, then under those, there is a panel dedicated to the canvas and adjustment, and under that, we have layers, channels, and paths. Let's say we have the intelligence of a goldfish and so we can't immediately find the various brushes or brush options in a dedicated window. If we go to the toolbar, these are the tools we will find:

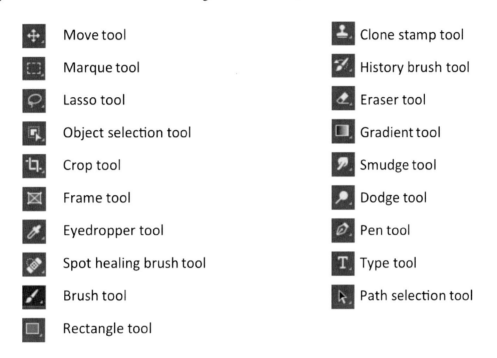

Figure 1.2 – Photoshop toolbar

This lets us know that this is undoubtedly a piece of software for photo editing, as we have six tools for selection and five tools not directly related to drawing (such as the clone stamp tool), and only six tools directly related to drawing.

If we right-click on the various tools, we can select other tools; let's call them **Sub Tools**.

Now let's focus on something more important—how the brushes are organized.

Brushes in Photoshop

Now let's assume that we have a greater degree of intelligence, we recognize the brush icon at the top (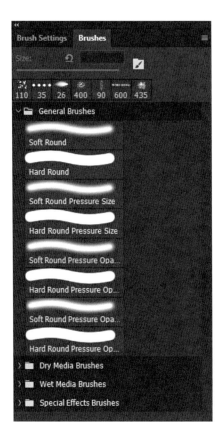), and we unlock the brushes. We will then see this:

Figure 1.3 – Brush window in Photoshop

We have brushes subdivided into folders, but here's something interesting—we have a list of the latest used brushes with the last size used.

Now let's talk about how the brushes work in relation to the environment:

- We can't add a shortcut to a single brush.

- We can't add a shortcut to a single brush folder.

- We can only add a shortcut that lets us go to the various tools in the toolbar. So, this means we can only add a shortcut to the **Brush tool** or **Mixer brush tool**.

- We can add a shortcut to scroll between the next and the previous brush.
- This brush list can't contain erasers or other tools.

If we needed to organize our brushes, we would need to put everything in **Brush tool**, and after that, we would need to organize the brushes using folders. Every time we need a brush, we need to scroll to find the folder we need to get our desired brush.

Now let's see how Krita presents its interface.

The Krita interface

We have something that at first seems pretty crowded, but in reality, it's pretty straightforward:

Figure 1.4 – Krita interface

On the right, we have color selection, tool options, and an overview/navigator section, and below that, we have layers and channels. Lastly, we have **Brush Presets** and **Brush presets History**. If we go and look at the toolbar, we will see those tools.

We have six groups of tools and six single tools:

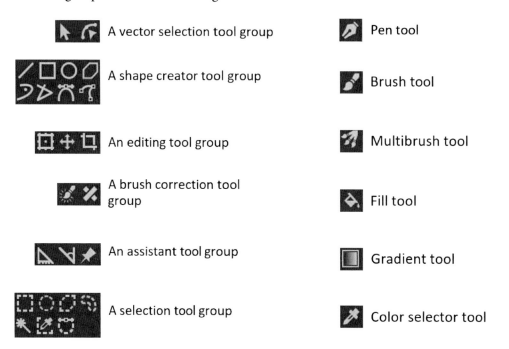

Figure 1.5 – Krita toolbar

We can see that out of 31 tools, only 2 tools are related to photo editing and all the rest are related to drawing with vectors (layers based on math functions) or rasters (layers based on pixel graphics). We can deduce that this software was always intended for illustration and drawing.

Now let's look at **Brush presets** and see how the brushes work in the Krita environment.

Brushes in Krita

The following screenshot shows the brush options within Krita:

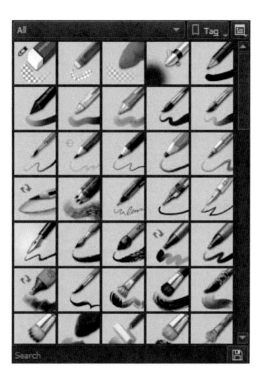

Figure 1.6 – Brushes in Krita

We can find a lot of interesting things:

- We can start by seeing that we don't have a distinction between brushes and erasers; we don't even have an eraser tool in the toolbar.

- Another point of interest is that the brushes are called brush presets, and you can toggle between these presets. So, you can create different presets based on what you need.

- We can add shortcuts to certain brush presets, giving us the ability to toggle between them.

- We can't add a shortcut to a single brush, at least not in the vanilla version.

- We can't put the shape tool or any selection tools in the brush presets.

Every time we need a brush, we will need to select a preset, via clicking or using a shortcut, and select the brush.

Now we have seen how two of the main pieces of software in this domain work in their native vanilla environments. We have seen how the workspace changes between photo editing software and pure illustration software. Now it's time for us to finally look at the environment of CSP and see how that works.

The CSP interface

When looking at CSP for the first time, it can seem a little bit intimidating, but there is a reason for this. Do you remember that Photoshop was created with a single target in mind? It is the same thing with Krita. In CSP, we have three target audiences—illustrators, comic artists, and animators. Consequently, CELSYS, the people who created CSP, don't know which one of those you are, so they give you all the windows that you would need for all of those jobs. Your first task is to remove everything you don't need:

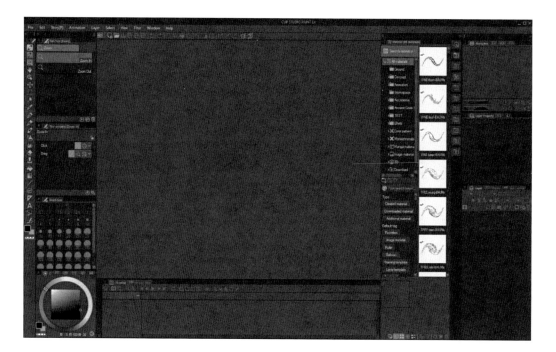

Figure 1.7 – CSP interface

Let's break down what options we have in the interface:

- **Left column**:

  a) **Sub Tool**

  b) **Tool property**

c) **Brush Size**

d) **Color Wheel, Color Slider, Color Set, Intermediate Color, Approximate Color, Color History**

- **Right column**:

- **Quick Access, Material palette**:

a) **Navigator, Sub View, Item Bank, Information**

b) **Layer Property, Search Layers, Animation Cels**

c) **Layer, History, Auto Action**

We have an astonishing number of windows—22 when you count the toolbar! We have triple the amount of information compared with what the other software we looked at offers, but we need to remember that this is a software that was designed to be used by three kinds of professionals. We will later learn how to be tidy and keep it all organized.

Now let's talk about the toolbar. In my view, the toolbar is the most misunderstood part of CSP.

This is because it works in a very different way to other toolbars in similar software:

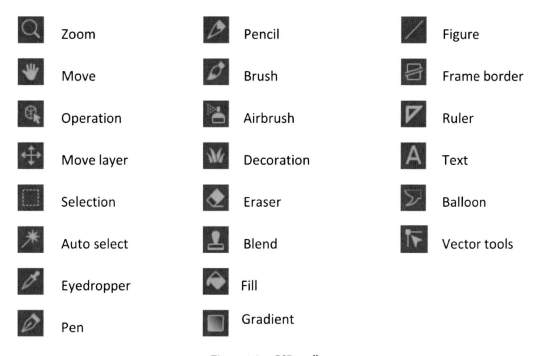

Zoom	Pencil	Figure
Move	Brush	Frame border
Operation	Airbrush	Ruler
Move layer	Decoration	Text
Selection	Eraser	Balloon
Auto select	Blend	Vector tools
Eyedropper	Fill	
Pen	Gradient	

Figure 1.8 – CSP toolbar

Right now, there isn't anything strange; it is more or less like what we have seen before.

We can see immediately that there aren't any advanced selection tools visible, and this means this isn't photo manipulation or correction software. I can tell you from experience that doing something such as *photobashing* (which we will cover in *Chapter 7, Making Your Own Illustration*) will land you in a world of pain and frustration.

> **Important Note**
>
> Doing concept art in CSP in a *photobashing* way is doable, but there are some caveats—and not just in terms of photo manipulation, as we will see.

In CSP, the **Tools** that you select in your **tool** palette are like big folders. This is what the **Tool** palette looks like:

Figure 1.9 – Tool palette

After you select a tool, you open a **Sub Tool** group that will show in the **Sub Tool** palette:

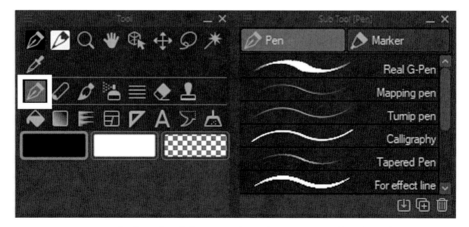

Figure 1.10 – Pen tool selected and the Pen Sub Tool group opened in the Sub Tool palette

Inside the **Sub Tool** group, you select a **Sub Tool**. This means that even if two tools are two different conceptual types, such as a **Text** tool and an **Object** tool, you can still group them together:

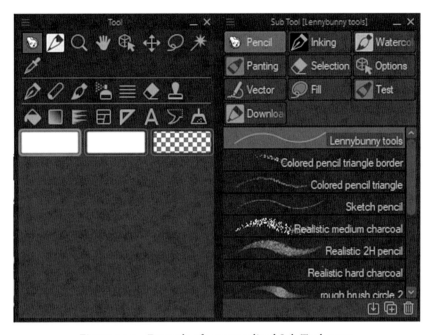

Figure 1.11 – Example of a personalized Sub Tool group

So, everything I usually need is in my personalized group, meaning, I don't need to change **Sub Tools** in the **Tool palette**. I have all I need at the tip of my fingertips, because as you will see in the next section, I can switch **Sub Tool** groups using a shortcut.

If you want to group something, just go to the **Sub Tool** window, click and drag the tool in the toolbar, and you will create a new **Sub Tool** group. Inside a group, you will find your tools.

CSP labels your tools in this way.

It means that when you select **Brush tool**, you don't change **Brush Tips**, like in Photoshop, but you completely change the tool.

Let's sum up the characteristics of tools in CSP:

- There is no major distinction between tools.

- You can add a shortcut for a precise **Sub Tool** group and that will let you return to the last group and **Sub Tool** you used.

- You can add a shortcut to one or multiple tools, giving you the ability to cycle between tools.

- All "brush" tools are interchangeable; you just need to change some options in **Brush settings**. I will explain which options are most useful in dedicated chapters later: you will find illustration brushes covered in *Chapter 6, Importing 3D Characters in CSP*, comic brushes in *Chapter 7, Making Your Own Illustration*, and concept art brushes in *Chapter 8, Creating Your Own Comic*.

As you can see, you can organize everything however you want, meaning you can create a single **Sub Tool** group with everything you need, and you can put the toolbar away and never let it see the light of day again.

It also means that you can *completely* discard everything you don't need, creating a laser-focused environment. Regarding this, there is some general advice that I can give you, and we'll explore this in the next section.

Setting up your workspace and mapping your shortcuts

My bachelor's degree was in painting, and I don't know why, but I often painted on a 2x1 m canvas. This gave me a muscle constriction in my shoulder nerves. Because of this, I learned the hard way that I needed to watch the ergonomics of my workspace. From the beginning of my digital career, I've used a tablet, a pen tablet, and a display tablet, and I've changed my workspace a lot. This will be the chapter in which I will share my thoughts with you on how to create a more enjoyable (and painless) environment.

Desk and chair

The first thing you need to consider is having a good chair, as you will probably sit in that chair for 2-3 hours at a time. You need to be comfortable, and having a bad chair can ruin you in the long run. If you have a chair that can't give you the right height, it will cause you a lot of problems with your back. Plus, a chair costs less than a desk usually, so it's the easier thing to buy, even if you're on a budget. Generally, you want something that lets you have your elbow at about 90° while you draw:

Figure 1.12 – On the left, we have a desk that is too low; this will give you neck pain. On the right, we have the opposite; this will give you elbow and neck pain

If your desk is too low, you can resolve this by stacking books to create the right height. Or, if you want something more refined, you could use some wood planks—screw them together and the job is done. For a desk that is too high, you just need a keyboard tray to put your pen tablet in. For the pen display user, you can use a *vesa mount* or a tablet holder.

Shortcuts

Shortcuts are important to cover, because we are not limited like we are in Photoshop, where *Ctrl + [key]* is the only option. We can use whatever key we want in whatever combination we want, with *Ctrl/Alt/Shift + [key]*. Just as an example, my **Undo** shortcut is *Ctrl + F12* and my **Redo** is *F12*. One exception is **Sub Tool**, for which you can only have a single-key shortcut without modifiers.

> **Tip**
> To add a shortcut, go to **File | Shortcuts settings**. You will have five options:
> **Main Menu**, **Pop-up palettes**, **Options**, **Tool**, **Auto Action**

We will explore shortcuts more in the upcoming sections, but before we do, we need to prioritize our shortcuts.

High priority:

- Switch main color and sub color
- Switch main color and transparent color

- Undo/redo

- Shortcut to your personal **Sub Tool** group

Low priority:

- Create new layer.

- Vector eraser: This eraser will work as a normal eraser in a non-vector layer, so it's better to have this shortcut than the normal eraser.

- A shortcut for your favorite selection tool.

- Increase/decrease brush size, for when you need to fine-tune the brush size.

Those are my recommended essential shortcuts. Now, if I listen carefully, I can hear you saying: "You know nothing! You haven't listed a zoom-in/zoom-out shortcut! What about the rotate tool? This book is garbage!" Hold your horses. There is a reason for this. A lot of those actions can be performed using modifiers in CSP.

Modifier shortcuts

The modifiers are *Ctrl*, *Shift*, *Alt*, and *Spacebar*, and they can be used in combination with each other. They let you temporarily select some tools:

- *Ctrl/Cmd* selects the **Object** tool.

- *Shift* creates a straight line. You create it by selecting the first point of the line, and after that, you select the end point of the line.

- *Alt/Opt* selects the **Color Picker** tool.

- *Spacebar* selects the **Hand** tool.

- *Ctrl/Cmd + Shift* enables the **Layer selection** tool.

- *Shift + Spacebar* rotates the canvas.

- *Ctrl/Cmd + Spacebar* is how you use the zoom-in/out tool. You need to click and scroll horizontally to make it work flawlessly.

    I really recommend that you train yourself to use the *Alt* modifier for the **Color Picker** tool rather than the button on your pen.

Now, if I listen carefully, I can hear the sound of silence saying that I am right.

Those are the shortcuts to use in order to have the bare-minimum workspace. If you want to add more shortcuts, feel free to do so, but the ones I recommended should be the first ones you map. Remember that the same key can give different results if you bind it with different modifiers.

Now let's talk about the various workspace scenarios in which you may find yourself.

> **Important Note**
> I will refer to all tech using generic terms, meaning that when I say "desktop computer," this means both PC and Mac, and so on.

Laptop + pen tablet

In this combo, you will have a device with an integrated keyboard, meaning that you will need to factor in the fact that all your shortcuts will be in front of the monitor:

Figure 1.13 – Laptop + pen tablet

I recommend, if possible, putting your tablet to the right or left of the laptop, because if you put everything in a straight line, you will be prone to hunching over and creating problems with your back.

Figure 1.14 – Example of hand position on the keyboard

My general advice is to keep your non-dominant hand on the keyboard, such that you can rest your thumb on the spacebar. In this way, you can press the modifiers with your thumb while easily reaching the other keys.

This is an example of how I do things on a QWERTY ITA keyboard:

Thumb	**Forefinger**	**Middle finger**	**Ring finger**	**Little finger**
Modifiers	R Undo	4 Increase brush size	3 Selection tool	Q
Spacebar	Cmd/Alt + R Redo	Cmd/Alt + 4 Decrease brush size	W	
X Switch to transparent color	T Subtool group	E Vector eraser		
C Switch to main/sub color	F Fill tool			

Figure 1.15 – Shortcut example for a right-handed user on a laptop keyboard

Q and W are purposely kept empty, and in the next chapter, we will explain why.

I would recommend going to the options of your pen in your graphic tablet settings and linking the button to **Pan/Zoom**. With this option, if you click the button without pressing the pen on the tablet, you can pan through the canvas, and if you press the pen on the tablet, you can zoom. In addition, if you press *Shift* while clicking the button on the pen, you can rotate the canvas.

Some pen tablets have shortcut buttons, and I recommend linking those buttons to shortcuts such as *Ctrl + T* (for **Transform**, say) for the shortcuts that require modifier + key. In this way, you can leave the tablet on the side and retain the ergonomics of your posture, because you don't need two hands to press those keys.

Two-in-one tablet

These are the worst to draw on if you think about the ergonomics, because usually you cannot comfortably access the keyboard and, unless you have something like the third option in the following figure, you don't even have a built-in stand to enable you to use the shortcuts:

Figure 1.16 – Example of a two-in-one tablet

In this case, I really recommend buying a tablet holder that lets you have the monitor however you want so you have a more comfortable drawing angle, and also a one-hand keyboard, possibly with programmable keys. Regarding one-hand keyboards, the official solution is the Clip Studio Tabmate, but a less official and much cheaper option is to buy a Bluetooth numpad and remap the keys using third-party software. I recommend searching for a tutorial online because it can be pretty convoluted if you're not tech-savvy.

Another trick is to use the **Quick Access** palette and put your most-used tools, options, or windows in there. For example, keep **Color Wheel** to the side of your non-dominant hand so you can click on the icons using your thumb. I recommend putting **Color Wheel**, **Tool Options**, and **Layer** in the **Quick Access** window. In this way, you can do all the operations you need with the thumb of your non-dominant hand:

Figure 1.17 – My Quick Access window; the window menu shortcuts are the lime green icons

In this way, every time I click this icon with my thumb, CSP will open the window I need under the pen.

Pen display + PC

This configuration is the best for good ergonomics, even when you use a pen tablet + PC:

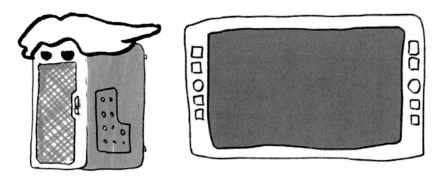

Figure 1.18 – PC and a pen display

My advice when using a pen display is to buy a *vesa mount* or tablet holder, based on the size of your display, so you can have the monitor where you find it most comfortable, giving you the option to work while standing and not hunching over.

Regarding shortcuts, I recommend this kind of setup:

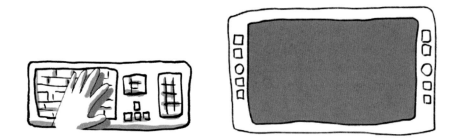

Figure 1.19 – Put your keyboard to the side of your non-dominant hand and have your hand in such a way that you can access Ctrl, Shift, and other modifiers

Find a position in which you can rest your hand comfortably on the keyboard and map the keys based on the laptop + pen tablet combo.

A good way to have a less-crowded shortcut environment is mapping one of the two buttons of your pen to **Pan/Zoom**, because it means you can easily rest your hand on the keyboard without having to move it away. If you don't do this, you will probably have to keep moving your hand away from the keyboard to the side buttons on your tablet. It is better to link the side buttons to something that doesn't require your dominant hand to move, such as the **New correction layer**.

If you have a *Wacom tablet,* I recommend that you link the second button to a radial menu and add options such as **Transform** and **On/Off ruler** to it, or whatever you find comfortable. This is a way to replace the missing lateral buttons on Wacom's new *Cintiq* line.

Here are the shortcuts I might use with my left hand on a Windows QWERTY ITA keyboard:

Thumb	Forefinger	Middle finger	Ring finger	Little finger
Modifiers	Backspace	F11	F10	The button under F9
	Hand tool	Redo	Increase brush size	Zoom tool
		Ctrl + F11	Ctrl + F11	0
		Undo	Decrease brush size	Vector eraser
		F12	F9	Ctrl + O
		Switch to main/sub color	Selection tool	New Layer
		Ctrl + F11		
		Switch to transparent color		

Figure 1.20 – Shortcut example for right-handed users for PC

Now we have set everything up, you are ready to create your next masterpiece, without sacrificing your back!

But wait, there's more! The next section contains some general advice regarding CSP that will help you create a more enjoyable workflow and workspace while drawing.

General CSP functions

In this section, we will learn how to have a clean interface and how to use **Quick Access** to have all the information you need. Plus, I will teach you how to use auto-actions to do away with the most tedious tasks, such as changing the color of your line. We will finish with learning how the **Color, Grayscale, and Monochrome** color modes in the layer properties can be used to your advantage and how to use the Material palette.

We haven't touched on one very important issue—creating a clean workspace.

A *workspace* refers to how windows are arranged, how you've set up your shortcuts, the unit of measurement used, and your command bar settings:

> **Tip**
> To change from dark mode to light mode, just go to **File | Preferences | Interface**.

Figure 1.21 – The command bar is practically a fixed quick access area
that is at the top of the workspace

Before modifying anything, it's best to save the workspace:

Figure 1.22 – Menu bar

Go to **Window | Workspace | Register Workspace**. Let's be a little bit narcissistic and name it after ourselves. In my case, I'll name it *Lennybunny workspace*. Now let's do some cleaning:

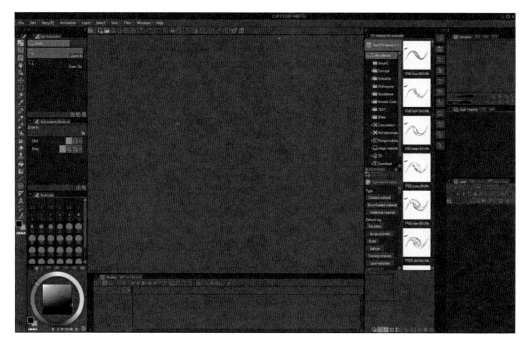

Figure 1.23 – CSP's basic interface

This is the basic interface. To remove something, you have two options—either clicking and dragging the window and pressing the **X** in the top right of the window, or going to **Window** and selecting/deselecting what you don't need. If you remove something in error, you need to come here to undo your mistake:

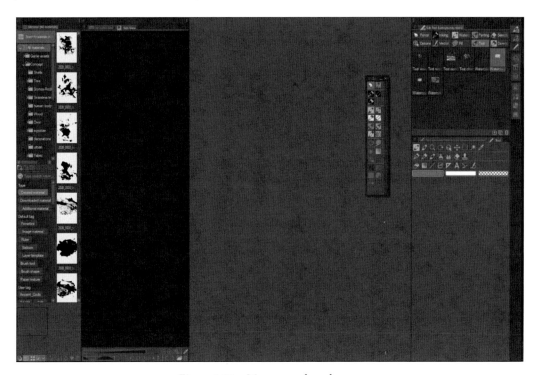

Figure 1.24 – My personal workspace

This is my personal workspace, and I will use it to explain a little bit of how CSP handles things. I've got the Material palette on the left for the quick click and drag of textures… or 3D materials… or whatever else. On the right, I've got all the options I need to work nested together. I don't need to have all the information at my disposal; I only need the information I need to change in a given moment. When I draw, I collapse everything and I just concentrate on the work I'm doing. If I need something, I click on the little icon and this will open my menu, or I use a shortcut to call that menu under my pen. In this way, I have a very clean interface.

The first most important thing to remember is that CSP lets you nest your windows:

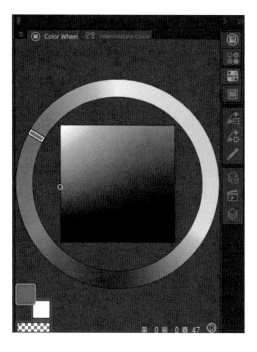

Figure 1.25 – Nested windows in CSP

The first way to collapse windows is by using the two arrows, ▬◢. If you press the single arrow, you will collapse the window into a small icon (the one on the right in the preceding figure), but if you press the double arrow, you collapse the entire window. To get it back, just click again on the double arrow. The first type of nesting is group window nesting. Note that there is a gray line between some of the icons—that gray line means that those are different window groups. The second type of nesting is between windows. In the example, **Intermediate Color** (the one with the grayed-out icon) is nested inside **Color Wheel**. If I click on the grayed-out icon, I will switch to that window.

A third way to organize windows is to display them as popups. This means that windows will open individually. This can be useful if you have a small monitor, such as with a 13" two-in-one tablet, and you can't have much information within a single space.

You can use this window nesting to organize your information into a less-crowded interface, because you can put all the information on one side and select only the information you need to change. For example, when I do an illustration and I want to concentrate on painting, I don't need to know which layer I am in all the time. I can't change layer unless I use the **Select layer** tool anyway. Instead, I just need **Color Wheel** and **Color Set** open as I am only using those two windows.

> **Tip**
>
> Another great trick to organize your workspace is linking your window to shortcuts. To do so, go to **File | Shortcut settings | Category: Pop-up Palettes**. In this way, every time you click on a shortcut, it will bring your pen over to the window. For example, I have the *9* key as a shortcut for **Sub Tool** group and *Ctrl + 9* for **Tool property**, so every time I need to change tool or change one of the options, I don't need to change the window I'm seeing and using.

Quick Access

If we look on the left, we have the **Quick Access** window, and this is one of the most underused windows for new users. It is useful because it is a fast way to get your most-used tools and options without creating shortcuts for everything.

To modify the **Quick Access** window, you need to press this icon:

Figure 1.26 – Icon for modifying the Quick Access window

In the top left of the window, you can click on **Quick Access**.

This is especially useful for tablet users, because you can add the windows you need as pop-up windows. For example, if you need **Color set**, just click on the icon in **Quick Access** and it will appear under your pen. Then, you select what you need, and after clicking somewhere else, it will disappear.

But having your favorite tools in one clickable place is not the best feature of the **Quick Access** window. In the **Quick Access** window, you can add layer options, create new correction layers, add filters, change file options or current drawing colors, and do basically anything else you can think of.

A neat little trick is that you can even add **Tool** in the toolbar. When you select the icon, it will go to the last used **Sub Tool** in that tool group. This can be used to switch between different types of brushes without crowding a tool group too much.

For example, I have these in the top section of my **Quick Access** window:

Figure 1.27 – Icons in my Quick Access window

These two icons let me toggle between my main brushes and my decoration brushes.

On the left, I have all my drawing/painting **Sub Tools**, and on the right, I have my decorations tool group, subdivided into various **Sub Tool** groups based on the decorations. Using this in tandem with my shortcut for the **Sub Tool** group, I can keep everything organized and within reach.

Auto Action

One last thing that we can add to **Quick Access** is **Auto Action**:

Figure 1.28 – Auto Action window

This is a recording of actions that will be done automatically once you click that little play button to the right of the bright red button. The difference between this bright red button and the bright red button often used as an apocalypse device in a spy movie is that when we press this button, it will start to record our actions.

For example, the selected auto action changes the color of my lineart (or whatever there is in the layer) using my selected color.

To recreate this auto action, you need to click on the button to the right of the play button, and this will create a new auto action. Name it *Change color*. After this, click on the big bright red button to make the sequence:

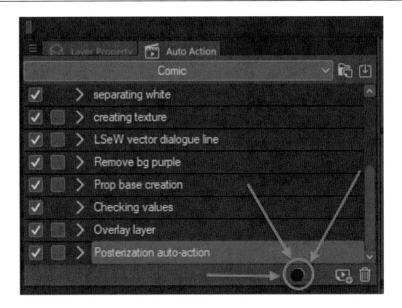

Figure 1.29 – This big bright red button

If you want to change only the color without changing the values of what you have, do this:

1. Go to **Layer | New Layer | New Raster Layer**, or you can just press ⬚ in the layer window.

2. Go to **Layer | Layer settings | Clip to layer below**, or you can just press ⬚ in the layer window.

3. Change **Blending mode** (which will look like this: ⬚ Normal ⬚) for the layer from **Normal** to **Color**.

4. Go to **Edit | Fill**.

5. Go to **Layer | Merge with layer below**.

If you want to change everything from color to values, do this:

1. Go to **Layer | Layer settings | Lock transparent pixel**, or click ⬚ in the layer window.

2. Go to **Edit | Fill**.

> **Important Note**
>
> We have seen the **Lock pixel** and **Clip to layer below** options, but what do they do exactly?
>
> **Lock pixel** literally locks the pixel, meaning that you can't draw outside of what you've already drawn; however, you can still erase.
>
> **Clip to layer below** means that you can only draw where there is something in the layer below.

Black and white pixels

We have talked about **Layer Property**, but there are three other really useful things to look at:

Figure 1.30 – Window with the layer properties

The first thing we need to notice is **Expression color**, where we can choose between **Color**, **Gray**, and **Monochrome**.

The color mode is easy to understand: it's the standard mode that will show you the image in colors. **Gray** and **Monochrome** transform an image into a grayscale or bitmap image, respectively:

Color mode   Gray mode   Monochrome mode

Figure 1.31 – Color modes

This means that if you need to see your image in grayscale or you need to create a bitmap image, you can do so with just one click and in a non-destructive way, because unless you click on **Apply expression color of preview**, you can always revert your changes.

The second thing to note (and I don't know who thought of it but I want to marry him/her) is an absolute lifesaver:

Figure 1.32 – Expression color interface in Gray mode

If we look to the right of **Gray** in the preceding figure, we can see a black box and a white box. If we click on the black box, only the black pixels will be visible:

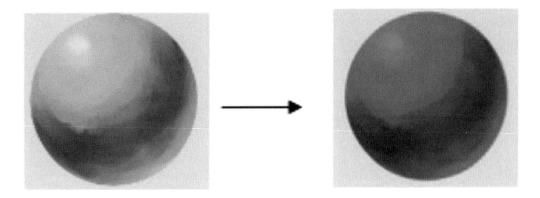

Figure 1.33 – Gray mode with only black pixels selected

We have put the orange base used for the sphere, under the **Gray** expression color. As you can see, we now have the darkest values applied to the sphere underneath the grayscale in a non-destructive way.

But what if we want a colored shadow and not that muddy brown? If we change the color as we did before, we can apply the grayscale and permanently change the expression color.

Now we arrive at the third useful feature inside **Layer Property**—the **Layer color** effect:

Figure 1.34 – Layer effect panel

If we click on the button highlighted with a red square, CSP will convert all black and white pixels to two colors of our choice:

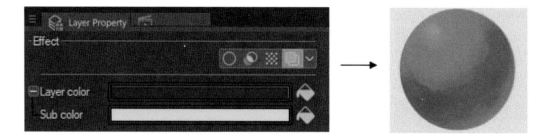

Figure 1.35 – The result of using the Layer color effect

Layer color controls the black pixels and **Sub color** controls the white pixels. This gives us complete freedom as to our basic values because it means that we can change the color of our values whenever we want.

Trying it yourself

Organizing the values:

Try to create an auto-action in which you convert your subject to grayscale and divide your dark values from your white values, all while maintaining your original subject.

Material palette – adding a material versus drawing an object

Now that we have talked about the layer properties, we need to talk about how to transform CSP from simple drawing software to a little war machine that will become better and better the more you use it. The **Material** palette is a way to store images/folders/textures/brush tips/whatever else you want inside CSP:

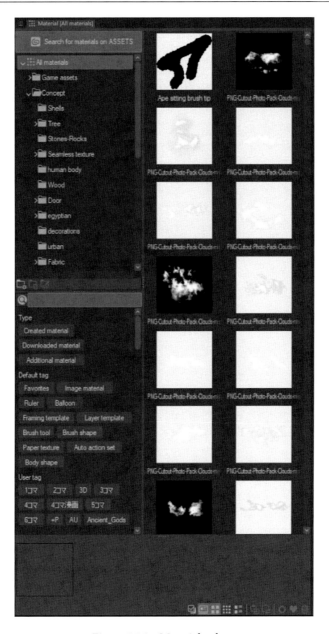

Figure 1.36 – Material palette

This is integrated offline, which means that you can access it even if you don't have internet, and it is a good way to organize textures, brush tips, and entire folders with subfolders and tags.

To add something to the **Material** palette, go to **Edit**. In the options in the following screenshot, there is **Register Material**; click on that and select **Image**:

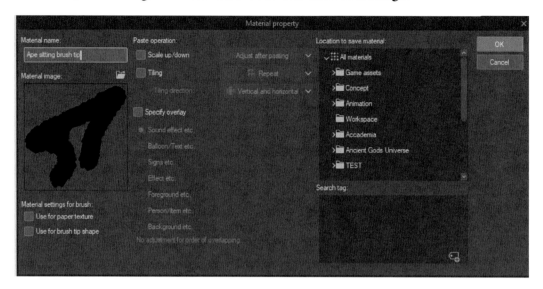

Figure 1.37 – The Material property window—every time you register a material, this will appear

You decide which folder you want to save to, add some tags, press **OK**, and you have your custom material.

Here is an example of why this is the best feature you will encounter using this software. Say I've bought some cut-out PNGs of some clouds, trees, and environments. I can add them to my material folder so that every time I need those PNGs, I don't need to import them in a folder into my PC; I just open the **Material property** window, click and drag, and I have the image pasted on my layer.

And if this isn't enough, CELSYS gives you 10 GB of free online backup storage, meaning that you can back up your materials online and download them on any PC you want. Therefore, even if your PC dies, you will not lose anything, and if you change your PC, you can download everything.

If you need to do an online backup of your materials, follow these steps. To use this feature, you need to open CSP and click on the blue cloud icon:

Figure 1.38 – Blue cloud icon in CSP

After this, you just need to click on **Cloud Settings** and select the option you prefer.

If you need to back up your work, you just need to click on **Manage works**, on the left:

Figure 1.39 – The Manage works icon

Now you just need to press this little button for every piece of work you want to back up:

Figure 1.40 – The Manage works cloud icon

The problem with materials is that you need time to make them, and sometimes you can spend more time on making a material than on creating a piece.

My advice to evade the problem is simple:

"Don't put anything in your materials that needs to be in perspective."

For example, it is useless to draw a chair and put it in my materials, because what if I need a different perspective? Or the chair I saved is not good enough for my illustration? I would spend more time creating a chair for every occasion than I would by just drawing one every time.

However, what about the decoration used on a chair? In that case, it is useful to save materials, because you would use a decoration even if it wasn't for a chair, and this will save you time in the long run.

But there is a little bit of an exception to this rule, and that is 3D objects. CSP lets you open 3D objects, save them in your materials, and reuse them whenever you want. We will see how to create them in *Chapter 3, Creating 3D Backgrounds in CSP*.

Your **Material** palette is also where everything you download from Clip Studio Assets will be kept, under **Material [Download]**. Thanks to the new update, you can directly download your brushes from this service using a convenient button in your **Sub Tool** group palette. We will take a look at this in the next section.

Adding a brush from Clip Studio Assets

Thanks to the May 2021 update, you can now directly add things from Clip Studio Assets, a free service from which you can download brushes, textures, materials, and more.

To do so, you just need to go to your **Sub Tool** group palette and go to the bottom. You will find a button called **Add sub tool**:

Figure 1.41 – Add sub tool button location

This will prompt you to a window using which you can add your most recently downloaded brushes:

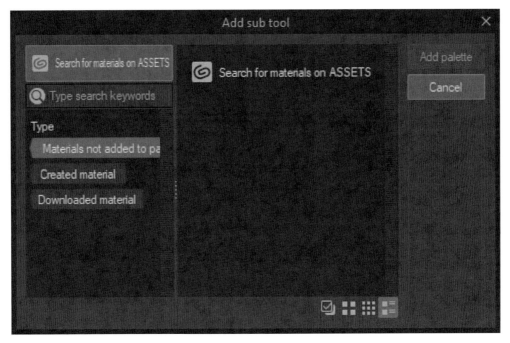

Figure 1.42 – The Add sub tool window

Here, under the **Type** section, you have three options:

- **Material not added to palette**: Here you will find every brush that you downloaded and never added to your **Sub Tool** palette.

- **Created material**: In here, you can find every brush that you have created and saved in your materials. Just click on a brush and click on **Register sub tool as material**.

- **Downloaded material**: In here, you can find all the brushes that you had at some point in your life, added to your **Sub tool** palette.

Let's say for the sake of this book that it's your first time opening CSP and you've never downloaded a brush. To start downloading something, follow these steps:

1. Click on the big button in the top-left corner named **Search for materials on ASSETS**. This will open Clip Studio Assets.

2. Now, just click on a brush that you like.

3. In the top-right corner, you can find a bright red button named **Download**. Click on that and your brush will be downloaded.

    This will add, without needing to close and reopen the **Add sub tool** window, the downloaded brush under the **Material not added to palette** type:

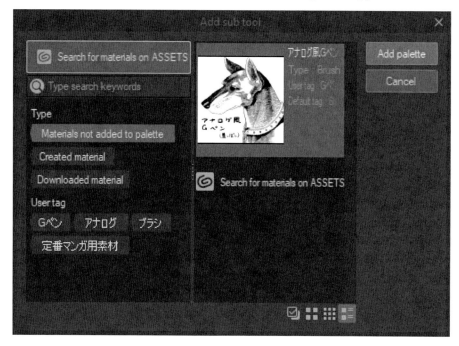

Figure 1.43 – The Add sub tool window with the newly downloaded brush

4. Now just click on **Add palette**, and you will have your new brush in your selected **Sub Tool** palette:

Figure 1.44 – My selected Sub Tool group with the new brush

In this way, you can easily add new brushes that you like—just don't start downloading a ton of brushes in one session… Not talking from personal experience, of course…

Summary

With this brief introduction, you've learned how CSP is different from other software, how it works on a basic level, and how to set up a more enjoyable environment in terms of your physical and digital workspaces.

In the next chapter, we will talk about how to create brushes.

2
Adding Brushes to CSP

In this chapter, you will learn how to create a brush and gain a basic understanding of how to create a brush in CSP, for decoration and general work. This is so that you can focus more on the fun stuff, such as drawing, thinking about composition or the color palette of your piece… or whatever part of the process it is that you like doing.

And as a bonus, as your benevolent/evil lord/teacher, I will give you a little homework for creating and understanding the options of a workhorse brush.

It's always a little bit daunting starting with new software, because you will find a lot of new, strange brushes that you're unfamiliar with. A workhorse brush is just a good, reliable brush that you can use for everything while you learn the basics of the software or drawing in general.

This chapter will cover the following topics:

- Creating a brush
- Decoration and texture brushes
- Workhorse brush

Creating a brush

Ironically, before talking about brushes, I need to talk about grayscale and give you some basic knowledge about it. This is because when you create a brush tip, you need to do it in grayscale mode. CSP can use images as brush tips, so, for example, if you need to create a forest and you have some tree png cutouts, you can add them to a brush and it will copy stamp those exact trees. But, if those trees were registered as a brush tip in grayscale mode, everything on the black-pixels side will be converted to **Main color** and every white pixel will be converted to **Sub color**. This can give you a lot of freedom in creating brushes with textures and color variation. The first thing you need to do is go to the **Sub Tool** group. Before following the steps, I recommend that you create a folder inside your Materials folder called Brush Tips. To do this, just right-click on the **Materials** folder and click on **New folder**. In this way, you will have all your brush tips cleanly organized. If you deem it necessary, you can even create subfolders based on the brush tips, such as Watercolor or Painting:

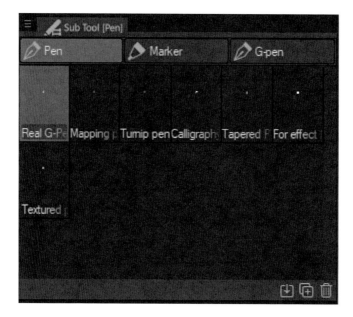

Figure 2.1 – The pen Sub Tool group

To create a new brush, follow these steps:

1. Go to the **Sub Tool** window and click on the following button and it will create a copy of the brush you selected. Rename it, and there you have your new brush:

Figure 2.2 – Create a copy of currently selected Sub Tool icon

2. Before changing our brush tip, we need to create one. The process is pretty straightforward. Create a new layer set by going to **Expression color | Gray** and drawing whatever you want.

3. Go to **Edit | Register Material | Image**.

    If you remember from the previous chapter, this will open this window:

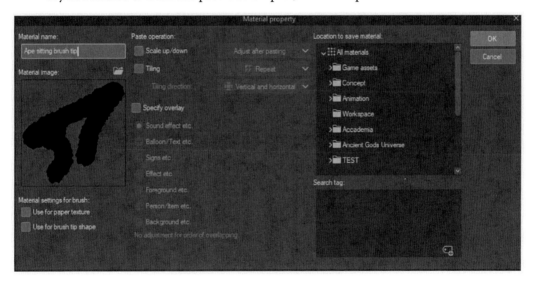

Figure 2.3 – Material property window

4. Give a name to your material, check the **Use for brush tip shape** box, select a folder **location** to save your material, and there you have it—your personal brush tip.

    Now… how can you apply your brush tip?

5. Go to the **Tool property** window and click on that little wrench in the bottom-right corner. This will give you access to all the brush options; go to **Brush tip**:

Figure 2.4 – The Tool property window

6. Click on **Material** (if it isn't already selected), and after this, double-click on the area in which there is written **Click here and add tip shape**. Now you just need to select your brush tip. And voilà… you just applied your first brush tip!

Figure 2.5 – The brush tip shape lets you use two things: a circle or custom brush tip

7. Now I have **Ape sitting brush**—I hope that you didn't follow me exactly and made something less silly…

Figure 2.6 – The result of using a custom brush tip

Before moving further, there is just one extra little bit of information. In CSP, you can now change how your brush cursor looks by just going to **File | Preferences | Cursor**:

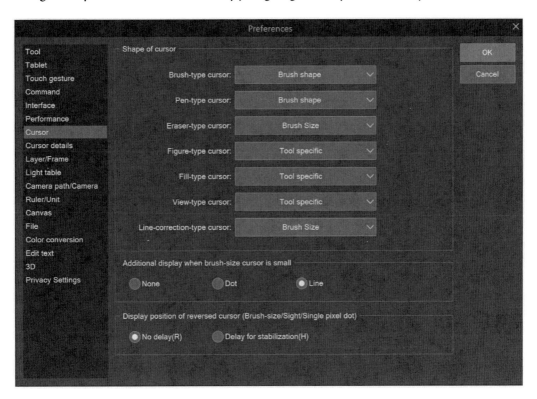

Figure 2.7 – Cursor shape options location

You have a pretty wide range of options for how your cursor will look while you work. Here's a list with some details:

- **Tool specific**: Your cursor will have the tool-like little symbol that you find in the **Tool** palette and the **Sub Tool** palette. An eraser will show a little eraser cursor—simple, no?

- **None**: You will have nothing, an invisible cursor. It's a strange feeling, to be honest. But if you can get used to it, it's the best option if you want to feel like you're painting in real life.

- **Cross**: You will have a little cross.

- **Triangle**: You will have a little triangle.

- **Dot**: You will have a little dot.

- **Single pixel dot**: You will have a very little dot, like, 1 px little.

- **Sight**: You will have a cross with a dot in the middle

- **Brush size**: This is the default mode for brush-related tools. You see your brush size as a circle that tells you the size of your brush.

- **Brush shape**: This is a new feature from the May 2021 update. You can have your cursor show your brush tips silhouettes, like in Photoshop. You can find your brush silhouette in the **Sub Tool Detail** palette, under the **Brush Size** section:

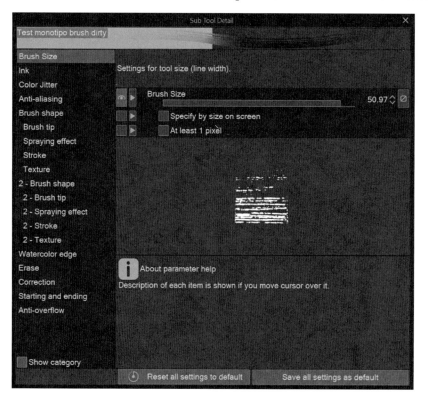

Figure 2.8 – Example of a brush silhouette and how it's seen on the canvas (right)

The other options are a combination of the groups I've just listed.

> **Little tips**
>
> If you feel like you're always cycling between the same brushes, thanks to the **Brush shape** cursor option, you can even remove the **Sub Tool** palette from your workspace. Just put every brush you need in a single group, bind a key to the shortcut for cycling between sub tools, and you can use the brush shape to recognize the brush you're using. You can find the shortcut under **File | Shortcut Settings | Category: Options | Sub Tool** palette.

And that is how you make a brush and change the look of your cursor. By using the same method that I showed you for creating a brush, you can create a decoration brush as well, as you will see in the next section.

Decoration and texture brushes

When I said "Your **first** brush tip" before, I was being serious, because you can apply more than one brush tip. The advantage of this is that you can create, as we will see in the dedicated chapter, a painting brush that doesn't rely on a texture, but only on the mark that makes on your canvas—just like a real brush. As a training ground, I will show how you can use this feature to create decoration and texture brushes that are randomized, giving you a different effect every time you draw.

Let's start with the basics, and ironically, we will start with tool options instead of brush tips. The following figure shows some flower decoration brush tips:

Figure 2.9 – Some book decorations

We will use these flower decoration brush tips as a base. Now, if we add them to the **Brush tip** tool option, this is what we will see in the brush preview:

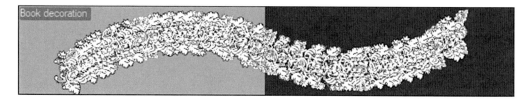

Figure 2.10 – This line is a preview of what you will see when you will use the brush

That's absolutely not what we want. To create a distinguishable pattern, we need to go to **Sub Tool Detail | Stroke**, and we need to check the **Ribbon** option. This option will give us this effect:

Figure 2.11 – An example of the ribbon effect

The **Ribbon** option creates a seamless pattern using your brush tips. Now we have another problem… these brush tips will repeat themselves in the same combination over and over:

Figure 2.12 – As you can see, there is a clear repetition; if you want this effect, you're good to go

Fortunately, we can change this easily—just return to **Stroke** and go to **Repeat method**:

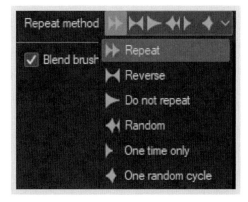

Figure 2.13 – The repeat methods you can choose from

We can change how these tips will repeat themselves. We will click on **Random**. This will mix your brush tips in a random pattern every time you draw.

> **Tip**
> If the brush tips are at the wrong angle, just go to **Brush tip | Angle** and change it there.

Now if we need a brush that has its size linked to the pen pressure, we just need to go to **Brush size** and click on this little button:

Figure 2.14 – Pen dynamic settings menu

This will open a menu in which we can link the brush size to the pen pressure, tilt of the pen, and velocity, or we can make it random.

> **Tip**
> Every time you see the pen dynamic settings button, it means that it is possible to link a value to a pen modifier. So, every time you see it, click on it and experiment with the possibilities.

To create a brush, all the options you need are here, in the **Sub Tool Detail** palette:

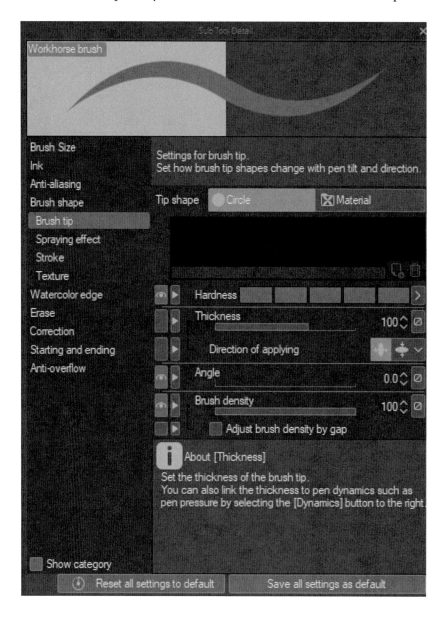

Figure 2.15 – Sub Tool Detail window

You will be surprised at how much you can do by only adding multiple brush tips and setting **Repeat method** to **Random**. I've created a lot of different brushes with only these two options.

But let's say we need to create a more complicated brush, such as a wood texture brush. For this wood texture brush, we need to create a seamless wood texture that randomizes itself every time. No problem, it is pretty straightforward and simple:

1. Let's start by creating a simple 10x10 cm canvas; just go to **File | New**. Remember to change **Basic expression color** to **Gray**.

    In this way, every time you create a new layer it will be in **Gray** mode. Now, just take a reference for creating some wood bark:

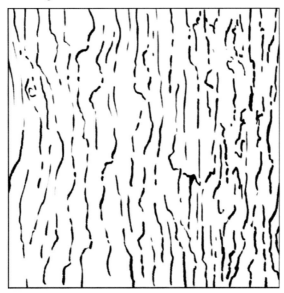

Figure 2.16 – The basic texture we have created

    This is mine. We don't shade it because it would be more problematic to create a seamless pattern. And usually, you need those texture/decoration brushes to have a good base to work on, rather than focusing on the end product. Now we need to tile it.

2. Right-click on the layer, and click on **Convert layer | Type | Image material layer**.

    Now, if we go to **Layer Property**, we will find this:

Figure 2.17 – Object tool option menu

Click on the small cube, then go to **Tool property** and click on **Tiling**. This will repeat the pattern in all directions. Now, without changing tool, click on the pattern and move it around:

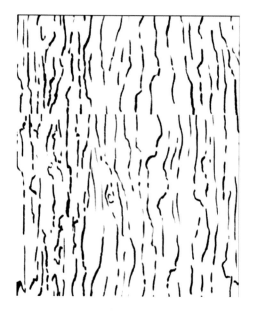 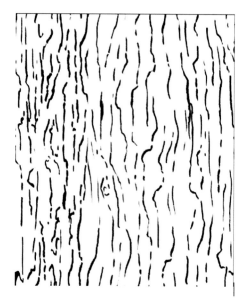

Figure 2.18 – On the left, we have the original image; on the right, the modified one

That's what happens when I move it—it's not seamless, and we can clearly see the cut of the repetition. But there is a pretty easy fix—just draw over it.

3. Create a new layer and start drawing where we can see the cut. When you have finished, merge it with the layer below. The result of this fix can be seen in the right-hand example of the previous figure.

    Now you just need to re-convert the layer and tile it again.

4. After this, move it a little bit or scale it to see whether everything is OK. If everything is OK (usually it is), undo all your movement by pressing *Ctrl + Z*.

5. After that, right-click on the layer window and click on **Merge visible layers**; check that **Expression color** in the **Layer Option** palette is still **Gray**, because sometimes when you merge the layers it will change to **Color**.

6. Now, register the material as a brush tip and you have your first texture brush tip. Yep, I said **first** again. You will need to redo this at least 4-5 times…

> **Tip**
>
> The preceding method can be used to create a seamless texture based on a photo. But for that, you will need to use the **Copy Stamp** tool to mask the cut in the texture.
> The **Copy Stamp** tool looks something like this:

Figure 2.19 – The Copy Stamp tool

Once you've made 4-5 texture brush tips, you'll need to apply them somewhere, no? But wait—we will not use a brush this time, but the **Straight line** tool. Why? You will see soon:

Figure 2.20 – The Sub Tool group for the figure drawing

If we go to **Sub Tool Details** for **Straight line**, we can see something familiar… Yes—we have the **Brush tip** setting; now redo the same thing you've done for the decoration brush. Now that you've done that, use it and create a straight line.

> **Tip**
>
> If you need a straight line when using a ruler or **Direct draw** tools, just press *Shift*.

Now, what will happen if we convert this line and tiling as we did before?

Instant random seamless wood texture…

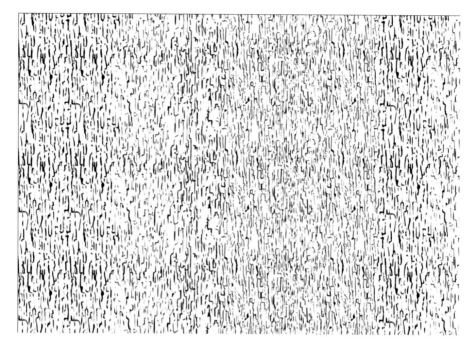

Figure 2.21 – Full-fledged random seamless texture

You can use this method to create practically anything that will require a seamless texture where you don't want obvious repetition in your texture. Examples of this could be seafoam, rocks, plaster, and so on.

> **Tip**
>
> Now, before continuing, I need you to think about this. A tool that is not directly a brush tool has brush tips, strokes, and spraying effect settings. So…
>
> Every tool that draws a line, such as the **Balloon** tool or the **Stream line** tool, has **Brush tip** settings. Basically, you can personalize every tool that draws something.

A little exercise for you. Take the **G-Pen** tool properties, go to **Ink**, and look at **Blending mode**; now do the same with **Hard eraser**. Do you see anything strange?

Blending mode in **Hard eraser** is set to **Cancel** but for **G-Pen** it's set to **Normal**. This means that every brush tool is an eraser, just with a different blending mode. In Photoshop, the eraser and the brush tool are two different tools, but in CSP they are the same, only with different settings.

Another way to erase is using the transparent color; it is the little bar under **Main color** and **Sub color**:

Figure 2.22 – Transparent color in the color wheel

The transparent color lets you transform every brush into an eraser in a quick way. You can select it in three ways:

1. Selecting the icon in the color wheel.

2. Color picking anywhere outside your canvas.

3. Using a shortcut. You can bind a shortcut to the transparent color by going to **File | Shortcut Settings | Options | Drawing Color**.

In my opinion, I prefer to use the transparent color rather than an eraser. I find it a lot faster than switching tools and it gives a more organic feeling.

As you can see in the next section, if you master only a few brushes, you can have a brush for every occasion without even changing tool.

Workhorse brush

When you're just starting to work with CSP, you can sometimes be overwhelmed by the number of brushes. My advice is to create a workhorse brush and use that until you feel more confident in your basic skills.

Showing and hiding options

Now, we've had a taste of the options in the brush engine of CSP, but wait—there is a lot more we can do. One of those things is showing and hiding options in the **Tool property** palette:

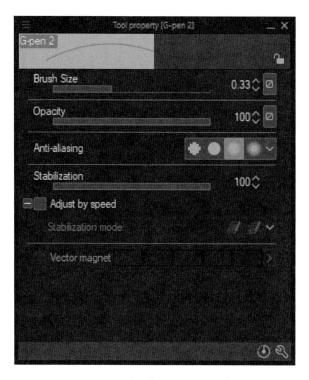

Figure 2.23 – Tool property window

For example, I don't want **Vector magnet**, because I don't usually use it. What do we need to do to hide it?

Click on that little wrench and go to **Sub Tool Detail**. Click on **Correction**, and now we can see a little eye icon over **Vector magnet**. We just need to click on that, and this will hide the **Vector magnet** option in the **Tool property** window:

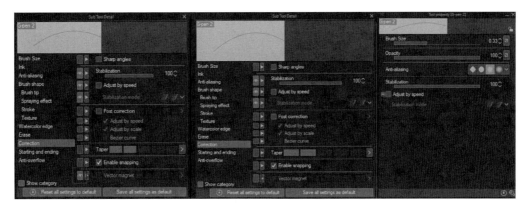

Figure 2.24 – We just hid Vector magnet from the Tool property window

This gives you a lot of flexibility regarding what you can change in a brush, without having to click on that little wrench icon every time.

Try it yourself

Now, as a little assignment, copy a basic circle-shaped brush, such as **Milli pen**. Navigate to **Sub Tool Detail** and try to show these options in the **Tool property** window of a new brush:

- **Brush Size** lets you choose the size of the brush.

- **Opacity** lets you chose the max alpha value of the color you can use while not removing the pen from the tablet.

- **Blending mode** lets you choose how the color reacts when you draw. For example, a **Multiply** blending mode will let you shift the color to black.

- **Color mixing** will activate the mixing of the color while you paint; these three options will control how it will mix:

  a) **Amount of paint**

  b) **Density of paint**

  c) **Color stretch**

- **Anti-aliasing** lets you have a harder or softer edge to your brush.

- **Brush shape** lets you choose the shape of the brush.

- **Angle** lets you decide the angle of the brush tip.

- **Brush density** is similar to **Opacity,** but with the difference that it lets you decide the degree of color buildup while you paint without removing the pen from the tablet. If you want a painterly effect, go for this option and not **Opacity**.

- **Stabilization** is an in-built stabilization that lets you decide how much you want to smooth your stroke.

Remember that you can find all of those options in the **Tool property** palette:

Figure 2.25 – Our Tool property window with all the options

Done? Good! Now, let's go to the next step.

Brush shape

Brush shape is a less-talked-about option in the CSP brush engine that can help you greatly, as it lets you save and load your brush options without going through your material brush tips and options.

Now, when using block colors or creating silhouettes, or if you want to have a certain degree of control when it comes to your shape edge, you need to toggle between some brushes. Usually, those are square, circle, and triangle brushes. With the **Brush shape** option, you can toggle between them with just a click:

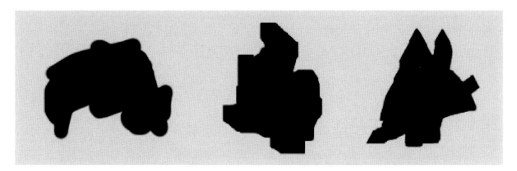

Figure 2.26 – From left to right, circle pen, square pen, and triangle pen

As you can see, those brushes give different characteristics to the edge of your shape. Which one to use is based completely on personal preferences… But how do we save and load the brush options? Let's take a look:

1. First of all, create a square and a triangle brush tip. I recommend using the **Polygon** tool:

Figure 2.27 – Tool property of the Polygon tool—if you switch between these options, you can have a square and a triangle

2. Now take your previously copied **Milli pen** and click on the usual little wrench icon, then go to the **Brush shape** option.

3. Now click on **Register to preset**. After this, click on that other little wrench icon below the brush shapes to change the name and call it Round Brush:

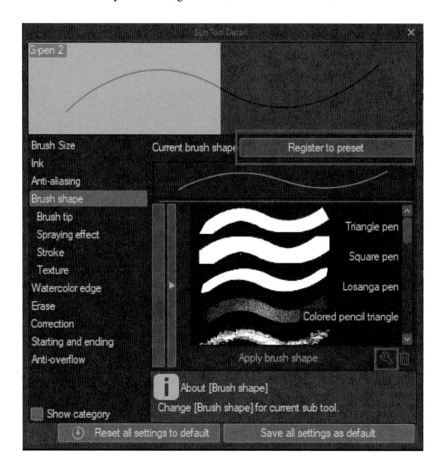

Figure 2.28 – Brush shape option

Now you've saved this brush shape.

4. Now go to **Brush tip** and add your square brush tip as a material.

5. Go to **Brush shape**, save it, and rename it Square Brush.

6. Now do the same thing with the triangle brush and rename it Triangle Brush.

Now, every time you need to change your brush tip, you just need to click on **Brush shape** in **Tool property** and you can change it. Plus, you have all the options to modify the type of brush you're using. You can also switch easily between an inking brush and a painting brush with a single click:

Figure 2.29 – Our workhorse tool property, as a reminder for the example

If you want to do this, it is a similar process to the steps previously followed. You just need to click on color mixing. And that's it, you have your painting brush.

Now, when I say "with a single click," I really mean it. You can link every window to a shortcut that will make that window appear under your pen.

To do so, you need to do the following:

1. Go to **File | Shortcut Settings**.

2. Click on **Setting area** and change it to **Pop-up palette**:

Figure 2.30 – Shortcut settings categories

3. Now select **Tool property** and bind it to a shortcut.

Now every time you press that shortcut, **Tool property** will come up right under your pen. This works for every window you can think of, from **Color Wheel** to **Layer**. This is a pretty unique feature of CSP that lets you hide a lot of information from your monitor, without it being out of reach. For example, I don't need **Color Wheel** all the time, only when I need to change the color. This is really useful if you have a small monitor or a dual-monitor setup.

We will see how to use this little workhorse brush in *Chapter 7, Making Your Own Illustration*, *Chapter 8, Creating Your Own Comic*, and *Chapter 9, Building Your Own Concept Art*.

Summary

With this chapter, you're fully equipped to create your own personal brushes to help speed up your process.

You can create a brush with multiple brush tips that you can use for decorations, such as the pattern of a dress, and not only for that but even for creating a randomized seamless texture, giving you a ready-made base to use for your illustrations.

And finally, you now know how to create a workhorse brush that you can use for every situation without changing tools, giving you the opportunity to focus on the creative process without thinking about the technical stuff.

In the next chapter, we will learn how to create a 3D object to speed up our work.

3
Creating 3D Backgrounds in CSP

We have learned the basics of how to create brushes for our artistic needs. But there is something that is not discussed so much in the western market, which is using 3D in **Clip Studio Paint** (**CSP**).

From this chapter through to *Chapter 6, Importing 3D Characters in CSP*, we will learn how to use 3D to boost our speed and creativity and cover all the options for importing and creating assets and how to use them.

The chapters up to *Chapter 6, Importing 3D Characters in CSP*, are not strictly essential to use CSP; you can make beautiful drawings even without 3D. But 3D in CSP is a lesser-known feature that can give you a huge boost in your productivity.

This chapter will cover the following topics:

- Working with 3D in CSP – pros and cons
- How to create a 3D mesh
- Adding 3D props to your CSP

Working with 3D in CSP – pros and cons

From 2018, we western users were finally able to use Modeler, with an official English release. This enabled us to create changeable 3D materials to use in CSP.

But there are some caveats that come along with the pros of using 3D materials, such as the time and effort we need to put in in order to create those basic objects and reusable scenes.

A quick summary of the pros and cons is as follows:

Pros:

- You can have reusable 3D assets from which you can extract lineart (*EX version*).
- You don't need to create AAA (Triple-A) game-level 3D object assets, so you don't need to worry about a lot of things. For example, all your models can just have texture painting on top of them.
- You can change and modify those assets, letting you create different situations with a single 3D material.
- They will speed up your workflow greatly, as you won't lose time sketching and setting a perspective grid.

Cons:

- **Clip Studio Modeler** (**CSM**), despite the name, is not modeling software, so you need to create the object somewhere else.
- You can't even select vertices, edges, or faces of the object.
- Because of how CSP and Modeler handle 3D, they can't read the UV mapping of the object, nor do they have a fully fledged render engine.
- You will spend a lot of time creating an object you can edit; if, for example, you want to change the color of a cube, you will need to create two different textures.

Before analyzing Modeler in detail, I want to share my rule of thumb with you. Deciding whether something is useful or not is based on this little question:

"What are the things that I can't do with this?"

I ask this question because it will give me a reasonable estimation of what the developer's priority was when creating this service, and help to define what the purpose of the tool is. Here is an example:

"In Photoshop, they don't have an option to simulate the amount of paint or the density, so they don't have emulating a real-life medium as a priority."

"In CSP, they don't have a magnetic lasso tool, so they don't have making a precise selection in a photo as a priority."

So, what's the purpose of Modeler? We know it is not modeling software, because it can't read UV mappings or select individual components of a mesh. It is not even 3D **baking** software because you can't render in it. So, what you can do there?

The only useful thing you can do is **import 3D objects in CSP**, so what does this mean? It means that everything revolves around this core concept. So, we need to ask ourselves the following:

"What can we do with 3D objects in CSP?"

We can use it, as we will see, to create assets to easily implement objects in our drawing, without worrying every time about creating a perspective grid or re-drawing an object every time we need it.

Take the following example:

Figure 3.1 – A simple 3D vase in CSP

If we take this vase I created, we can see a little bit of what we can do in CSP. If we look at the command bar under the object, we can see two or three icons that are extremely important. This is because they give you the following options:

- ▣ : This lets you use different camera presets, letting you choose between different camera presets.

- ▣ : This lets you choose between different material presets; in other words, it lets you choose different textures.

- ▣ : This lets you choose between different layout presets, meaning that you can switch between different composite scenes that you have recorded.

- ▣ : This lets you use the moveable parts of your object, using a slider that you set up in CSM.

So, in CSM, we can give 3D objects different presets, and we can toggle between them in CSP. So now that we know what purpose CSM was created for, we can look at the pipeline for creating a usable 3D object in CSP.

First of all, we need to create an object (also called a mesh in other software). Every movable/changeable part needs to be on its own separate "layer." After this, if we want to apply a texture, we need to use UV mapping on the mesh, export the image, and reapply it on the mesh. After this, we export in either `.OBJ` or `.FBX` format (`.FBX` works a little bit better). Next, you import the object in CSM and set up all of the presets. Then you can save it as a material in CSP.

Now you're done, and you have your 3D object.

If you want a static 3D object, you just need to click and drag it into CSP and save it as a material.

Now we can see it is not a really fast process. So, it's pretty useful asking ourselves "Is all of this really worth it?" It depends.

If you do all of this to create a single object that you will use a single time, you just wasted 3–4 hours of your life. But if you have a recurring background in your comic and you need to draw it in various shots with various camera angles… well now 3–4 hours of your time to set up all of this is more acceptable. So, it all depends on what you need to do.

My general advice is this: if you have a recurring prop in your comic or your illustrations, such as a chair or a sword, or something like that, make it a 3D asset with 2–3 variations of the object. This will take you 1 hour at the most if you're fast; if not, it may take approximately 2 hours to set up.

When it comes to the details of the object, use this simple rule:

"Create the least detailed object you can create while still being useful to you."

If I need a bamboo chair, is it really useful for me to model all the bamboo texture, considering that I will need to rasterize my object in CSP? No, it's not. Because unless we are making an illustration of 3,000x3,000 px in which we can only see the chair, I'm pretty sure that all those details will be lost because of a lack of resolution, and no, you can't increase the resolution of your canvas until it will be shown for two reasons:

- Your computer will explode.
- The viewer will need 5–10 minutes to load your image.

So, it's a really bad idea.

Now, what you can realistically do is create a base chair shape and apply a texture to it. In this way, you save time and don't use too much energy on details. That's the strength of using 3D in CSP—you can concentrate on the main focus and subject of your work.

Just a word of advice: before starting, save your texture file as a CSP file and store it somewhere. You will understand why we need to do this in the *Adding 3D props to your CSP* section:

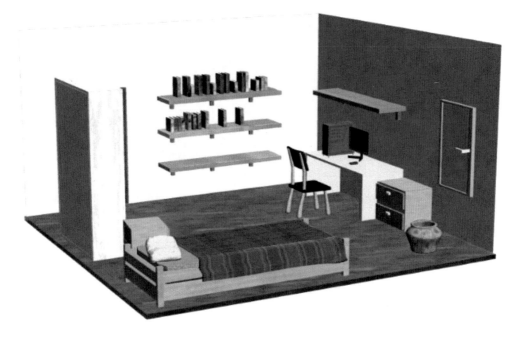

Figure 3.2 – A vase in perspective with a scene

We will learn how to create that vase in this chapter. As you can see, the texture is visible but not in a way in which you can see every single decoration applied. So that's why I'm telling you to not create highly detailed objects… because, simply put, it will not matter.

In the next section, I will show you how to create two simple objects, a die and a vase, and how to be sure they are shown properly in CSP.

How to create a 3D mesh

Because CSM is not a full-fledged 3D software, it means that we need to use another software to create our basic mesh. I will use Blender to do it, for a few simple reasons: it is free and is not so demanding regarding specs, plus there are a lot of free add-ons that you can use to speed up the process, and some of them are even pre-installed. When you open Blender for the first time, you will see the following screen:

Figure 3.3 – Blender 2.9. To remove the little start screen, just click somewhere in the software

We will create a **die**, because it will let you understand a lot of how 3D works, and a **vase** (because I've used it so many times as a reference… so why not?).

Remember this: we don't need to be the guys from the *Flipped Normals* or *Blender Guru* YouTube channels, but I recommend watching their videos. We just need a basic, simple mesh that we can unwrap easily and apply a texture over. CSP doesn't have a proper render engine, meaning it is useless trying to create a really complicated mesh with a lot of details. Before we start, let's check out the Blender interface so that we can get familiar with the software we'll be using.

Blender interface

Blender seems a little bit intimidating at the beginning, because there is a lot to assimilate and it is usually a new type of software for an illustrator. The following screenshot shows Blender in Object Mode:

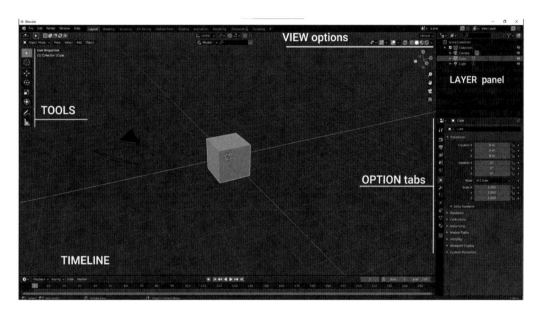

Figure 3.4 – Blender interface in Object Mode

But rest assured, for what we need we can easily disregard 99% of what we see for two reasons:

- We don't need all those tools; we will do something called **hard surface modeling** on a really basic level so we will only need basic tools such as **Extrude** or **Inset**.

- Blender is a really shortcut-based software, so we will not really use a lot of those icons. Ironically speaking, talking about the shortcuts is talking about the interface.

Click the little arrow near the two circles as shown in the preceding figure, as in there you can find the view options. Click on **Face Orientation**:

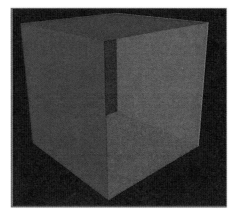

Figure 3.10 – Our cube with Face Orientation activated

If it's red, it's in the wrong direction; every red face needs to be on the inside. But what happens if our face is inverted?

Figure 3.11 – Whole cube with an inverted face

We go to **Edit Mode**, and we press *3* or click the **Face** button in the top-left corner of our screen:

Figure 3.12 – Option to select vertices edges, or faces

The **middle mouse button** (**MMB**) is used for panning, zooming, and rotating your view in this 3D space. It's like the spacebar in CSP but for the 3D world.

Here are the ways in which you can use the MMB:

- *MMB* without anything lets you rotate the view.
- *MMB + Shift* lets you pan the view.
- Scrolling the *MMB*, or *MMB + Ctrl*, lets you zoom in/zoom out.

If you don't have a mouse, or if you're using a pen, do the following:

1. Go to **Edit**.
2. Click on **Preferences**.
3. Go to **Interface**.
4. Click on **Emulate 3 button mouse**.

In this way, when you press *Alt* + **left mouse button** (**LMB**), it will simulate the MMB, so to pan the view, you will need to press *Shift + Alt + LMB,* and to rotate the view, just *Alt + LMB*.

The next most important part is understanding the axes. We have the *X* (red), *Y* (green), and *Z* (blue) axes. The first two let us work in the horizontal space, and the third one is for the height. Every time we scale, rotate, or move an object, we will use those axes.

To do so, you just need to select your object with the *LMB*. After this, you can use these shortcuts:

- *G* for moving
- *R* for rotating
- *S* for scaling

After this, you just need to press *Z*, *X*, or *Y* and it will snap to the relevant axis, or you can just use the *MMB*.

We will work in two modes, **Object Mode** and **Edit Mode**. To toggle between them, you just need to press the *Tab* key. The main difference is this: in the first one you change the whole object—in fact, you can only move, rotate, and scale the object. In the second one, you can change the vertices, edges, and faces of the object. But what are they?

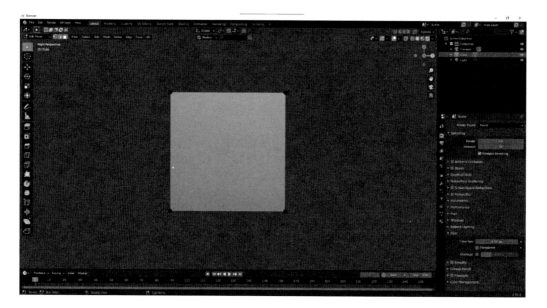

Figure 3.7 – Blender Edit Mode interface

The preceding figure shows a square with four big black points. Those points are our **vertices**. The vertices are the "corners" of a face, and the **edges** are the lines that connect two vertices. The **face** is the "closed" space between at least three vertices; where there is a face, the light will not pass.

Now, before continuing, I need to explain something really important. **Faces have an orientation.**

If we take our previous cube and we remove a face, we can see that it's empty inside:

Figure 3.8 – Our basic cube without a face

This means that our faces that compose the cube have an outside and an inside. If we flip those two values in error while creating our mesh, it will not render properly.

In layman's terms, when 3D software creates a 2D image, it will take a light source and it will see where the light bounces off. This informs the software how you want to visualize an object. It answers questions such as *How much of the surface is rough? It is shiny? Does it emit light?* and so on.

> **Important Note: Mesh**
>
> No… I'm not talking about hair extensions. In 3D software, a **mesh** is, in layman's terms, the object. So, every time you see the word mesh, it's referring to an option that will be applied to the vertices, edges, and faces selected.

So, the right orientation will allow the light to bounce off correctly, and the wrong side will let the light pass through. Or at least that's what will happen in CSP.

How can we find out whether the face is in the right orientation? Just click on that little arrow next to the intersected circle:

Figure 3.9 – Viewport options

Click the little arrow near the two circles as shown in the preceding figure, as in there you can find the view options. Click on **Face Orientation**:

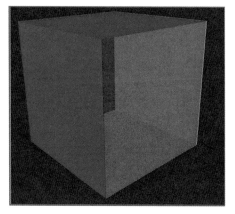

Figure 3.10 – Our cube with Face Orientation activated

If it's red, it's in the wrong direction; every red face needs to be on the inside. But what happens if our face is inverted?

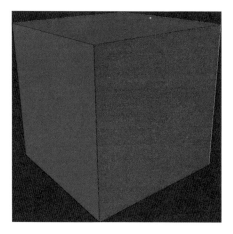

Figure 3.11 – Whole cube with an inverted face

We go to **Edit Mode**, and we press *3* or click the **Face** button in the top-left corner of our screen:

Figure 3.12 – Option to select vertices edges, or faces

After this, click on the face of interest and press *Shift + N*. This will flip it back to blue. Now you have a completely blue cube! 99% of the problems you can have in CSP with 3D models are caused by this little face orientation error.

Now, with that being said, let's start creating our first model.

Creating a die

Now, open up a new document in Blender by pressing *Ctrl/Cmd + N* and clicking on **General**.

This will open up a file with a cube. OK, we have our die base the right way. Isn't it easy?

But let's say we cancel it by error, and we need a new cube. Press *Shift + A* and click on **Mesh** and then on **Cube**. Now we've created our first cube. Every time you need to add a mesh, just press *Shift + A* and add the mesh you need.

After this, we press *Tab* to enter **Edit Mode**. Now we will do something called UV unwrapping.

Now, what's UV unwrapping? It is practically taking a 3D object and flattening it into a 2D surface:

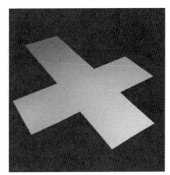

Figure 3.13 – A cube flattened into a cross shape in a 2D shape

This gives us the possibility to use a 2D painting software, such as CSP, to paint a texture over it.

So, how we do it? We will use something called **Mark Seam** in **Edit Mode**. Practically speaking, Mark Seam tells the software where to cut the box.

Before starting, know that there isn't, at least for what we need, a "right" way do to it. There is a "clean" and a "dirty" way to do it:

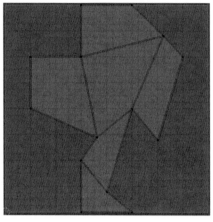

Figure 3.14 – A clean (left) and a dirty (right) unwrapping

The "clean" way creates a UV unwrapping that is less distorted and lets you control the painting part in a more streamlined way. Follow these steps for the "clean" method:

1. Click on the cube.

2. Press *Tab*.

3. Press *2* to select the edges.

4. Select the edge you need to create a cross-like section:

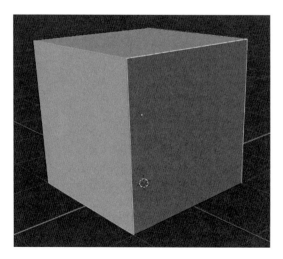

Figure 3.15 – The orange lines are the necessary edges

5. Now press the **right mouse button (RMB)** and click on **Mark Seam**.

6. Click on **UV**, and then click on **Unwrap**.

7. Now go to **UV Editing**:

Figure 3.16 – Contextual menu

8. Press *A* to select everything or click on this little fella, 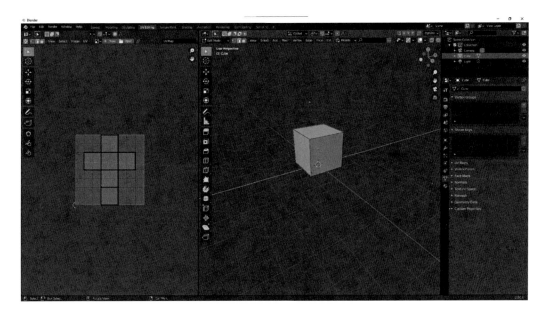, which is in the top-left corner:

Figure 3.17 – UV Editing workspace

Now, on the left, you will have your 2D image "ready" to be painted, but before doing it we need to export it. Fortunately, this is pretty easy; we just need to click on **UV** above the image and click on **Export UV layout**. Save it wherever you want, and you will have a transparent PNG with all the reference lines:

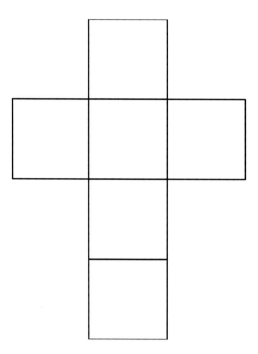

Figure 3.18 – Our guidelines for the UV unwrapping

Now we just need to create the texture for our die, the little points displayed on the faces. Let's open up CSP and open with it our UV image.

Important Note

In the case where you import a PNG in CSP and you need to add a background, you can use a **Fill** layer or a **Paper** layer. To do so, just go to **Layer** in the menu and select **New Layer | Fill/Paper**.

There are various ways to be precise in CSP, and my favorite is by using the grid. But before using it, we need to set it. These are the grid settings used by me:

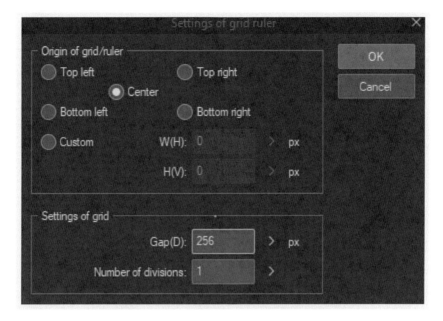

Figure 3.19 – Grid settings. Don't copy the values

This will give us a good frame in which we can work with a good degree of precision:

1. Go to **View** and select **Grid Settings**.

2. Click on **Center**.

3. Set **Number of divisions** to 1, for now.

4. For **Gap**, you need to scale up/down the value until the lines of the grid match the lines of the UV lines.

5. Set **Number of divisions** to 4.

6. Now just click **OK** and you're all set up.

7. Now, go to **View** and click on **Grid**. After activating it control on **View** if at the bottom of the menu the **Snap to Grid** option is checked:

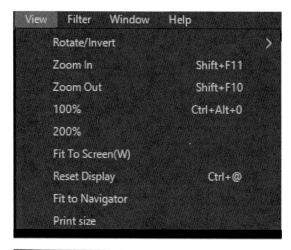

Figure 3.20 – Snap to Grid location

Now, to create a new layer, take the **Polygon/Square/Circle** tool and use it to create the numbers on the die. Remember that if the **Adjust angle after fixed** option is checked, you will need to click twice in order to create the shape. If there is no fill, you just need to go to the tool option and above all the options there is **Line/Fill**. Click on the far-left option.

> **Important Note**
>
> If you want to create a shape from the center of the shape, just click on our usual little wrench icon to access all the options, click on **Shape Operation**, and click on **Start from Center**.

Now we just need to create a layer below our die and fill it with the color we want our die to be. I've opted for a desaturated cream color. Deactivate the layer for the UV guidelines and export it as a .png file. For professional texture making, games, and animations, there are other types of file formats, but for our needs, the old, reliable .png is good enough. You can see the texture of my cube in the following figure:

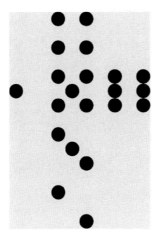

Figure 3.21 – My cube texture

To apply the texture to the cube, we will need to return to Blender. Fortunately, this is pretty straightforward. You just need to go to the **OPTION** tab, under the layers, and click on this icon, ▣, for the **Material palette**. This will open the Material palette, the tool that decides the look of your object. In this menu, you can add and modify the materials. Every object in Blender has a material; it's what decides the roughness, specularity, or color of an object. This is what the Material palette looks like without any material:

Figure 3.22 – Material palette, without a material

If you see something like in the preceding figure, just click on **New**, and this will add a new material. This is what the Material palette looks like with a material:

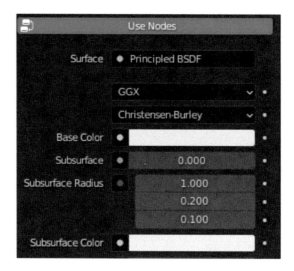

Figure 3.23 – Material palette, with a material

After adding a basic material, click on the yellow button on the right of **Base Color**, and this will open a little menu. Under **Texture**, click on **Image texture**. Now click on **Open** and select your die image:

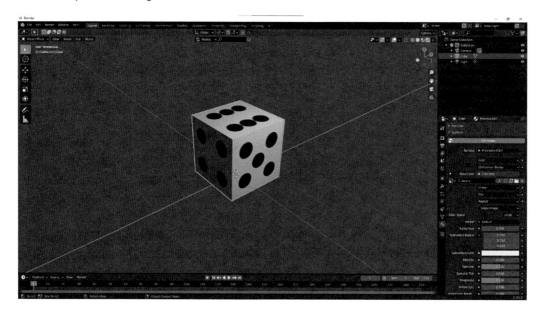

Figure 3.24 – The interface with our little cute die

This is my result; your result may be different based on what you wanted to make…

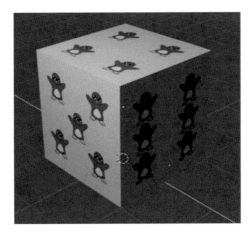

Figure 3.25 – An alternative die

For another example, here's a die with cute penguins… because we can! Deal with it.

> **Tip**
>
> If you want to add bevels to your die, you need to click on that little blue wrench above the Material palette. After clicking on it, click on **Add modifier** and click on **Bevel**. The **Amount** parameter indicates how big you want your bevels; **Segments** indicates how refined they will be. The difference between **Vertices** and **Edge** is that the first one will be applied on the angles, and the other to the edges.

As you can see in the next figure, we added some bevels and removed the edges, creating a child-safe die:

Figure 3.26 – On the left we have vertices and on the right, edges, each with bevels applied

Now we know how to do a cube. But let's make something a little less angular and softer… such as a vase.

Creating a vase

Now, let's model something more complicated, a vase, which will look as in the following figure:

Figure 3.27 – A simple vase created in Blender

Let's get started by following these steps:

1. Add a cylinder; if you don't remember how, just click *Shift + A*, then **Mesh**, then click on **Cylinder**:

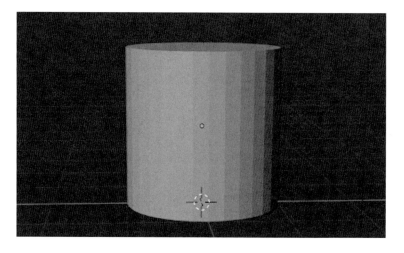

Figure 3.28 – A simple cylinder in Blender

We now have our little cylinder, but if that's a vase, I'm an eggplant dressed as a human. Now we need to give it a vase shape.

2. To do so, go to **Edit Mode** by pressing *Tab*:

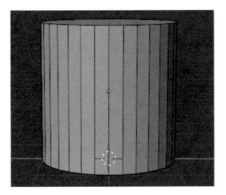

Figure 3.29 – Our cylinder in Edit Mode

Let's create a little bit of roundness in this cylinder.

3. Press *Ctrl + R*, and this will activate the **Loop Cut** tool, 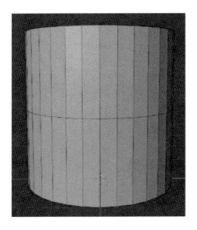, giving us the ability to add an edge loop.

    Clicking with the *LMB* and then clicking the *RMB* will give a nice cut in the middle of the mesh.

4. Now we just need to press *Alt + LMB* to select what we created; if you have previously checked the **Emulate three mouse button** option, you just need to double-click on the edge:

Figure 3.30 – Our cylinder with the edge loop selected

5.   Now press *S* and it will scale the edge loop:

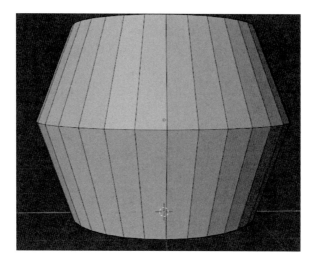

Figure 3.31 – Our cylinder with the scaled edge loop

6.   Now we need to do the same where we want the bevel of our vase:

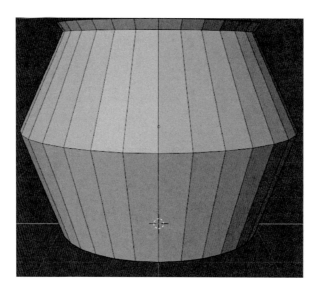

Figure 3.32 – The vase with a bevel

7.   Now we will need to give more body to that little bevel on the entrance of the vase. Let's move our view to see the top of the vase.

8. Press *3*.

9. Click on the top face:

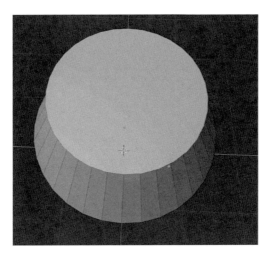

Figure 3.33 – Our top face

10. Press *I* for inset:

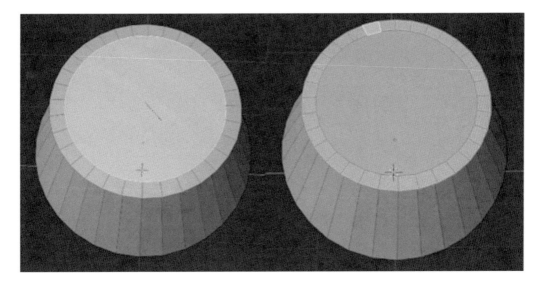

Figure 3.34 – Our inset face

11. Adjust the inset settings to the level of bevel you want. Now we need to extrude the bevel we created. If you press *I* for inset what do you need to press for extrude? Obviously, *Alt + E*… Select **Extrude along normals**:

Figure 3.35 – Our extruded bevel

For the rest of this exercise, it would be better to use Wireframe mode with X-Ray toggled on. Press *Z* and select **Wireframe**. If **X-Ray** is not active, press *Alt + Z*.

Now we need to select the big round face inside the bevel, and we will need to create the inside of the vase. After selecting it, you can see at the top right a little gizmo:

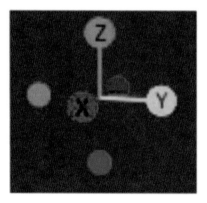

Figure 3.36 – Blender gizmo to navigate the camera

If you press one of the colored balls, the view will be snapped to an orthogonal view on that axis.

For what we need to do, we need to press on that little red ball. Doing so will let us see the following:

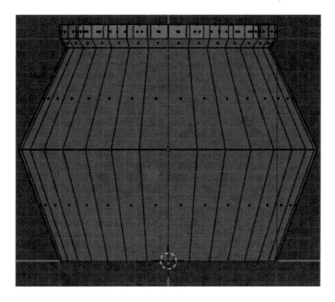

Figure 3.37 – Our view in an X-axis orthogonal view

Now we just need to extrude our face and try to align it on that middle line. If you press *Ctrl* while clicking, it will snap the movement to the grid. After this, scale it until you're satisfied with the width of the inside of the vase:

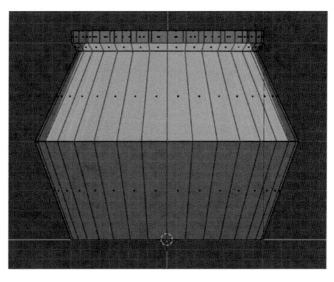

Figure 3.38 – Our vase after extruding the inside

Now let's do it one more time to create the base of the inside. It will overflow a little bit, so scale it with *S* until it's inside the vase:

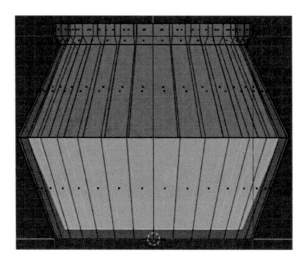

Figure 3.39 – The rest of the inside of our vase

Now return to **Solid view** mode, press *Z*, and select **Solid**. Before creating our UV mapping, we need to give a little bit more roundness to our vase. To do so… guess what? We will go to our little blue wrench bar, **Add modifier | Subdivision Surface**:

Figure 3.40 – The result of our subdivision surface

As we can see, there are some jagged lines in there, plus the bevel is too round. Fortunately, there is a quick fix. Let's do that:

1. Go to **Edit Mode**.

2. Press *Ctrl + R* to enter loop cut.

3. Put a loop cut just above the base:

Figure 3.41 – As you can see, the jagged lines disappear

4. Now do the same thing with the base of the bevel:

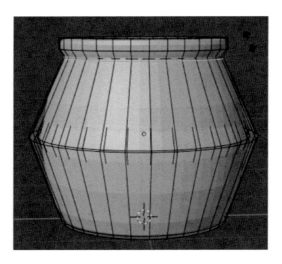

Figure 3.42 – The bevel is a little bit tighter

5.   Do the same everywhere you want a tighter angle.

We will do the same with all the parts that seem a little bit loose and scale when needed. This is what the final vase looks like:

Figure 3.43 – My final result

Now we need to UV unwrap this vase. *Breathe in…* Now, there is no "easy" way to do it. It takes a lot of trial and error; it's impossible to have a "clean" UV if you're a beginner because you don't know how Blender will read your inputs. So, don't be discouraged and just experiment a little bit.

My advice is to make a copy of your object by just using the old, reliable *Ctrl/Cmd + C* and *Ctrl/Cmd + V*. Re-click the object and move it somewhere, and press *G* to unwrap it, so you have a backup copy:

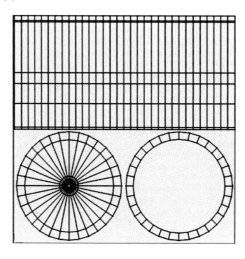

Figure 3.44 – Our basic UV unwrapping

We can't use the autogenerated UV because the interior and exterior are on the same plane, and that's something that we don't want. The cuts I've made are the red lines and are mirrored between the axes:

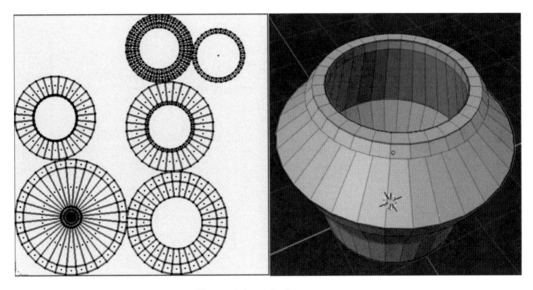

Figure 3.45 – My first attempt

Now, this doesn't work because some geometry is too small to be effective. This means that the texture will be compressed in those smaller points and it will be stretched on the bigger faces. This is what I did on my second attempt:

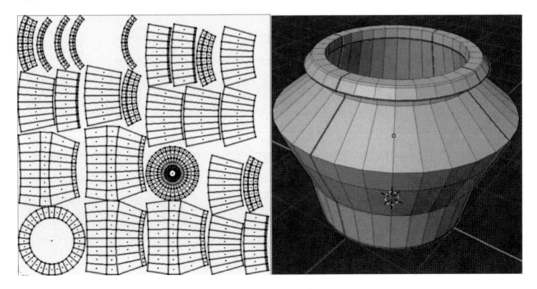

Figure 3.46 – My second attempt

To put it simply, this is too overcrowded. It's difficult to keep in mind what's what, and although it may be usable, we would surely benefit from a cleaner UV map. This is what I did on my third attempt:

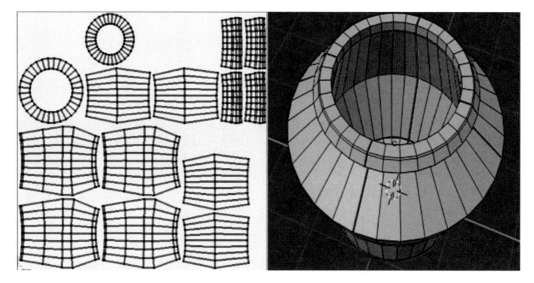

Figure 3.47 – My third attempt

This is a pretty satisfactory result; we know what's what, and nothing is too small. In the case of a more complex object, I will probably need 5–6 tries. It's normal to not get it right on the first attempt; it is all part of the process. So, don't be hard on yourself.

Now let's go to CSP and add colors and a texture. This time, we will try to add a seamless texture to it.

To do so, take a seamless texture of your choice; I've used *Painted Plaster 6* from *CC0 Textures*, which is a free texture website:

1. Open up your UV image with the UV layout, just as we did with the die.

2. Add a color that will be a good base for our texture. In my case, this is desaturated ivory.

3. Take your texture and go to **Edit | Transform and Mesh Transformation**. This will create some lattice points that you can use to transform the texture and adapt it however you want to a surface.

4. Now add, using **Tool Property**, the exact amount of vertical and horizontal lines that one of your UV map islands has. As an example, one slice of the vase has one horizontal line and seven vertical lines:

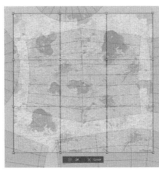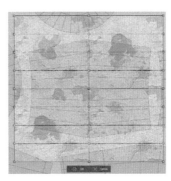

Figure 3.48 – In my UV island, I have one horizontal line and seven vertical lines

5. After this, we need to take all those little dots and align them with the UV island:

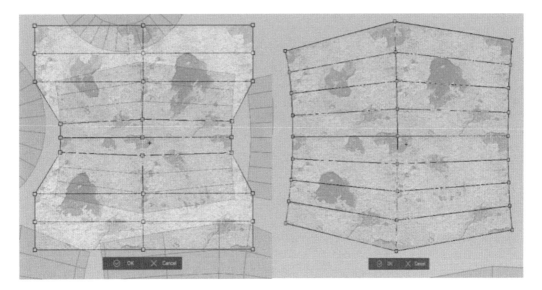

Figure 3.49 – Our texture aligned with the UV island

6. Now do the same for every island type and copy and paste the result where needed.

In the following exercise, you will learn a pretty neat trick to use in CSP for your object textures.

Try it yourself

As you can see, you have a lot of islands sometimes... and it can be a little bit tedious to apply a change to all of them without creating problems. But while working with CSP, I discovered a little trick:

1. After creating one island, go into its layer, right-click on the layer, and select **File Object**.
2. Click on **Convert Layer to file object**.
3. Now copy and paste the result where needed.
4. Now, right-click on the file object you've created and select **File Object** and then **Open file of file object**.
5. Modify the file that you opened, and then save it.

What happened in your UV unwrapped texture?

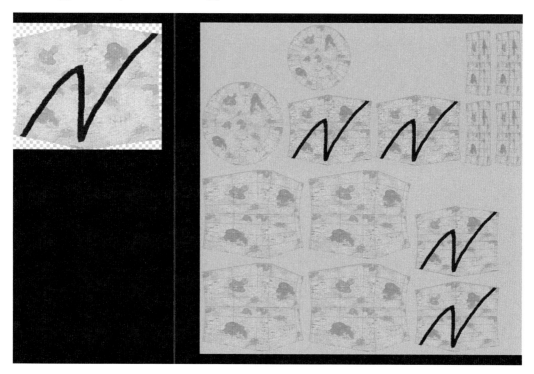

Figure 3.50 – My texture (right) and my file object (left)

As you can see, every change I make to the file object will be applied to every copy of that file object. This gives you the ability to make one-time changes without worrying about reapplying every island precisely. This is what my final vase looks like:

Figure 3.51 – My final result

Now apply it on Blender as we did for the die:

1. Go to the **Material palette**.

2. Click on the yellow button on the left of **Base Color**.

3. Click on **Image texture**.

4. Click on **Open** to add the texture.

Now we have not one, but two 3D objects to add to our CSP Material palette. Next, we will see how to import them into CSP.

Adding 3D props to your CSP

We have finally created two objects that we can import in CSP. But before opening CSP, we need to open CSM and import the object, making sure that everything is fine, and then add the objects as materials for CSP.

Adding them to Modeler is pretty straightforward:

1. In Blender, click on the object.

2. Go to **File** and then to **Export**.

3. Click on **FBX**.

4. On the right, select **Limit to Selected object**.

5. Save it in the same folder that you saved the texture used. This step is really important. If you don't do it, CSP and Modeler will not read the object correctly.

6. Now you need to open Modeler:

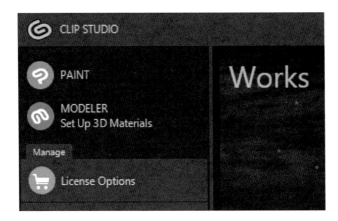

Figure 3.52 – To open Modeler, you need to open the Clip Studio launcher and click on MODELER

After opening it, you will see the following screen:

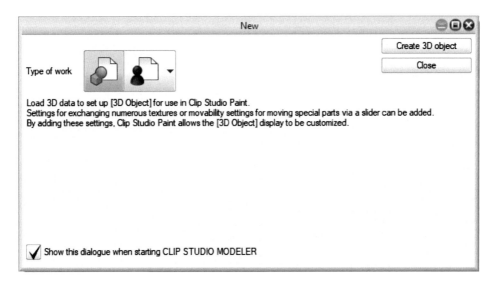

Figure 3.53 – Starting screen of Modeler

7. Click on **Create 3D object**.

8. In **Object configuration**, click on the little tree, and after that click on the little folder below (not the one with the smile):

Figure 3.54 – Object configuration window in Modeler

9. Now you just need to select your FBX object:

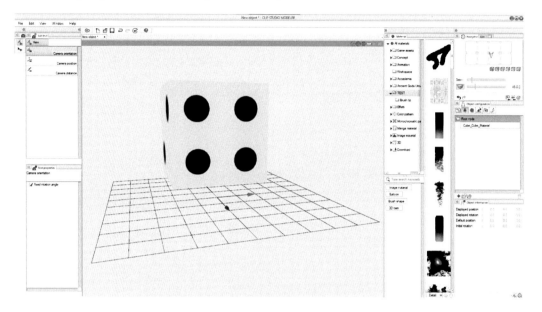

Figure 3.55 – Our Modeler interface with our cube

10. If your little gizmo for moving the cube is not centered in the object, you just need to click **Move part origin point** on the left window in the **Move palette**.

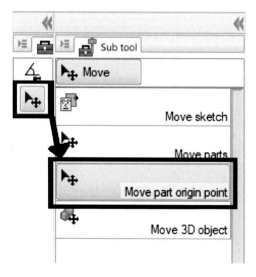

Figure 3.56 – Move part origin point location

11. After this, click on that little central gray box, as shown in the following figure:

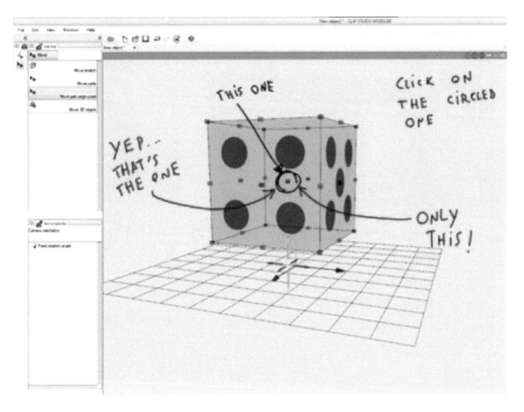

Figure 3.57 – Changing the origin of our object

But our cube is a little bit bland. So, why don't we add another material?

12. Click on the icon next to the tree, that little strange sphere known as the Material palette.

13. Now click on the little folder called **Default material**, and click on the little icon below to make a copy of it.

Every copy is a different material that you can toggle on CSP:

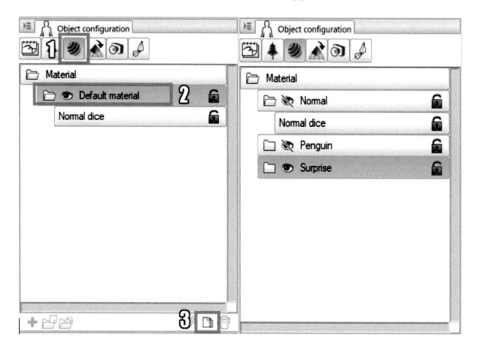

Figure 3.58 – How to make copies of materials

14. Next, you just need to click on that little folder icon and under the **Object configuration** window there is the **Object information** window. In there, click on that little icon with the CSP logo:

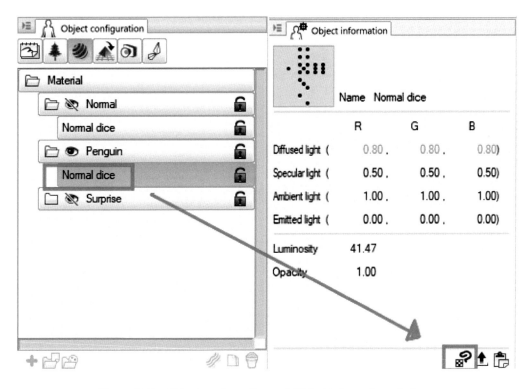

Figure 3.59 – Object configuration and Object information windows

With this, we will open CSP to modify our texture. You will see a preview of that in CSM. So, if I upload my penguin die texture on the file opened in CSP, this is what I will see in Modeler:

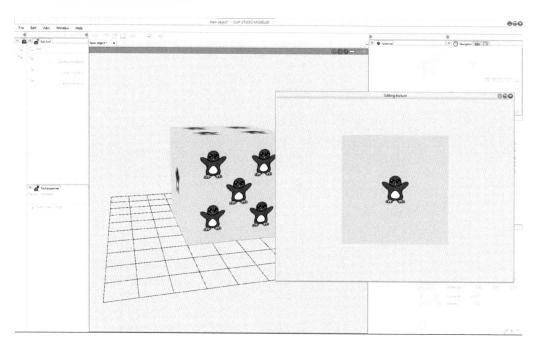

Figure 3.60 – Modeler interface with the texture preview

> **Tip**
> To set your material thumbnail, you just need to double-click on the thumbnail in the **Object information** window. This will open a 3D view of the object that you can change with the mouse buttons. Click on **Complete** and you're done.

15. To import the die, in CSP you just need to go to **File** and click on **Register as new material** and select the folder you want. And that is it… that's how you add a 3D object in CSP.

16. Now you just need to click and drag in CSP and you will have your 3D object.

    To toggle between the materials you've created, you just need to press this little icon: .

The following figure shows a bodybuilder die created by me:

Figure 3.61 – Our final result in CSP with a bodybuilder die… you're welcome

As you can see, you can go full crazy with how you show your personality even with simple objects. And that's the point of those objects, giving a quick personal flavor to your drawing. As an example, when you buy beef/vegetable broth, do you eat it on its own? No… you add something else, such as red pepper, dried garlic, some chopped vegetables/meat, tortellini… Great, now I'm hungry.

The point is, you modify something standard to give it a more personal flavor.

Summary

In this chapter, you've learned, quite frankly, a lot of complicated stuff. But don't worry, it will get even more advanced in the next chapters!

You've learned how to do some basic navigation in Blender, giving you the ability to stand on your own two feet and understand more advanced stuff, and do some basic troubleshooting with face orientation.

This was explained by guiding you step by step through creating two objects, a die and a vase, which are examples of hard surface modeling, or in another term, non-organic modeling. With those two objects, you learned how to add an object to your Blender scene, extruding and cutting the movement of your objects and vertices/edges/faces.

You also learned how to add textures via UV unwrapping by unpacking an object in a 2D space in a clean way, and then editing it in CSM.

In the next chapter, we will see how to create editable scenes in CSM. Don't worry—it's mostly easy.

4

Using Your 3D Props to Create a Scene

Clip Studio Modeler (CSM) lets you import static single objects and create a complete editable scene that you can change in **Clip Studio Paint (CSP)** with only a few clicks. Thanks to this, you can create 3D props to reuse in your drawings and work.

In this chapter, I will show you what Clip Studio Assets is, a free service that you can use to cover your weaknesses by downloading assets such as brushes or textures.

After this, I will show you how to create a single object, a drawer, from scratch using Blender and how to import it into Modeler, and we will then move on to a more complex scene.

In these two cases, I will show you how to create an editable scene, which is the goal of this chapter. This will give you the ability to create 3D props and a scene on your own that you can use for your work, with the possibility to change the angles of the camera, the position of the object, and textures.

This chapter will cover the following topics:

- Introduction to Clip Studio Assets
- Creating a 3D real-life scene for your work
- Creating a 3D fantasy scene for your work

Technical requirements

We will use the following in this chapter:

- Clip Studio Paint
- Clip Studio Modeler
- Blender

Introduction to Clip Studio Assets

Before going into detail into how to create a reusable scene, we need to spend some time discussing *Clip Studio Assets*, a free service that **Celsys** gives you. It is a place in which users can share the materials they have created, and it is also a good place to find single 3D objects to add to your scene for little narrative details. This is what a Clip Studio Assets screen looks like:

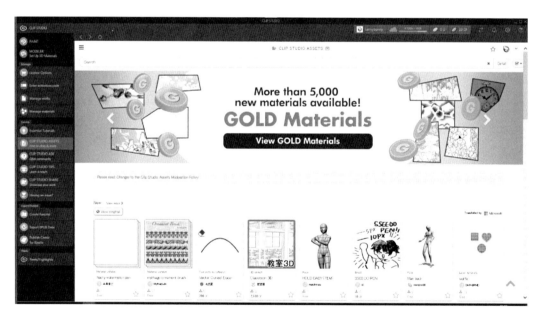

Figure 4.1 – Clip Studio Assets screen

To open the Clip Studio Assets service, you need to open Clip Studio with the following icon and click on **Clip Studio Assets**:

Figure 4.2 – Clip Studio logo

Here, you can find three types of materials, including reusable objects such as brush tips, 3D models, and image sets:

- **Free materials**: The name is self-explanatory.

- **Clippy materials**: Clippy is a non-purchasable currency inside the store. You can obtain it only through being gifted Clippy, selling an asset, or being a gold member.

- **Gold materials**: These are easy to understand. You pay some money, you receive some gold, and you buy the material.

For a purchase, you can use both currencies, but it will cost more in Clippy currency.

For the purpose of this chapter, we will only look at 3D assets. To do so, you need to go to the bar at the top of the window and click on the **Detail** button:

Figure 4.3 – In the top corner, under your avatar, you can find the Detail button

After this, select the **3D object** tag:

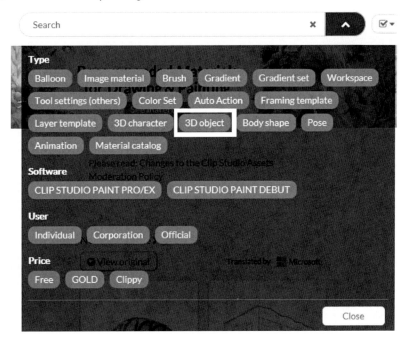

Figure 4.4 – Clip Studio Assets tags

Now, why am I telling you to do this? Because it is pretty much impossible that you will always have the time to model everything, so sometimes you will need to use premade assets.

For example, there is a castle provided as a free material (content ID: `1770016`, `1770045`, `1770044`). Do I know how to model a 3D medieval castle? No... absolutely not. So, I just download it and whenever I need it, I just put it in.

Premade assets are something that you download when you don't know how to model an object, or if you're in a pinch and can't do it by yourself.

Important note

The content ID is a series of seven digits that define a *material* in *Assets*. You can search for a material using those digits. Whenever you download a material, you can find it in the **Material palette** under **Download**.

But sometimes we need to create composite reusable scenes. In these cases, we can't use premade assets.

In layman's terms, you can't use them to build a reusable scene. But, truth be told, you can download a series of 3D objects in Assets, compose the scene in CSP, record the 3D layer as a material, and use it whenever you want. But this method lacks two crucial options:

- You can't change the texture of an object.

- You can't hide and unhide an object from your scene.

So, you can use premade assets to add details, but for the main structure of the scene, we will need to turn to plan B—also known as **Blender**. We will be using the 3D software to import the materials we need.

Now, if you don't mind having an untextured object, you can download a 3D object from a website. I prefer using **Sketchfab** and **BlenderKit**, but you can use whatever you want; just remember to save it as `OBJ` or `FBX`, because those are the file types that CSM can read.

However, if you need a specific object for a specific scene and you need it to be textured, you need to create it as we saw in the previous chapter.

I really recommend that before continuing, you create a folder wherever you want on your computer, calling it `CSM Scene` and creating a subfolder called `3D materials` inside it.

Now create two subfolders inside `3D materials` called `Realistic Room` and `Fantasy landscape`.

It is essential that everything is organized because we will need to create a lot of 3D objects and we can't have them scattered across our computer. Plus, if you remember, all the textures need to be in the same folder as the object. Next, we will see how to create a real-life scene for your work.

Creating a 3D real-life scene for your work

After you've made a 3D object, you can use it however you want in whatever angle you want.

As you can see in *Figure 4.5*, *Figure 4.6*, *Figure 4.7*, and *Figure 4.8*, I've created a simple room that I can reuse from various angles, without worrying about tracing perspective lines or adding the same textures every time.

It seems like a really advanced technique, but as you will see, those are all practically glorified cubes:

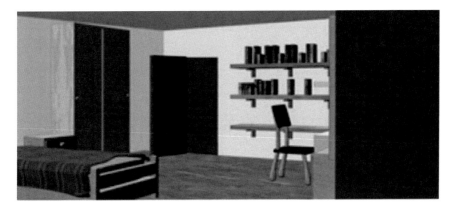

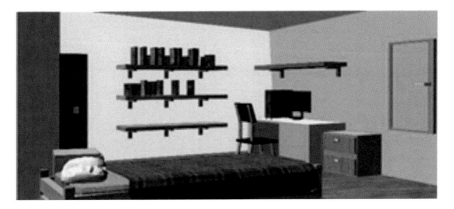

Figure 4.5 – 3D scene in different perspectives

Another thing you can do is change the colors using the **Line conversion** layer option, but this is only for EX users. This will separate your image into various tones that you can change later:

Figure 4.6 – 3D image with a simple line conversion (only in the EX version), with adjusted color

You can import and use 3D images in CSP even with the PRO version, but you can extract lines only in the EX version, which is done by going to **Layer | Convert to lines and tones**:

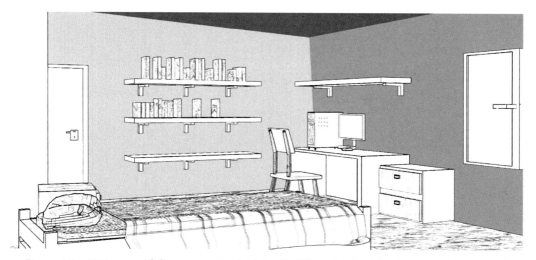

Figure 4.7 – 3D image with line conversion (only in the EX version), with only extract line selected

Something else that you can do, even with the PRO version, is "posterize" your image. In short, you duplicate your layer based on how many tones you want. In *Figure 4.8*, I duplicated it around five times. After that, just go to the **Layer property** palette and set **Expression color** to **Monochrome**, and click on the black square so you will only have the black pixels. Now just play around with **Color threshold** and **Alpha threshold** until you have a silhouette you like. Next, just play around with the **Layer color** option and you're done:

Figure 4.8 – 3D image with a posterization auto-action, created by me

As you can see, there is a huge array of possibilities with 3D, even without painting over it.

But I must admit… it's a lot of work, and when I say a lot, I mean it. That room in *Figure 4.5* took me around 6–7 hours to make, and I can't possibly show you how to model everything for two simple reasons:

- It will take more pages than you could possibly read while keeping your concentration.

- Everything you see in that scene is a glorified cube, and I changed every shape using only **Extrude, Inset, Separate/Join**, and **Move**. So, after two or three objects, I would be repeating myself and I will bore you to death. Even if you're a complete beginner, you can make a whole world using only those four tools, and I'm pretty sure of it because the first 3D artists for games used only those tools.

So, how can I demonstrate my process to you? I will take only a *drawer*, and I will show you how to model it. Everything else will use the same exact tools.

How to create a drawer

I know that a lot of people right now will be overwhelmed by this huge information dump regarding 3D objects, but trust me, you can do it. You can create those 3D objects, because it's not complex; you just need to perform some actions that you're not familiar with, which is why they seem complex. Don't worry if you don't make a "cool" drawer from the get-go. We all start from level 0.

First, let's open up Blender and save our Blender file in the `Realistic Room` folder you've created as `Room` (or whatever you want).

That being said, let's start. The first step is having measurements. Blender lets you work with precise measurements. Every time you look at a number related to location and scale, those numbers are in meters or inches:

Figure 4.9 – Scene properties with units of measure

If you want to change the units of measurement, go to **Scene Properties** and click on **Units**. You can switch between **Metric** and **Imperial**.

So, the first thing we need to do is measure our drawer. There are multiple ways of doing this, and the simplest one is measuring one you have at home, or going to an IKEA or somewhere like that with a ruler and measuring the drawers there. Don't worry, they give you paper rulers there, so in a way they must be expecting you to do this!

Another, less embarrassing way is using the image provided by the seller to have a general idea of the proportions of the drawer. It is usually better to have a frontal and lateral view of the object.

After deciding on the height, width, and depth of our drawer, we create a cube and input those values in the **Object properties** tab under the **Scale** option:

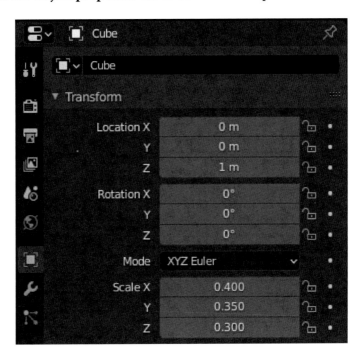

Figure 4.10 – Object properties with the measurements, in meters, of my drawer.
Don't copy them; use your own drawer

> **Tip**
> A really simple way to put an object on the ground is by copying the **Scale Z** value to the **Location Z** value. In this way, you're adding the height of the object to its Z location, in other words, the height of your scene. In CSM, the height is the Y location.

Next, let's create the base of the drawer.

The base of the drawer

Now we have our cube with our measurements. Let's go to Edit Mode by pressing *Tab*. This is what the cube would look like in Edit Mode:

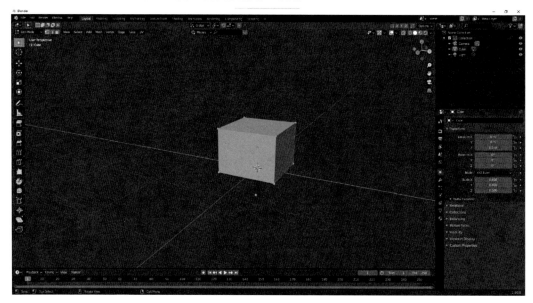

Figure 4.11 – Our cube in Edit Mode

Let's start sculpting the drawer by following these steps:

1. The first thing we need to do is divide the height in two. To do so, just press *Ctrl + R* to activate the edge loop tool:

Figure 4.12 – Edge loop tool icon

2. Press the **left mouse button** (**LMB**) when you see a horizontal yellow line. Now scroll with the mouse until you have two lines. Click the LMB again to confirm it:

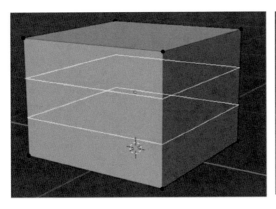

Figure 4.13 – Our cube with a horizontal subdivision

3.   Now, just press *S* to scale and press *Z* to lock it on the *Z* axis. Now, we just need to create a little horizontal space between the top face and the bottom face:

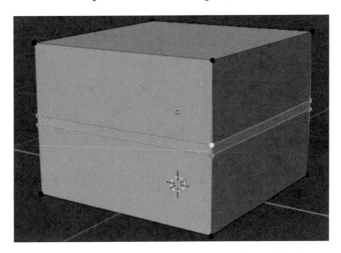

Figure 4.14 – Our cube with space between the two big faces

4.   The next step is pretty easy—just select the two big faces and press *I* to inset those faces, using the inset tool:

Figure 4.15 – Inset tool icon

This is what our cube will look like:

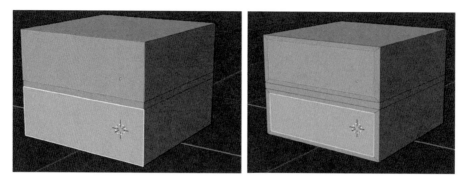

Figure 4.16 – Our cube with the inset faces

5. With those inset faces selected, press *E* to extrude them, and we will extrude them inside the cube:

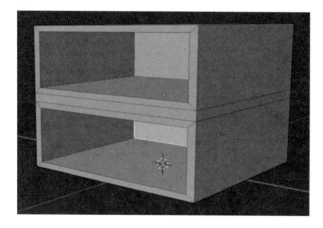

Figure 4.17 – Our extruded face

Now take a deep breath… a really deep breath. We will need to take a lot of steps to make the movable part of the drawer. Don't worry, it is easy, just a lot of unfamiliar steps, so follow along closely.

The movable part of the drawer

I will show you how to make the top drawer. After seeing my process, try to do the same with the bottom drawer.

These are the steps to follow for creating the moving top drawer:

1. We need to select the inside face of our drawer:

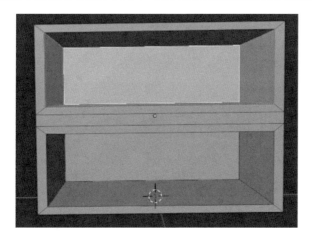

Figure 4.18 – Our drawer with the inside face selected

2. After this, we need to press *Shift + D*. This will make a copy of our selected faces. When you copy an element in Blender, you move it wherever you move your mouse. Press the **right mouse button (RMB)** to erase any movement, such as rotating or moving along the axis, you could have made while copying it. This will give you a copy that is located in the same exact spot as your copied element.

3. Now, press *P* and click on **Selection**. Now you've got your drawer.

4. Press *Tab* so you're in Object Mode, which is the mode with fewer tools. Click on your drawer and press *Tab* again so that you're now in Edit Mode.

    Now we just need to close the front side of our drawer.

5. To do so, just click on both the side edges and press *F* to *fill* that space and create a face between those two edges:

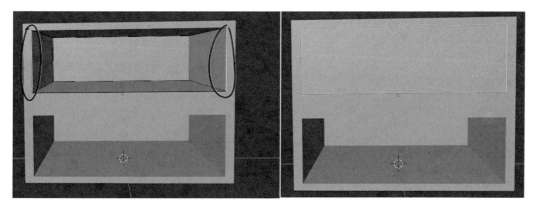

Figure 4.19 – Our closed drawer

6. Press *Tab* to go to Object Mode, and press *G* so we can move our drawer a little bit further. Remember that clicking on the **middle mouse button** (**MMB**) will snap it to the axis:

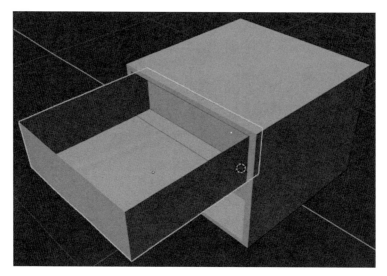

Figure 4.20 – Our drawers with the top drawer extended

Now we need to create the interior of the top drawer, just to add a little bit of thickness to it. It's pretty fast and easy, so don't worry.

First, we need to create a *roof* to our drawer; we will do the same thing we did before.

7. Select the two edges and press *F*.

8. Now press *I* to inset the face we just created.

9. Press *E* and extrude it a little bit inside itself:

Figure 4.21 – Our final result

Now let's create a handle for our drawer.

Details – the handle

Creating the handle for the drawer is quite easy. Follow these steps to create one:

1. Press *Ctrl + R*, and scroll with the mouse wheel until you have two lines that follow along all of the object:

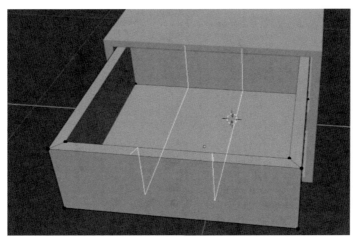

Figure 4.22 – A common "error"

If your two yellow lines turn out like they are in the preceding figure, a common troubleshooting tip is to just press *A* and after that *M*, and then click on **By distance**:

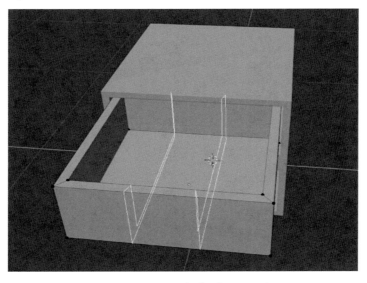

Figure 4.23 – A good edge loop preview

2. Click the LMB to confirm the numbers of loop cuts, and then click it again to confirm the location.

3. Now, redo the same thing for the height. You will have a little square in the middle of the front face—select it and scale it. Remember that if you press the MMB it will snap to one of the axes:

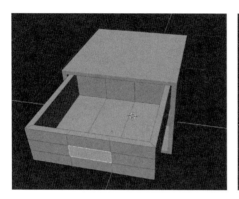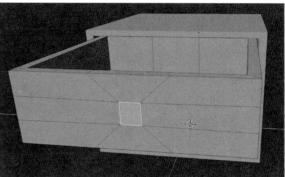

Figure 4.24 – Our little handle in the making

4. Now guess what we will do? We will extrude it and scale it—a lot of times:

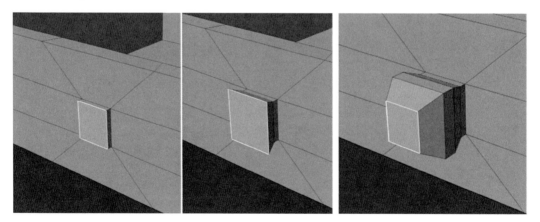

Figure 4.25 – Extrude, scale if it is too big or small, and extrude again, until you're satisfied

We have just finished our handle, meaning that we have finished our drawer. Redo the same thing with the bottom drawer, and we have finished our drawer! This is the finished look of our drawer:

Figure 4.26 – Our beautiful mouse-made drawer

Now we just need to UV unwrap, flattening our drawer in a 2D space, but before that, press *A* and then *Ctrl + A* in Object Mode and select **All transform**. This will apply all the transformations we made. Now, a little important next step is to click on **Object**, in the little top-left menu:

Figure 4.27 – Object menu location

Click on **Origin | Set Origin to geometry**, while all objects are selected.

The last step before UV unwrapping is parenting the movable drawer to the base. Parenting in Blender is like a little duck that sees its mother for the first time, screams "MOMMY!", imprints on her, and does everything its ducky mommy does. So, what do we do?

We first need to select the little duck, which is our movable drawer, and after that, we select our duckling mommy, which is the big box, and we click on *Ctrl + P* (as in controlling parent) and click on **Object (Keep Transform)**. Now, every time you do something to mommy, the little drawer will do the same.

Now we can UV unwrap this. I want you to do this step by yourself; I know you can do it. Use the previous chapter as a reference:

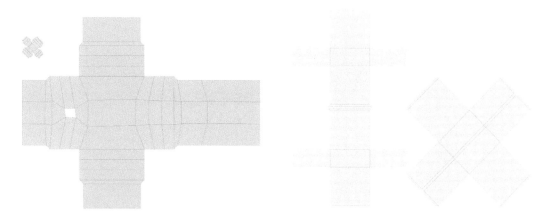

Figure 4.28 – My UV unwrapped object

You can use my UV unwrapped drawer as a reference. As you can see, they have practically the same unwrapping of a cube, just with different proportions. So, if you can do a cube, you can do this—I believe in you.

Now, managing every single texture in your scene is… impossible, frankly speaking. You will need to have at least 30 different images and every time you will need to open, edit, and close it. So, what we do? We will put every texture we need in a single big image.

Packing UV unwrapping

After you've unwrapped everything, we need to put all of those images into a single giant one. I must say, this step is pretty easy, so let's get started:

1.   Go to **Object Mode** and press *A* to select all:

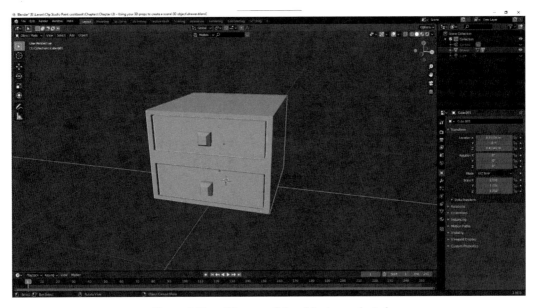

Figure 4.29 – All parts of the object are selected

2.   Go to the UV unwrapping tab.

3.   Press *A* again to select all:

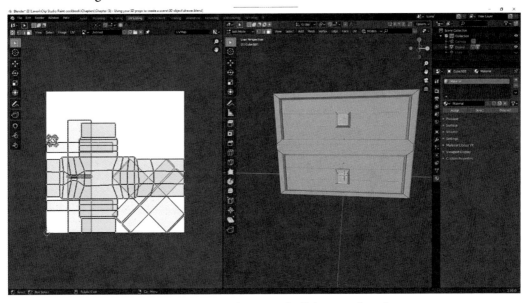

Figure 4.30 – Our drawer with all the UV selected

4. Now just go to **UV | Pack Islands**:

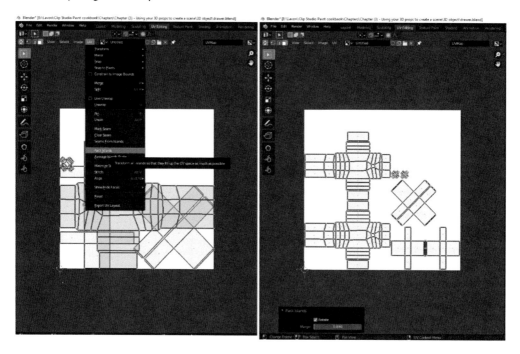

Figure 4.31 – All our UVs are now in the same image and in a clean way

5. Now we do the same exact procedure as in the previous chapter to create a texture. Select everything in the UV image by pressing *A*, and go to **UV | Export UV Layout**.

Remember to save it in the same folder as your 3D object; in this case, it's our Room Realistic folder.

Applying the same texture to different objects

Using a single image texture for different objects is pretty straightforward. First, we open our exported UV layout in CSP. If your UV layout is completely transparent, just add a white fill in a layer below our UV unwrapped image:

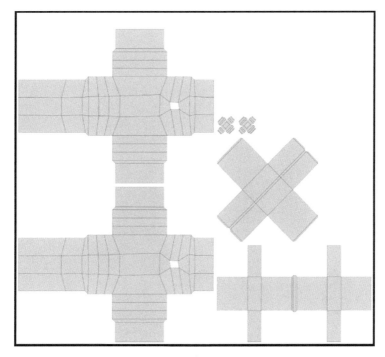

Figure 4.32 – Our drawer UV unwrap

Make a copy of the image before modifying it—this will help us later and then follow these steps:

1. Select outside the gray area; remember to select even in those little white squares. Press *Shift* + **the auto-select tool** (the magic wand) to select multiple things.

2. Click on this little fella, ▨, in the contextual menu, to invert the selection.

3. Now mask the selection by pressing the highlighted icon in the following screenshot:

Figure 4.33 – Layer window

Now you have your UV masked, meaning you can now paint over them easily. At this stage, I would advise you to use a bright color that can be easily selected with the magic wand:

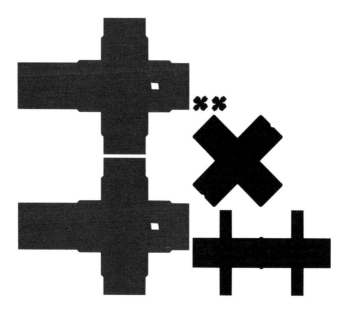

Figure 4.34 – An example of coloring for base mapping

4. Now save it in the same folder as the object, so in the `Realistic Room` folder.

5. Then return to Blender.

6. We need to go into **Object Mode** and we need to select our big base cube drawer. Go to **Material Properties** and click on that little material highlighted by a square in the following figure. The black box above **Preview** in the screenshot is named **Drawer**; yours will be named **Material** or something similar… and guess what you will need to do? Rename it `Drawer`:

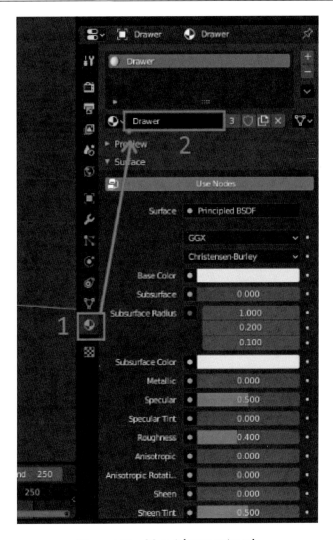

Figure 4.35 – Material properties tab

Now here comes the cool part: you can assign the material you've created. Yes, you've just created and renamed a material… and you didn't even know! For the next step, select the top drawer, and in the **Material** tab, select **Drawer**:

Figure 4.36 – List of materials in the Material tab

Do the same with the bottom drawer. This will link all those objects with the same material. So, if you apply a texture, it will be shown in all those objects. Here, let me show you!

Figure 4.37 – Our object is textured

To apply the texture, refer to the previous chapter. This will be your task for this chapter. Try to apply the texture by yourself; you should have a single image as shown in the following figure, in which every texture is in a single image:

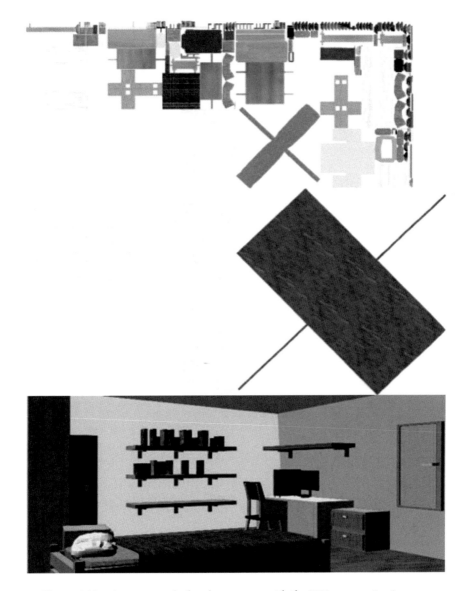

Figure 4.38 – As an example, here's my room with the UV unwrapping image

For the rest of the room, just apply the same method we used for the drawer to everything else. You can do this for objects from the bed to the door. After you have UV unwrapped everything, remember to select all of the objects and click on **UV | Pack Island**. So, with this little section, you now know how to have a single image texture for all of your scenes, meaning that you don't need to have a ton of files—you just need two files, that is, your 3D object and your texture. In the next section, we will take a look at how to edit an object in Modeler.

Editing an object in Modeler

Now, finally, we are at the meaty part of our chapter. Ironically, it will be pretty fast. If you don't remember how to import a material, go back to the previous chapter.

In this section, we will see how to add movement to our 3D props and create different textures for our object.

I will use the drawer as an example, but we would use the same procedure for the whole room:

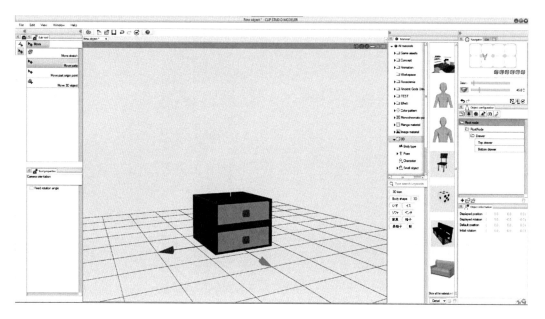

Figure 4.39 – CSM with our drawer

Before "animating" the drawer, we need to set up the materials for further editing. Let's get started:

1. First, we save the file in the `Realistic Room` folder just in case everything crashes. What if your cat chews on the power cord of your PC and you lose everything?

2. After saving the file, go to the **Material** tab in the **Object configuration** window and click on **Merge same material**. This will merge any duplicate materials, giving you only one global material, meaning that when you edit the texture, it will change everything in the scene:

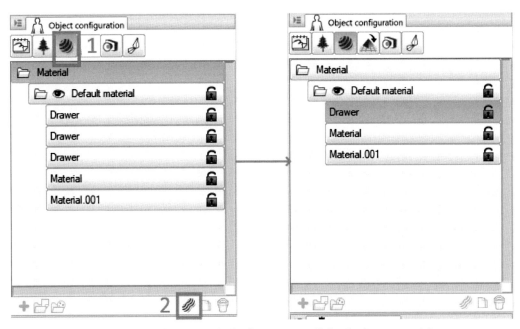

Figure 4.40 – The Material tab after merging all the duplicate materials

3. Now that we have a single texture for everything, duplicate the material by clicking on the highlighted icon in the following figure:

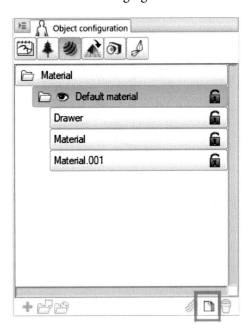

Figure 4.41 – The Material tab

4. Now, double-click on the material you copied and write something such as `Wood texture`, `Metal texture`, or `Cat texture A`, whatever you want.

This is just so you can recognize it. Why is all of this important? Because now every time you need to add a new texture, you copy the default material with all the bright colors that let you color pick them easily, and you can change it easily. You can select only one color in all the canvas using the color gamut selection, and to do so, go to **Selection | Select Color Gamut…**:

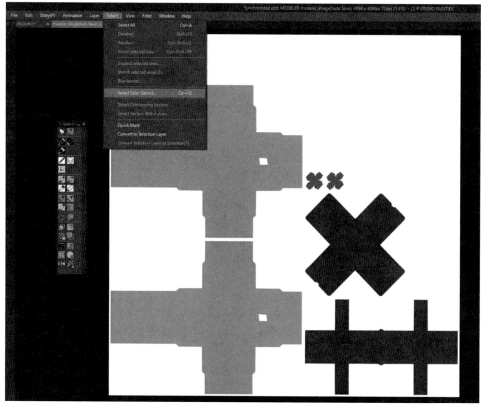

Figure 4.42 – Select Color Gamut location and options

Now, every time you need to change the color or apply a texture, they will be automatically masked:

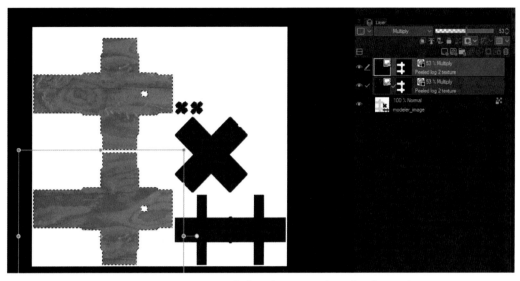

Figure 4.43 – My texture image with the selection made with Select Color Gamut

This allows us to make easy changes to our texture while not destroying the possibility to *Ctrl + Z* (undo) ourselves out of problems. Now, it's time to animate the object.

Animating our object

Strictly speaking, this is not animating in itself, but it's a way of changing the location of some parts of the object, and linking that movement to a slider—so I suppose it is animation, after all!

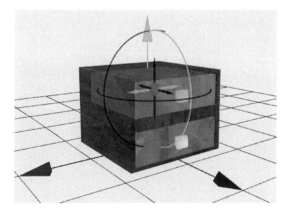

Figure 4.44 – Drawer with the top drawer selected

To animate our drawer, follow these steps:

1. Select what you want to animate; in my case, it's the top drawer.

2. Go to the **Movability** tab in the **Object configuration** window and click on the little plus sign (**Add new**) at the bottom.

3. Double-click on the new **Movability** "layer" and rename it `Top drawer`:

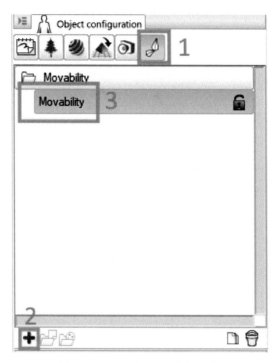

Figure 4.45 – The Movability tab

4. Now go to the **Object information** window, where you will see a little slider. We need to crank it all the way to the right:

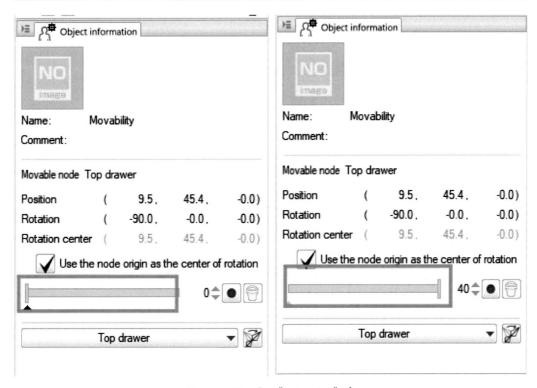

Figure 4.46 – Our "animation" tab

5.   Now we take our top drawer, and we move it until it's completely open:

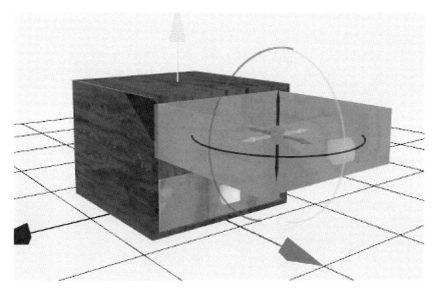

Figure 4.47 – Our top drawer open

6.   Now click on that little black circle on the right of the slider, which will record your movement:

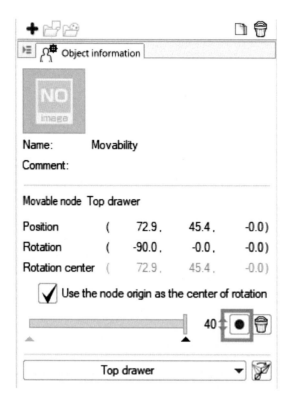

Figure 4.48 – Just press the record button

You now have an animation! Every time you move the slider, the drawer will open. Do the same with the bottom drawer:

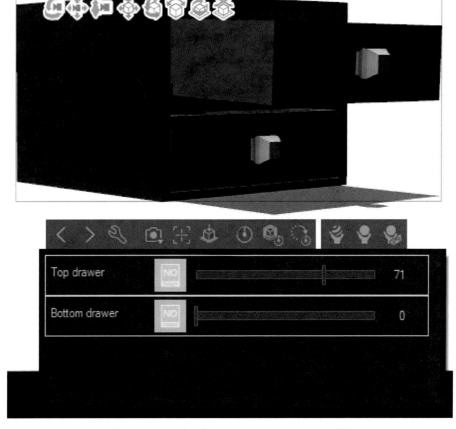

Figure 4.49 – Our drawer with movement in CSP

In this section, we learned how to create a basic prop, a drawer, starting from modeling it, and then after that texturing it, creating movable parts, and then creating a changeable texture in Modeler. The same steps are applied to every other piece of furniture you need to create.

In the next section, I will show you how to set up a little fantasy town street.

Creating a 3D fantasy scene for your work

In this section, we will learn how to make an easily editable fantasy scene, delving a little bit more into the options you can use in Modeler.

Now, there is only one thing remaining to talk about in Modeler—the **Layout** tab.

Before going on, I must warn you that I will not explain to you how to make a fantasy building for two simple reasons:

- There are better tutorials online for this, and they exceed what I can explain to you while keeping it simple and concise in a compact chapter. A good YouTube channel to start off with is the one called *Grant Abbitt* (`https://www.youtube.com/channel/UCZFUrFoqvqlN8seaAeEwjlw`).

- Everything I would show you would be a cube with makeup:

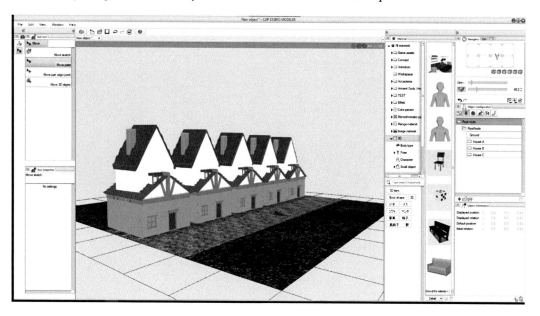

Figure 4.50 – My fantasy 3D scene in CSM

As you can see from the preceding figure, we have a lot of perfectly equal houses stacked on top of one another. With those, we just failed our architecture finals and we need to retake the course. Dammit…

But fortunately, we are not architects. What we need to do is to go to the **Layout** tab in the **Object configuration** window and add a new layout:

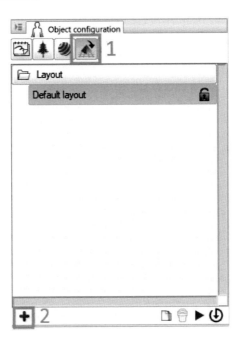

Figure 4.51 – The Layout tab

A layout is like a switch that lets you choose what to see and what to hide.

What we will do is select our newly created layout and go to the **Object information** window. Click on **Set display state of node**, which will open a window where you decide what to hide and what to show:

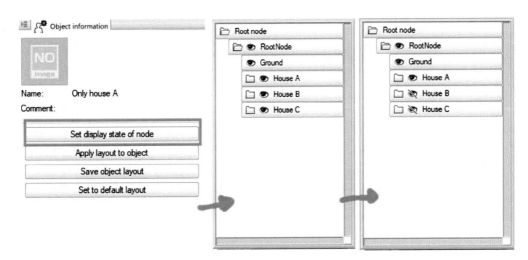

Figure 4.52 – Setting a display state of nodes with my choices

Now click on **Save object layout** to confirm your choices. This is what my final fantasy 3D scene looks like:

Figure 4.53 – My final result

You can use this technique to create different settings inside the same material file. The following figure displays the same fantasy scene but with different building layouts:

Figure 4.54 – An example of different building layouts

If we combine this technique with the technique I've taught for animating an object, you can create an infinite amount of assets:

Figure 4.55 – An example of layout and animation options

As you can see, the (3D) world is yours to be modified to your needs. Don't fear failure… it is not "difficult" per se, it is just something with a lot of steps that you're unfamiliar with. I have used Blender for approximately 4 months, and in those 4 months I have successfully made those houses, and I'm not the brightest tool in the shed, OK? So, don't worry—you can do it, possibly even faster than I can!

Figure 4.56 – A quick sketch in CSP using the 3D objects as a reference

As you can see, a 3D scene is never good by itself, but it lets you speed up your drawing. For example, *Figure 4.50* was done in around half an hour. This gives you a lot of flexibility for creating cities with similar buildings.

With this, we have finished this chapter, and now you know how to use CSM for interior and exterior scenes.

Summary

In this chapter, we have finalized what we can do with CSM and how to use it to improve the speed of our work, using animated objects and different layouts. We used a drawer to explain how to create complex objects that you can then use in Modeler.

Also, you've learned how to use different objects to create a changeable scene in Modeler.

You were introduced to Clip Studio Assets, a service that you can use to download different materials that you can use to complement your scene.

In the next chapter, you will learn how to create from the ground up a 3D character in Blender that you can import in CSM and CSP.

5
Implementing 3D Characters in CSP

In this chapter, we will see how to create a basic human character. We will learn how to make it pose in the next chapter: *Chapter 6, Importing 3D Characters in CSP*. Now, creating a character and making it pose may sound like a daunting task. But don't worry, it's just that you need to follow some steps that you're not familiar with. But I can assure you, you will have all the tools to make a character in Blender.

Being able to create a 3D character to use in **Clip Studio Paint** (**CSP**) is one of the biggest advantages there is to using CSP. This is because it means you can put your recurring character in a scene, and without needing to check for proportions or perspective, you're ready to ink and color them.

But as you will see, it's a lengthy process; it requires 5–6 hours to make a character, but the payoff is huge.

So don't worry, and follow me along in this chapter on how to create a 3D character in Blender.

This chapter will cover the following topics:

- Creating a sculpting base
- Creating the base
- Sculpting the mesh
- Retopoing the mesh
- Adding the details

By the end of this chapter, you will be able to create a 3D character that you can use in CSP.

Technical requirements

For this chapter, you will only need Blender and a turnaround of a character; you can create the turnaround using CSP.

Creating a sculpting base

In this section, we will see how to create a base mesh for our character.

In regards to characters, Modeler works in a similar way to LEGO; you have different pieces with different textures, and CSP turns those objects/textures on and off.

What does this mean for us? It means that we will need to create those parts of the character as different objects. So, we will be creating the following:

- Body
- Head
- Hair
- Clothes
- Details (if necessary)

Another thing I need to clarify is that you can create and import the characters in CSP and pose them even with just a PRO license, but remember that if you want to use **Convert to lines and tones** on the layer or the old **Convert to lines** feature, or if you want to extract the lines from a 3D model, you need the EX version.

Different methods

OK… make a cup of tea and take a deep breath because we will need to take a lot of steps. These are going to be simple steps, but there are a lot of them. You're relaxed? Good… let's go!

As I said in the previous chapter, Modeler can't model from scratch, so we will need to use the old, reliable plan B, that is, Blender.

So, open the software and erase the cube.

There are a lot of ways to create a basic human figure, but usually the main ones are these two, at least from what I know:

- Using metaballs/basic geometry to create a human-shaped thing
- Using vertices to create a stickman, and after that adding a **Skin** modifier and editing it

The first one is really easy; you create a sphere, you move it, you rotate it, you add a cube, and so on, until you have a basic human shape. After that, you sculpt the zone you need. It's tiresome, but it doesn't add anything new to what we have learned so far.

The second one is faster—a lot faster… but it can be a little bit unreliable. The following figure shows a human figure created using the first method, in which I created a basic mannequin using basic geometry, such as spheres and cylinders:

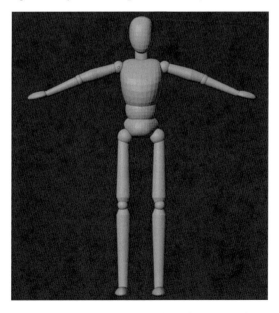

Figure 5.1 – An example of the first method

The following figure shows a human character created using the second method, in which I added a **Skin** modifier to a stickman:

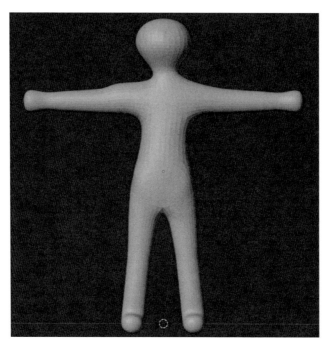

Figure 5.2 – An example of the second method

Just to let you understand the difference, the first type took me approximately 20 minutes, while the second one took me 5 minutes, or maybe less.

Now, you can do what you want. If you're an absolute beginner, I would really advise you to use the first method, because it lets you be really precise with your character proportions. The second method is good if you've got some experience in sculpting.

Because I'm not a good sculptor, I prefer to use an in-between way, in which I use the second method for the body and arms, but for the face, neck, legs, and hands, I prefer the first method.

Before starting, I need to warn you that I activated the *Object: Bool Tool* add-on. This add-on simplifies Boolean operations, such as union and difference, because you can do Boolean operations without using modifiers.

> **Important Note**
>
> Blender is a powerful and customizable tool, and for that, you have small add-ons that you can activate or deactivate.
>
> To do so, you just need to go to **Edit | Preferences | Add-ons**. There, you will find a list of different add-ons. Just check the little box on the left and you can activate/deactivate the add-on. Trust me, this thing is a rabbit hole.

Adding references

Now, I will add the main character of my new Bunnyfable, *Pipotto Fattaposta: The Smith Pendant*, as a reference. For that, I've created a complete character sheet, something that you always need to do with a recurring character:

Figure 5.3 – Pipotto complete character sheet in an A pose

Now just separate the front view and the profile view into individual images. Just remember that the front needs to be in a **T** pose, as you can see in the following figure:

Figure 5.4 – Our character in a frontal T pose and profile

Now, let's open up Blender. If you go to the upper-right corner, you can find a little gizmo:

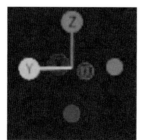

Figure 5.5 – Blender gizmo

You can use this gizmo to rotate the view. If you don't like using the middle mouse button, clicking on one of those little balls lets you have a perfect orthographic view of that axis. So, every time I say red sphere, green sphere, or blue sphere, I am referring to those spheres.

Now, to add a reference image, follow these steps:

1. Click on the red sphere.

2. Press *Shift + A* to add a new object to your scene.

3. Click on **Image | Reference**.

4. Select your image and align it:

Figure 5.6 – My frontal view aligned

5. Click on the green sphere and do the same with your side view of the character:

Figure 5.7 – All the reference sets in place

An extra step you can do is to add transparency to the reference images; this is not necessary but it can help.

6. Go to the **Image Properties** tab, check the **Transparency** box, and reduce the opacity:

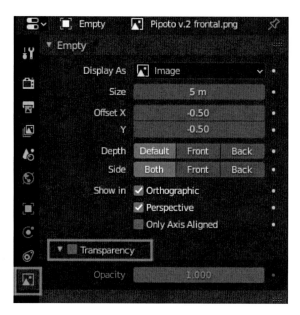

Figure 5.8 – Image Properties tab

Now, before adding the body, we need to block the selection of the reference images, because we don't want them to get selected by mistake:

1. Click on that little funnel icon, **Filter**, in the layer window in the top-right corner.

2. Select the little arrow and choose **Selectable**.

3. Click on the newly shown arrow to lock the selection of those images:

Figure 5.9 – Layer window

With this, we have set up all we need to create our character. In the next section, we will see how to create a basic 3D mesh.

Creating the base

In this section, you will learn the steps to create a basic mesh for your character that you can use to refine your 3D model and create an exportable file.

Body

Now for creating the body:

1. Click *Shift* + *A* to add a new object.

2. Add a plane.

3. Go to **Edit Mode**.

4. Press *A* to select everything.

5. Press *M*, as in merge, and click on **Center**.

This will give you a single vertex. Now it's time to create a base skeleton, which is pretty easy:

1. Press the red sphere. Take this single lonely vertex and put it at the center of the hip bone.

2. Press *G* (move) and *Z* to snap it to the *Z* axis and go where you need to put it.

3. Press **left mouse button** (**LMB**) to confirm. With this you will confirm the vertex position; that little orange point in the image is the vertex:

Figure 5.10 – My character with the little vertex on the hip bone

The rest is easy.

4. Go to **Edit Mode**, click on the vertex, press *E* to extrude, and create a basic skeleton for the body and the arms.

The logic of how to put the vertex at the right height with the right width is pretty easy, and later, when we add a **Skin** modifier, we will be able to increase or decrease the size of the skin wherever we have put a vertex. In the following figure, you can see where generally to put your vertex:

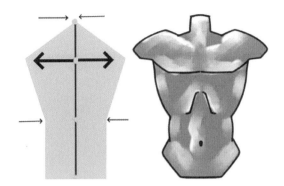

Figure 5.11 – The basic logic to add a vertex

Now we just need to add, with the same thinking, the vertex for the arm:

Figure 5.12 – Vertex basic skeleton

Now we go to that little blue wrench, the **Modifier** section, and we will add three modifiers. We will add them in a precise order, that is, the **Mirror** modifier (remember to check the clipping), the **Skin** modifier, and **Subdivision Surface**. This is because Blender activates those modifiers in order of activation, which means that it will apply the **Skin** modifier after the **Mirror** modifier. This will prevent errors. The following figure displays the character with all the applied modifiers:

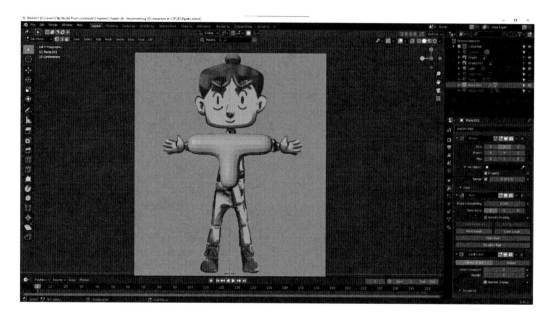

Figure 5.13 – My character with all the modifiers

Now we go to **Edit Mode**, press *Z*, and select **Wireframe** mode, and we will select the vertex where we need to puff or reduce the **Skin** modifier. We select it and press *Ctrl + A*. In cases where you need to create more vertices in an edge to create a smoother transition, just press *Ctrl + R* and *LMB* to confirm. With this, you've just attached a skin to your character:

Figure 5.14 – My finished body

Next, let's move to the hands.

Hands

Now we need to work on the hands. To do so, just create a cube, and remember to press *Shift* + *A* in **Object Mode** and select **Mesh | Cube**.

Now, we just align this cube with our drawing, and remember to press *G* to move and *S* to scale. To do so, you just need to click on the highlighted color picker, which will let you select an object in your scene:

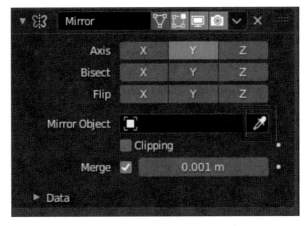

Figure 5.15 – Mirror modifier and eyedropper

Now we add a **Mirror** modifier to our cube-hand-ish object, and we will mirror it, using the body as a center. To do so, just add a normal **Mirror** modifier and click on that little eyedropper shown in the preceding figure, and select the body:

Figure 5.16 – Our hand aligned and mirrored

Now we can go to **Edit Mode** and create a basic hand shape. Now, what is the bare minimum of subdivisions we need to make to create a basic hand shape?

If we consider that a finger needs to be a single face, and you need to create a small face between fingers… that's how many we will have. This totals seven horizontal and three vertical subdivisions:

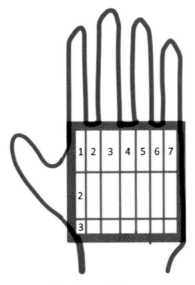

Figure 5.17 – The bare minimum subdivision

To do this, we just need to press *Ctrl + R* and scroll the mouse wheel until we have the desired subdivisions:

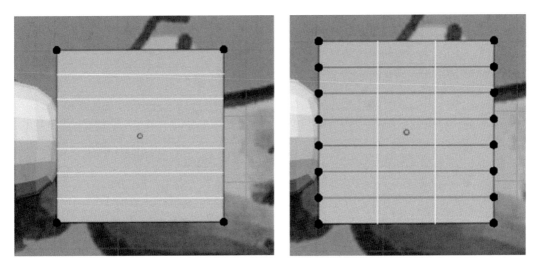

Figure 5.18 – Our cube with the necessary subdivisions

Now, while in **Edit Mode**, go to **Wireframe** mode. To do so, just press *Z* and select **Wireframe** mode, and model all the vertices until we have a basic palm shape. This is what it will look like:

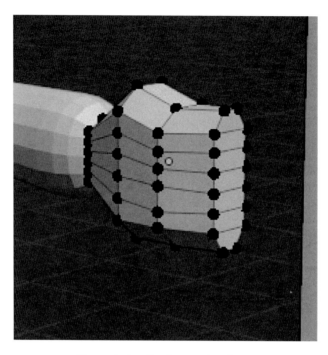

Figure 5.19 – Our basic palm shape

Now, the rest is easy. We select the face we need (remember to press *3* to switch to **Face select**) and we extrude the selected faces to create the fingers. We will need to do it three times for the fingers, because they have three segments, and two times for the thumb, because it only has two segments:

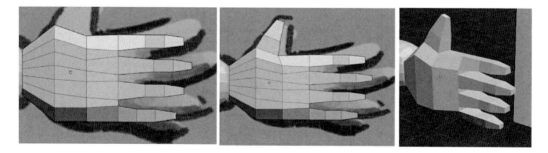

Figure 5.20 – Our finished hand

Remember to scale and rotate the face so you have better proportions. Now we will add a **Subdivision Surface** modifier.

Legs

For the legs, we will do something really easy: we will create spheres for the joint and cylinders for the thighs and the rest of the leg. For the feet, we will use a cube and we will modify it to create a more foot-like shape:

Figure 5.21 – Pipotto with the modeled legs

For creating the legs, I didn't add anything new; I just added a sphere, a cylinder, and a cube and moved them around and edited them as we have seen in this chapter and the previous chapter.

Joining all the pieces together

Before joining all the parts, we will need to apply the **Subdivision Surface** modifier to the body. To do this, follow these steps:

1. Go to **Object Mode**.

2. Select the body.

3. Hover your mouse above the **Subdivision Surface** modifier and press *Ctrl + A*.

Now we need to click on the body, and we will create a **Boolean** modifier. This modifier acts as a union/difference/intersect operation in Illustrator or Affinity Designer. *Figure 5.22* shows the **Boolean** modifier:

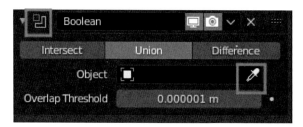

Figure 5.22 – The Boolean modifier

As you can see, the icon in the upper-left corner is red, because we didn't tell Blender the object we want to add/unify or intersect with. To do so, we use that little eyedropper tool. With the eyedropper, select the hand and apply the modifier:

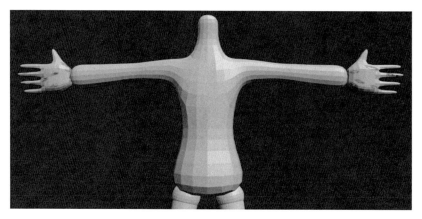

Figure 5.23 – Our body with hands joined to it

Your hands will probably have some artifacts; this is because Blender "duplicated" your hands, meaning that there are two objects in the same space. To remove them, just go to the layer window and hide them by clicking on the eye icon:

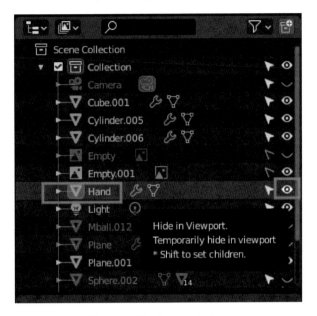

Figure 5.24 – Layer window

This is the "standard" way of doing this, but if you have activated the *Object: Bool Tool* add-on, you just need to do the following:

1. Select all the objects you need to join.

2. Go to **Object** in the menu.

3. Click on **Bool Tool**.

4. Click on **Union**:

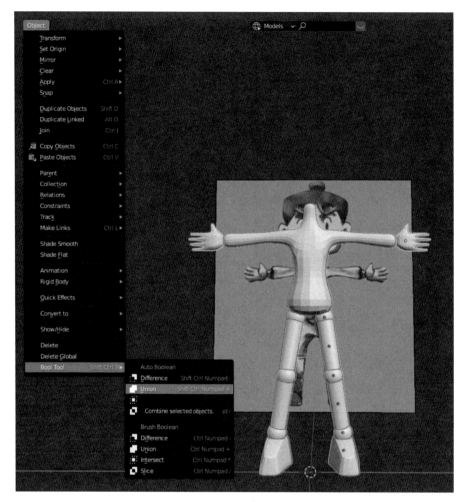

Figure 5.25 – Bool Tool | Union location

Now all our single objects have joined together to become one headless body.

> **Important Note**
>
> The main difference between **Bool Tool** and the **Boolean** modifier is that with the add-on, if you have, as an example, two spheres that intersect with each other, that intersection will remain. But with the **Boolean** modifier, the two spheres will not have intersecting geometry. This distinction is a little bit useless for our topic, but is something that you need to know as general knowledge, if you want to do something else in 3D.

Head

The head will be pretty simple; you just need to add a sphere and position it where the head should be. Remember to check with the frontal and profile view to see whether you're centering the head properly:

Figure 5.26 – My final base body

OK, finished with this head section… if only all the chapters were so simple…

Now, with this, you learned all the steps necessary for creating a base 3D mesh for your characters. Now the next step is adding details.

Sculpting the mesh

In this section, we will learn how to add details to our mannequin using the Blender sculpting tool.

We will first sculpt the face and then we will see why going for full extra details is not always a good idea. After this, we will move toward the hair. Remember that hairs need to be a single object for importing correctly in Modeler. If you want to go a little bit deeper regarding how to create hairs, I recommend you go to a YouTube channel named *Yansculpt* and check out his *Easiest Way To Create Hair in Blender - 5 Minute Tutorial* video (`https://www.youtube.com/watch?v=BqWYgrXw7Jk`). At the end of the section, we will see how to create clothes for our character.

Face

Now, before starting, take that front view image and put it in front of the mesh, and reduce the opacity to approximately `0.1`. Remember to lock it from selection again. Chop chop! We don't have all day.

In this way, you can see where the main features are, while still being able to see the object:

Figure 5.27 – Our model with a transparent front view

Now you will ask yourself: "Why didn't we modify the head?" We didn't modify the sphere to adapt it to the face because we will sculpt it… it's pretty easy to do. Select the sphere of the head and go to **Sculpting**:

Figure 5.28 – Where to find the sculpting mode

Another way to do this is by pressing *Ctrl/Cmd + Tab* and clicking on **Sculpt Mode**. If you can only see **Object Mode** while pressing *Ctrl + Tab*, it is because you didn't select the sphere.

Now the rest is pretty easy but we need to make sure of a couple of things. The first and most essential is that the **Mirror** and **Dyntopo** (*dynamic topology*) options are turned on. Sometimes, when you press *Ctrl + Z*, this option turns off—so keep that in mind and look at the **Dyntopo** option if something doesn't work right. Those options are located near the gizmo I've shown you:

Figure 5.29 – Mirror and Dyntopo options

I've selected **Y** as the mirror axis, because my character is mirrored on the *Y* axis. So, just change between *X* or *Y* and based on that, the active axis is highlighted in blue.

If you click on **Dyntopo**, you can see the options within it. Now, the first thing we need to do is change **Detailing**. You need to change it from **Relative Detail**, a mode in which the resolution of the brush stroke is based on how much you zoom in, to **Constant Detail**, in which the resolution of the brush stroke is constant. The **Resolution** option is the "definition" of your brush stroke. The higher it is, the more defined it will be. As you can see in *Figure 5.30*, the right brushstroke has a lot more definition than the left one:

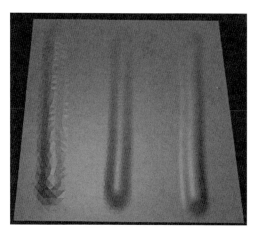

Figure 5.30 – Our brushstroke with a resolution set at 15,30,60

You can go really high on the resolution… but do you really want to do that? Absolutely not. The higher you go, the more RAM your PC will need to keep track of all the details. So, if you have a potato PC, there is a danger it may become this:

Figure 5.31 – A badly baked potato—unfortunately, my lunch. We all make mistakes…

I hope I've been pretty clear on why you shouldn't put too high a number on **Resolution**. For what we need to do, 15 is plenty:

Figure 5.32 – Mirror and Dyntopo changed options

Now, there are some basic shortcuts we need to keep in mind:

- While pressing *Shift*, you smooth the surface of the object.

- While pressing *Ctrl*, you remove part of the object.

- *F* is the shortcut of the brush size.

- *Shift + F* is for changing the strength of the brush.

These are the brushes that we will use:

- **Elastic Deform**: This brush is for making small changes without adding or removing things.

- **Draw**: The basic drawing brush. It's more or less like sculpting with a g-pen brush.

- **Clay Strips**: A square brush… easy.

Now we will use Elastic Deform to change the basic form of that sphere so that it looks similar to the reference picture:

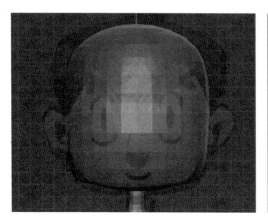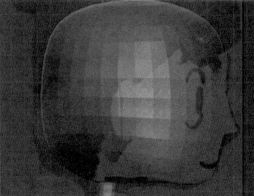

Figure 5.33 – Our face with the front and profile aligned

Now, here, you can take Clay Strips or the Draw brush; this part is based on your preferences and what you like from your brush.

We will sculpt the nose and the ears. We don't need to make Michelangelo envious, but you could say that even being able to 3D sculpt would make him envious… but, getting back on track. We just need a basic shape—nothing too fancy. This is what the sculpted face looks like:

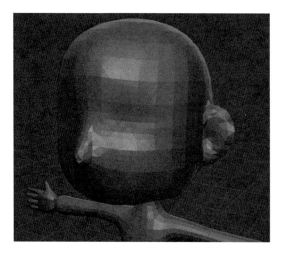

Figure 5.34 – The basic sculpted head shape

I used the Draw brush and Elastic Deform to make all of this, so you don't need anything fancy and don't worry if you don't succeed the first time. This is my third attempt—sometimes I either forget to mirror, or Dyntopo is deactivated. So don't worry, take all the time you need. Now, for the next step, we will be a little bit of a hairstylist, because we will put some hairs on that head.

Hair

The hair is pretty straightforward; my character practically has box-shaped hair. So, what did I do?

Figure 5.35 – Pipotto head details

I created a box and aligned it with my character's head. After aligning it, I went to **Edit Mode** and I started to **Move** (*G*), **Rotate** (*R*), and **Extrude** (*E*) until I was satisfied with the results. In *Figure 5.36*, you can see my process:

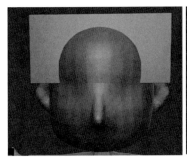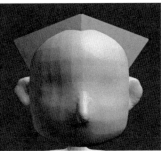

Figure 5.36 – My process for the hair. In the last step, I've applied a subdivision surface

For the little ball on the back of the head, I just added a sphere and joined it with a **Boolean** modifier to the rest of the hair, and this is what it looks like:

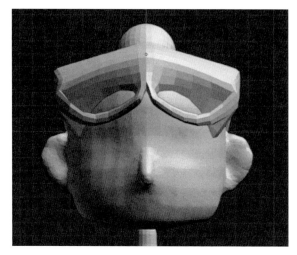

Figure 5.37 – My final hair

Now that we have finished our work as a hairstylist, we need to put some clothes on our character—we can't let him walk naked, can we?

Clothing

Now, the clothing is pretty easy. We have a shirt, trousers, and a cape:

Figure 5.38 – Pipotto character sheet

For creating a shirt and trousers, I need to introduce to you a new friend. The **Shrinkwrap** modifier is a modifier that will glue whatever you want to the surface of an object. This is what the modifier looks like:

Figure 5.39 – Shrinkwrap modifier

We just need to create a plane and put it near the body, by pressing *Shift + A* and selecting **Mesh | Plane**. Now we just need to click on that little eyedropper and select our body, and voilà! The plane I just created will stick to the body:

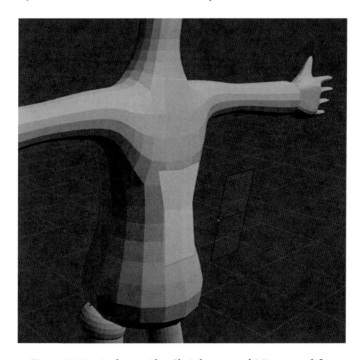

Figure 5.40 – A plane with a Shrinkwrap and Mirror modifier

Now we just need to change some settings on the **Shrinkwrap** modifier and we can start creating the shirt. Change **Snap Mode** from **On Surface** to **Outside Surface** and change **Offset** from 0 to 0.01:

Figure 5.41 – Shrinkwrap modifier with new settings

We can finally start creating our shirt, but there is a method to extruding the faces and creating the shirt. We will need to follow the body's "muscle lines":

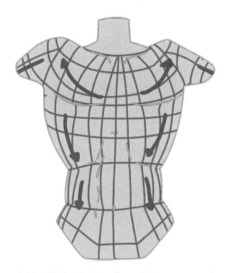

Figure 5.42 – "Muscle lines" used for creating the shirt

But before doing this, I would recommend putting the color of the object on **Random**. This means that every new object will have a random color, letting you see what you're doing with fewer problems.

To do this, click on that little arrow on the menu in the top-right corner and click on **Random**. If you want to change it back, just click on **Object**:

Figure 5.43 – Shading options

This will add random color to our objects, giving us a cleaner environment:

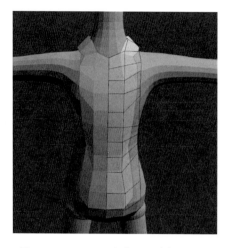

Figure 5.44 – Muscle lines of the torso

Now we continue with this method until we have made the whole of the torso.

A little exercise for you: try to mirror the shirt on the back using the body as a point of symmetry.

To make the sleeves, just select the edges near the shoulder and extrude them all the way down to the wrist. Apply the **Mirror** modifier, and you've finished with the shirt:

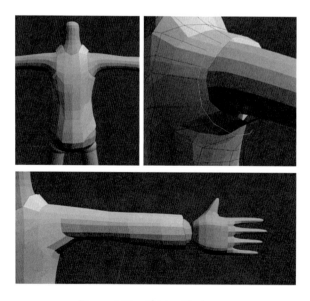

Figure 5.45 – Shirt with sleeves

Now repeat the same thing for the trousers and this is how it should look:

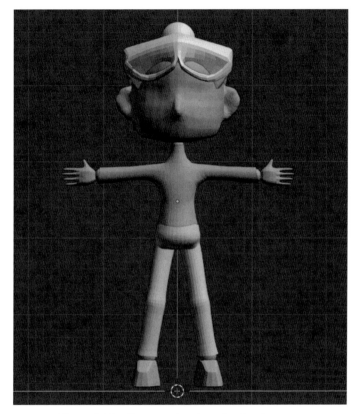

Figure 5.46 – Our complete base for the character

But you could say that those are not remotely close to the clothing I designed for the character; for example, I didn't even make the cape because we don't have a way to animate the cape in CSP, so it's better to just draw it. And you're right, because I need to modify the clothes a little bit after applying the **Shrinkwrap** modifier. But don't do it yet, because what we just did is practically **retopoing** the mesh. And this brings us to the next section.

Retopoing the mesh

Now, before starting, I need to specify this. This is not a retopo tutorial for games or animation, but for importing 3D character models in Modeler. I'm not a retopo expert—at best, I'm a retopo amateur. I only know what works for importing into Modeler. Nothing more, nothing less.

What do we mean by **retopoing the mesh**? This action is creating a cleaner arrangement for the faces so it's easier to animate, move, and UV unwrap the object. We do this because when we do all the operations that I've told you about in this chapter, the geometry of our object can start losing any kind of sense. As you can see in *Figure 5.47*, the shirt is a lot cleaner than the body we sculpted:

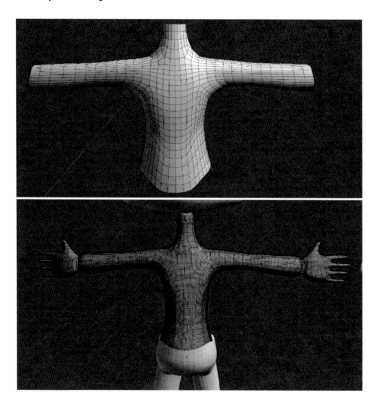

Figure 5.47 – Above there is the shirt, below there is the body we have created

As you can see in the figure, it's even impossible to see the geometry of the base body. So, what can we do? We can create a plane, snap it to the body, and redo the body—but we need to be careful regarding the muscle lines and geometry. Sounds difficult, eh? Well, it would be if it wasn't for the fact that you just did that for the shirt. So, I know for sure that you can do it.

Just redo the same thing, or you can always *copy* and *paste* the shirt and continue from there. I don't judge… just remember to reduce the **Offset** value to a number below the 1 for the shirt.

Retopoing hands

This is how I retopo hands:

1. I start with the thumb, making a little ring around it:

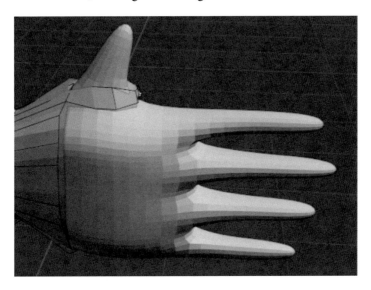

Figure 5.48 – The hand with a thumb ring

2. After this, I follow the palm of the hand without worrying about the other fingers:

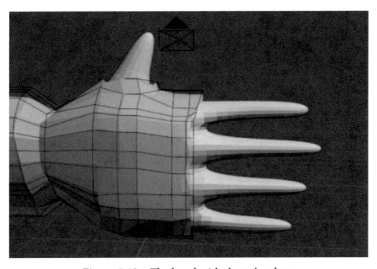

Figure 5.49 – The hand with the palm done

3. Then I create the same ring I did for the thumb for the other fingers:

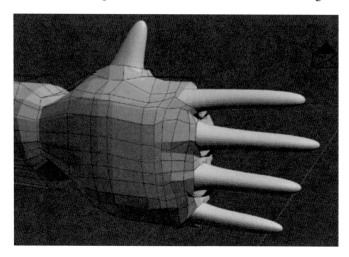

Figure 5.50 – The hand with all the finger rings done

4. Now we will extrude the fingers while keeping the anatomy of the phalanges in mind:

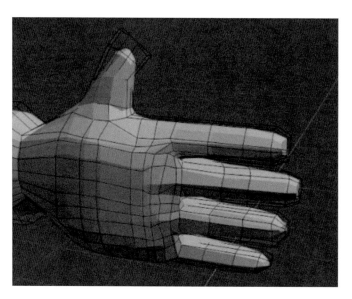

Figure 5.51 – The hand complete

And it's done! Let see how we can retopo the feet in the next section.

Retopoing feet

The feet are pretty easy because we will not model the toes, but we will model them as a base for the shoes, because Modeler doesn't even let you animate toes. So, for retopologing the feet, we just need to cover them with a basic topology. We use the same steps for the hands, but without the fingers:

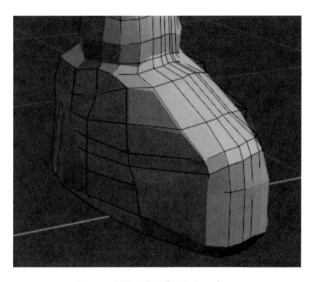

Figure 5.52 – Our basic topology

Let's move on to the head.

Retopoing the head

The head is a little bit different from a normal retopology, because Modeler creates expressions by applying different textures, plus the head in Modeler is a separate object, and it is not attached to the body. So, we don't need to think about the eyelids or whether the face is connected in the right way to the body.

More or less, the muscle lines are the ones shown in the next figure:

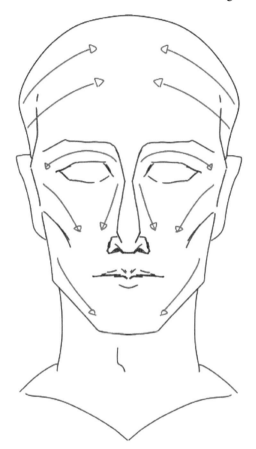

Figure 5.53 – Face muscle lines

Now we will just do what we did previously with the hands and feet:

1. Create a plane.

2. Align the plane where we want to start.

3. Add a **Mirror** modifier with the face as a point of symmetry.

4. Add a **Shrinkwrap** modifier.

5. Start to extrude, move, and rotate the edges until you cover all the face:

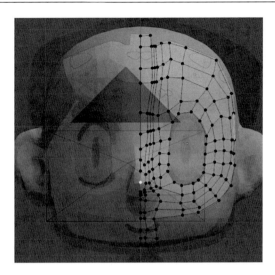

Figure 5.54 – An example of the retopo of the face following the "muscle lines" of the head

Once you retopo the head, the entire character will look something like this:

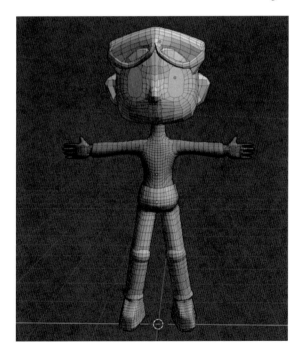

Figure 5.55 – Our finished retopo

With this, we have completed our character. Now, we just need to fine-tune our character.

Adding the details

Adding the details is pretty easy: we just need to apply the modifiers and fine-tune the geometry.

For applying all the modifiers, you need to do it in this order:

- **Shrinkwrap**

- **Subdivision Surface** (if you used it)

- The **Mirror** modifier is the last one we will apply, after editing all the small details, such as changing the shirt neck and sleeves size and the geometry of the shoes.

For adding some details, you just need to select the vertices and move them or resize them:

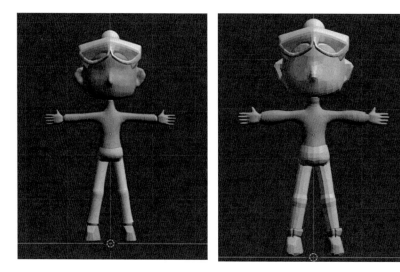

Figure 5.56 – The character after some small adjustments

Summary

In this chapter, you learned how to apply a reference to your Blender scene and two different methods for how to create a basic mesh to use for your character. In addition to this, you learned how to use the basic sculpting tools of Blender to refine your character model and a basic retopo introduction, using the "body lines."

Plus, I've introduced you to Boolean operations and how not to make a baked potato.

In the next chapter, we will see how to add textures and import your character to Clip Studio Modeler, and import it from Modeler to CSP.

6
Importing 3D Characters in CSP

In the previous chapter, I showed you how to create a character from scratch. In this chapter, I will show you how to import that character into **Clip Studio Paint** (**CSP**), starting with the nightmare-inducing UV unwrapping. After this, I will show you how to create a moveable character using a base skeleton; fortunately for you, a lot of the hard stuff is dealt with by Blender automatically. Later in the chapter, we will learn how to import this moveable character into **Clip Studio Modeler** (**CSM**), with the possibility of adding various facial expressions and poses. As a bonus, I will throw in a way to easily close multiple internet tabs.

This chapter will cover the following topics:

- Preparing the mesh for importing in Modeler
- Importing the character in Modeler

By the end of the chapter, you will have a finished textured and editable character in your materials.

Preparing the mesh to be imported in Modeler

Now we need to prepare this glorified potato of a character to be imported into Modeler. I'm the creator so I can call him a glorified potato… I know what will happen to the character when I'm done. So, I know for sure he is a glorified potato.

In this section, we will create all the cuts needed for the unwrapping of the entire model and we will rig it. Rigging is a fancy way to say that we will put digital bones in our model.

UV unwrapping

Now, take a deep breath because this will take a little while. The first thing I need to clarify is that you need to create a single image texture for every object. The process is different from the room or the fantasy landscape we created in *Chapter 4, Using Your 3D Props to Create a Scene*, where we created a single image texture for everything.

Here are some points to note before we get started. For body texturing, we want to avoid making a lot of cuts, because in organic texturing you could see a little deformation in the colors or texture everywhere you cut. So, we need to make the least amount of cuts possible and place them in positions that are difficult to see.

Now, let's start with the easiest one to unwrap, that is, the head. Why do I say it is the easiest? Because on the head, the cuts are easy to make. We only need to put one long vertical cut that goes from the base of the hairline to the base of the neck. You can refer to the following figure:

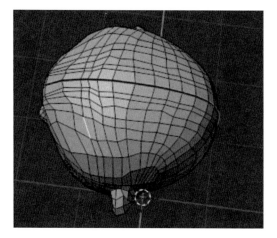 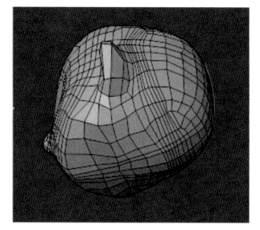

Figure 6.1 – Head with the cuts; practically speaking you've created
Aang from Avatar: The Last Airbender

As you can see, it's pretty easy. Now, this will be your result:

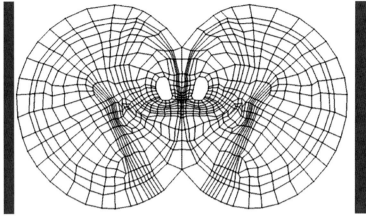

Figure 6.2 – Your UV unwrapped head

I swear it will always be creepy no matter how many times I see it. It stares into your soul…

Now save the UV layout; remember to press *A* to select all, before going to **UV | Export UV layout**.

Now, for the body, we will start with the easy part, the shoes, by creating a cut to separate the shoes from the rest of the body. We will cut (with the same precision as a drunken surgeon) the space that connects the shoes to the rest of the body. Refer to the following figure:

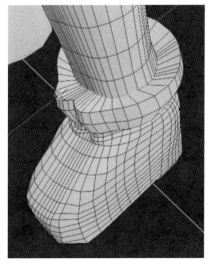

Figure 6.3 – Shoe separated from the leg

We will cut the rest of the shoe with the same cut of a real-life shoe; in my case, this is a medieval leather one:

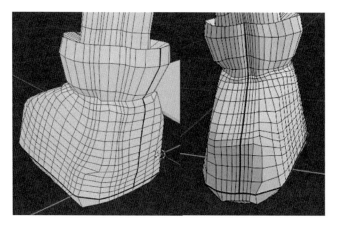

Figure 6.4 – My shoe with all the cuts

Now let's move on to the rest of the body. We will do this in the same way as we did the head, but in this case, we need to separate the hands from the rest of the body. So, we will make a cut right up until the height of the wrist. After this, we need to cut the hand in half while keeping part of the edge near the fingertip uncut. It's a little bit difficult to explain without showing you, so I hope the following figure helps you to understand:

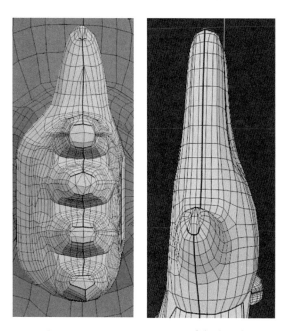

Figure 6.5 – UV unwrapping of the hand

The process for the rest of the body is pretty easy. Simply go through the following steps:

1. Cut the underside of the arm as shown in the following figure:

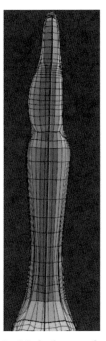

Figure 6.6 – Marked seams for the arm

2. Follow the cut made on the arm and cut until you arrive at the start of the leg:

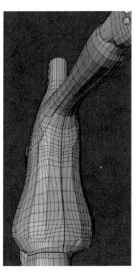

Figure 6.7 – Marked seams for the torso

3.   Now make a cut on the edge loop that separates the hip from the leg:

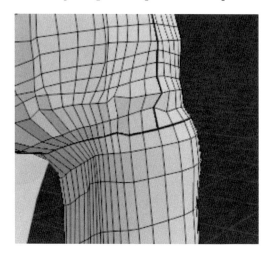

Figure 6.8 – Marked seams for the hip

4.   Now make a cut on the inside of the leg:

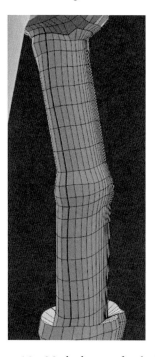

Figure 6.9 – Marked seams for the leg

5. If you used a Mirror modifier for this operation, this is the time to apply it:

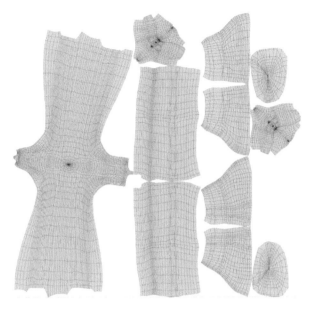

Figure 6.10 – The final UV unwrapped body: red is the shoes, UV blue is the skin

Now it's time for the clothing. We will use the same method that we used for the shoes; just follow the sewing line of a real piece of clothing and you will be fine:

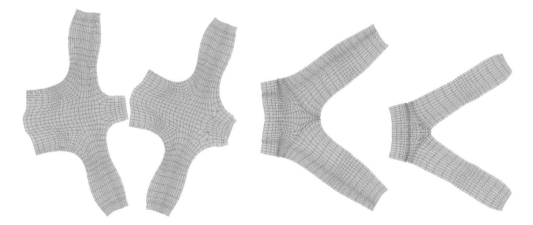

Figure 6.11 – UV unwrapped shirt and trousers

Now, before doing the hair, take a deep breath, because it is one of those UV unwrapping processes for which there isn't a correct way of doing it, but you can clearly see if you did something wrong. The UV map in *Figure 6.11* was my sixth attempt at unwrapping. You will need to do some experimentation.

Here, I've made a cut on the little pom-pom on the head and made some cuts that would keep the strands of hair:

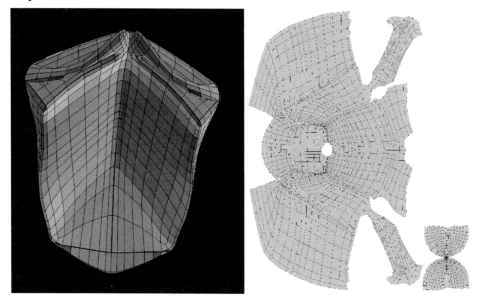

Figure 6.12 – UV unwrap of the hair

Now that we have created every cut we need and created all the UV unwrapping, we need to put a skeleton in the body of our character, the rig, and using it, we can animate the model.

Rigging the character

Now, we have come to the last part of this 3D Blender adventure. After this, we will work only in CSM and CSP.

Rigging, in layman's terms, is digitally giving our object a skeleton and using that skeleton to move a bunch of vertices.

Fortunately, there is an add-on in Blender that creates that for us automatically, so your brain doesn't transform itself into a baked potato trying to do it. The add-on is called *Rigify*, so go ahead and activate it. After activating it, follow these steps:

1. Press *Shift + A* and you will find a section called **Armature**. Go in there and click on **Human (Meta-Rig)**:

Figure 6.13 – Armature menu

This will create this really cute skeleton, with what looks like a set of nipples:

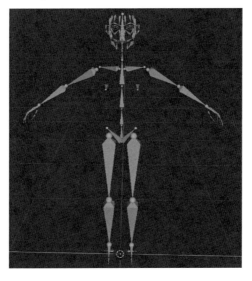

Figure 6.14 – Our basic skeleton

First things first—we need to scale the skeleton to be the same size as our character.

2. Go to **Object Mode** and select the skeleton, and press *S* to scale it. Use the clavicle as a reference:

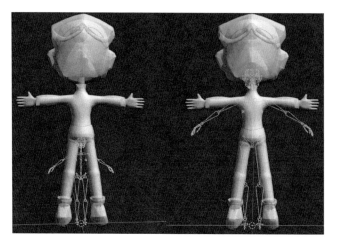

Figure 6.15 – The skeleton scaled to the height of the model

3. Now we need to do some cleanup. We need to remove all the bones I've selected in the next figure. To do so, you just need to go to **Edit Mode** and select all the bones you want to delete:

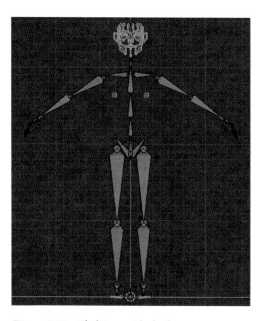

Figure 6.16 – Skeleton with the bones to remove

4. Behind the facial expression bones there is a big bone; remove that one, too:

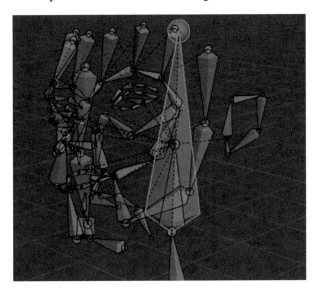

Figure 6.17 – The bone inside the head to remove

This is what our final skeleton will look like:

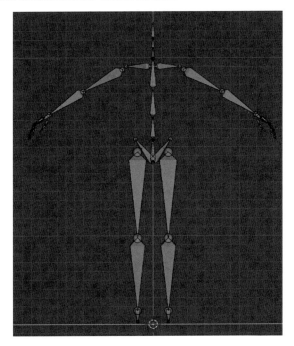

Figure 6.18 – Our final skeleton

5. Now, while staying in Edit Mode, we need to align all the bones to our character. The commands are the same as always: **Move** (*G*) and **Rotate** (*R*). The bones don't scale.

    Before starting, it's best that you activate the mirror to do the same changes on both sides.

    To do so, you just need to click on **Active Tool Settings**. Go under **Options** and click on **X-Axis Mirror**:

Figure 6.19 – Active Tool Settings location

Now we can align without worrying about having to do the same thing twice:

Figure 6.20 – The character with all the bones aligned

There are a few extra steps here before putting everything together in one happy family. We need to separate the **head bone** (as it is known in Blender) from the rest of the skeleton. It's like when we separated the drawer in *Chapter 4, Using Your 3D Props to Create a Scene.*

6.   Go to **Edit Mode,** and after selecting the skeleton, select the head bone, or in other terms, the skull, and then press *P* and click on **Separate bone** to separate the head bone from the rest.

Now we need to do something really simple—we need to parent the skeleton to our character; in other words, if we move the rig, we will move our character.

I swear I don't know who made Rigify, but I want to marry them and shower them with all the love they deserve, and you will understand why when you go through the following steps:

1.   Select everything you need, just by clicking and dragging the mouse over the character for the body:

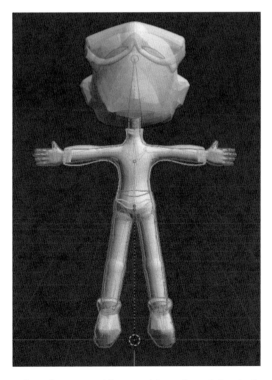

Figure 6.21 – Our character with everything selected for rigging the bones

2. Now press *Ctrl + P* and select **With Automatic Weights**:

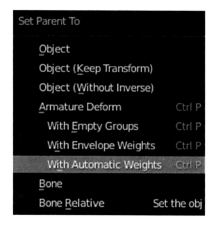

Figure 6.22 – Parenting option

3. Do the same for the head.

    And you are done!

Now you have a fully rigged character without having to create a rig or paint the weights of those bones. Trust me, if I needed to explain that, it would take at least another chapter. So, let's thank the Blender and Rigify creators!

With this we have a fully movable character; now we just need to add it to CSP via CSM.

Importing the character in to Modeler

This is where the magic happens. In this section, we will export our rigged model to Modeler, and we will add the base textures to our character and various expressions that will bring our character to life.

Exporting the object

Now, this is the easy part. You need to export these objects (body, clothing, face, hair) in FBX. Every time you do this, you'll need to export the skeleton with the rest of the object. It will be broken down as follows:

- Body and clothing in a single export
- Hair
- Head

Just remember that when you export in FBX, you need to go to **File** and then **Export**, and in the menu on the right, you need to remember to check the **Selected Objects** option. This will export only what you've selected. To know what you need to select, refer to the previous list. In the following figure, you can see the **Export** options, remember to check **Selected Objects**:

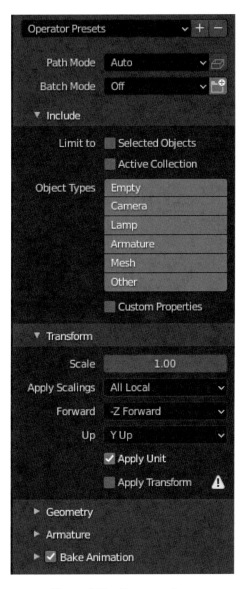

Figure 6.23 – Export options

Remember to put all the exported objects and the textures in the same folder.

Importing the character in Modeler

Now comes the simple part—importing it all in Modeler. Let's open it up and select **Create 3D character**:

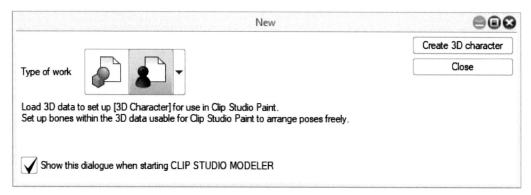

Figure 6.24 – Modeler startup screen

Now, all the dirty work will be done in the **Character configuration** and **Character information** tabs on the right-hand side. This is highlighted in the following figure; a more detailed version is shown in *Figure 6.26*:

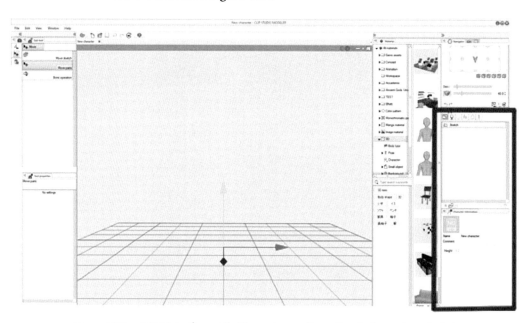

Figure 6.25 – CSM interface with Character configuration/information circled

Before moving on, let's be on the same page regarding the icons. In the **Character configuration** tab, we have five icons, and clicking on them will let you toggle between the folders in which you will put all the objects we have created:

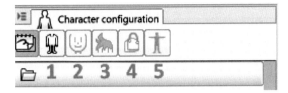

Figure 6.26 – Character configuration tab

The numbers in the preceding screenshot correspond to the following tabs:

1. **Body tab**
2. **Face tab**
3. **Hair tab**
4. **Details tab**
5. **Pose tab**

Now, go to the first tab, the **Body** tab, and import the body of our character here:

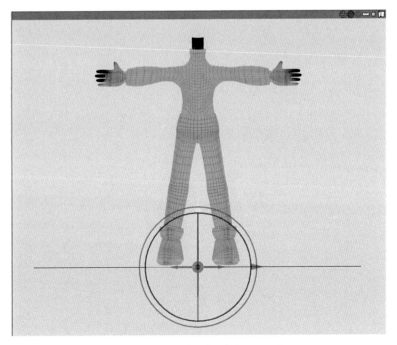

Figure 6.27 – Our body imported

Your character will probably be a giant that will take up all the space in your grid. To change this, you need to go to **Character information**, open your **Body** folder, and click on **Physics settings**. In the **Character information** tab, there is a **Height** option, with the measurement in centimeters:

Figure 6.28 – Character height settings

My Pipotto is a whopping 337 cm in height! He could be the perfect basketball player; if I set it up at 100 cm, he would be small… if I wanted to punish him, I could put the cookie jar on a higher shelf.

Now you need to click on the main body folder, the one with the eye on the left. In the **Character information** tab, you will find an icon with a bone. You need to pick that bone; this will start the procedure to translate your skeleton into something that Modeler can read, that is, **Perform Standard Bone Mapping**:

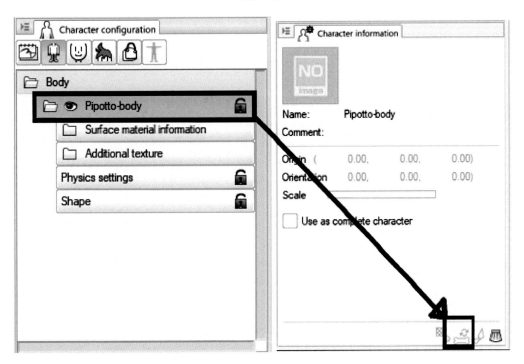

Figure 6.29 – Standard bone mapping location

Before starting, Modeler will pop up this warning:

Figure 6.30 – Modeler bone warning

In simple terms, it means that it will apply all the changes you've made to rotation, height, and so on to the model permanently. Don't worry, you can press **OK** without too many worries:

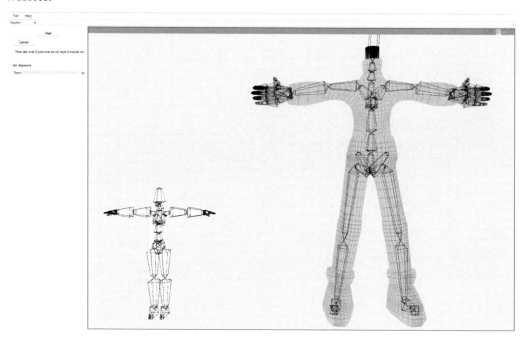

Figure 6.31 – Modeler arm alignment window

The first step that we need to do is align the arms of the little fella in the left corner to the arms of our bigger character. This can be done by using the slider called **Arm alignment**, which can be found in the top corner.

In this case, both characters are doing a fine T pose, so we can click **Next**:

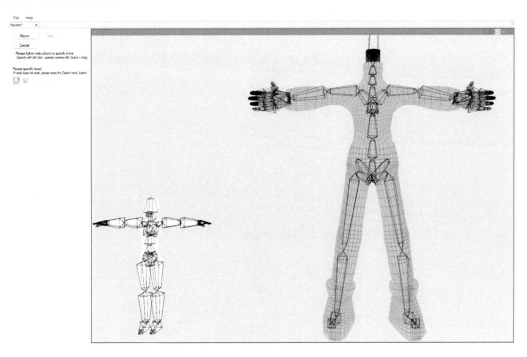

Figure 6.32 – Modeler bone selection

Now we can start with mapping our bones to the default CSP bones:

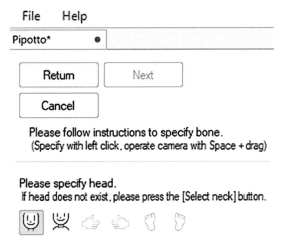

Figure 6.33 – Modeler bone selection detail

Now, this is where the magic happens. The first thing we need to do is click on the second icon, the one with the red neck area, because we don't have a head. This will start the procedure of linking the bones you created in Blender with the standard ones used in CSP. We will start with the neck bones, and finish with the feet ones. This is an automatic process, so after selecting the bones you need, you just need to click **Next** and it will go to the next step:

1. Now we need to select the neck bone:

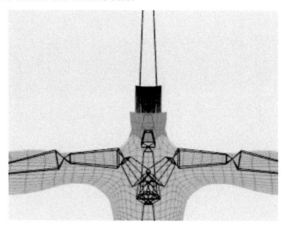

Figure 6.34 – Modeler neck bone

2. Now select the right arm. If you're unsure about the right/left orientation, look at the little character in the bottom corner. Seeing it lets us know that the right and left are inverted from our perspective, because they're based on the perspective of our character:

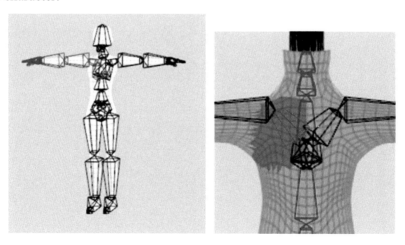

Figure 6.35 – CSM right orientation and right arm bone

3. Now we need to select the left arm:

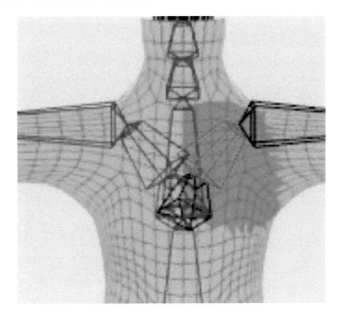

Figure 6.36 – Left arm bone

4. Now we need to select the right leg:

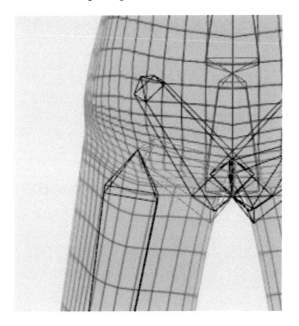

Figure 6.37 – Right leg bone

5. Now the left leg:

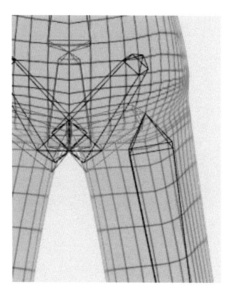

Figure 6.38 – Left leg bone

6. Now click on **Next**.

This will activate a test window in which you can test the bones you just created with your character. Just click on the dark-gray icons of people doing… I don't know. I am accepting suggestions on what they are doing!

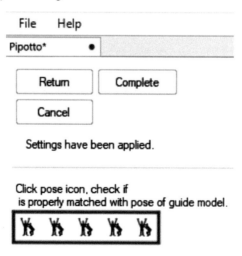

Figure 6.39 – Pose tester

You need to click on one of the poses and see whether the bones work right.

The green object is where the part should be. If there is some small difference, there are no problems; the most important thing is that the general pose is there and working:

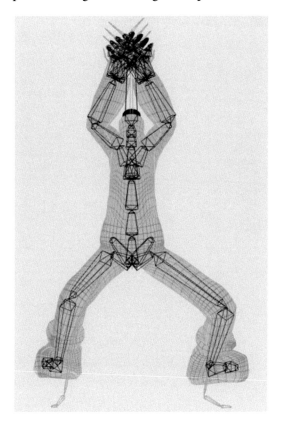

Figure 6.40 – Bone testing in "DO YOU EVEN POSE?" style

Now we just need to click on **Complete** and we are done.

Important note

If the bones shown in Modeler are not aligned to your character, it means you didn't export it with the right rotation from Blender. So, you need to return to Blender and rotate it and export it again.

In the final stage, if the poses don't work, it is usually because you've inverted the right hand/leg bones with the left hand/leg bones. Nothing serious, you just need to go to a previous step and click the correct ones.

If you're sure you've selected them correctly, it means that your character has the wrong orientation and is flipped. Just go to Blender and rotate it by 180°, export it again, and you're good to go.

Now the rest is pretty easy. We need to play LEGO with our character and go to the **Face** tab and import the head, then go to the **Hair** tab and import the hair:

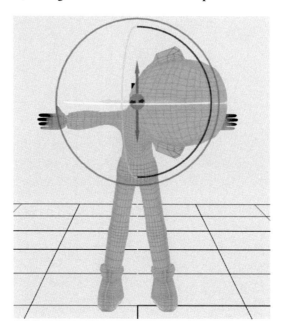

Figure 6.41 – A problem importing the head

In the case that something like what is shown in the preceding figure happens, don't worry—select **Move Parts** in the toolbar on the left and rotate/move it until it's in the right position:

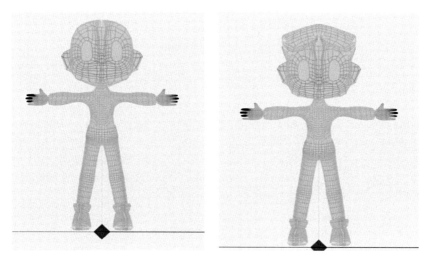

Figure 6.42 – Our character with the correct head and hair

> **Important note**
> If CSM tells you that the 3D model can't be used, it is because you didn't export the bones along with the object.

Texturing the body

Now, take a deep breath, because this will be a semi-long process. First, we need to texture paint the body. We do this by going through these steps:

1. Go to the **Body** tab.

2. Click on the **Surface material information** folder.

3. Select the material with which you want to start; in my case, this would be the body material.

4. Go to the **Character information** tab.

5. Click on the icon with the CSP logo.

This will open an instance of CSP in which we can paint the skin and anything else we want to paint:

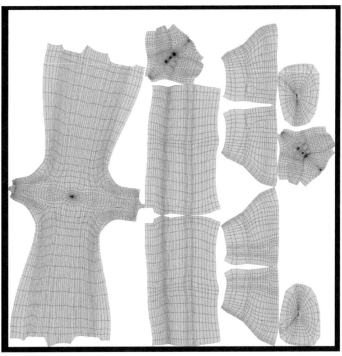

Figure 6.43 – CSP instance of the texture for the body

The advantage of doing the texture painting here is that we can use the tools of CSP while having a live preview of what we're doing. For example, I've filled the image with blue and it will appear in the **Editing texture** preview, as shown in the following figure:

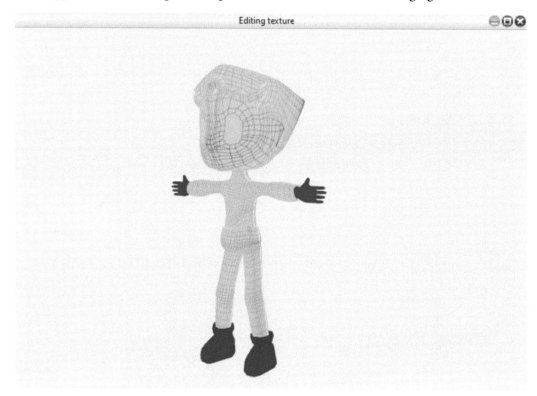

Figure 6.44 – Editing texture preview

Now we need to isolate everything that is a texture from the rest. It's pretty easy:

1. In CSP, go to **Select** in the top toolbar menu:

Figure 6.45 – Top toolbar menu

2. Select **Color gamut**.

3. Select the white of the texture image.

4. Create a new layer.

5. Go to **Layer**, in the preceding menu, and click on **Layer Mask | Mask Outside the selection**.

Now we just need to paint the basic skin and shoe tones:

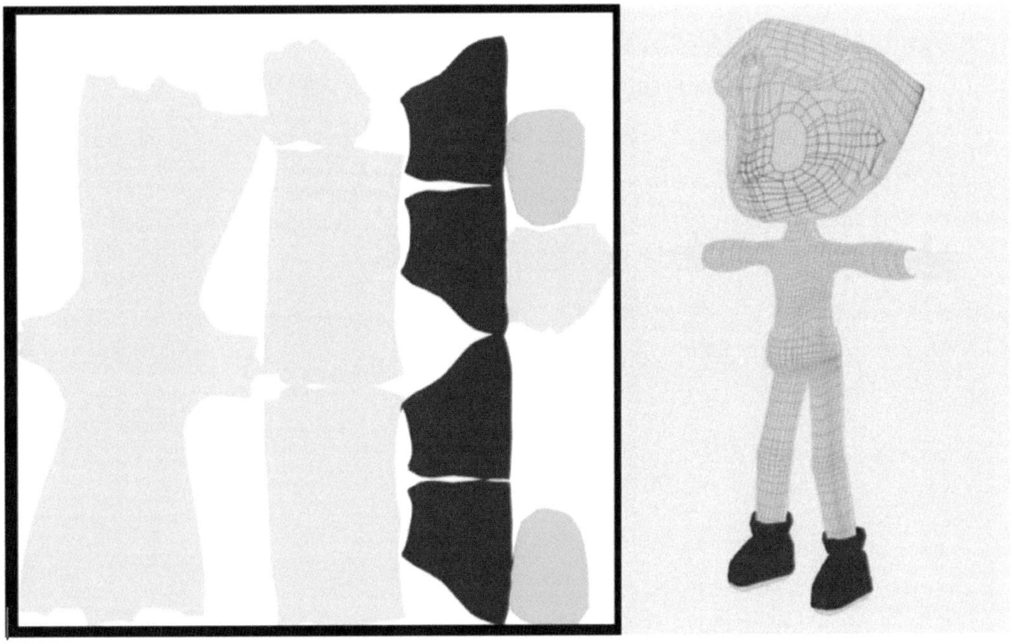

Figure 6.46 – Our basic colors put in place

Now we need to put the UV lines on top of the layers and change the **Blending Mode** setting of the layer from **Normal** to **Multiply**.

Now, to see what we're doing, we will change its opacity to something such as 10 or 20, so we can see where we are painting when zooming in. Remember to deactivate the UV layer before closing the CSP instance, because now we will paint some occlusion shadow and details.

Let's start with the occlusion shadow. This is a shadow where we know for sure the light will not hit, for example, the part of the arm inside the shirt.

We create a new layer and start painting the shadow.

> **Tip**
> If you're unsure where you're painting, use a bright color so you can easily notice it on the model. After this, just create a new layer and paint the color you need.

After doing the occlusion shadow, we start painting the details for the skin. Here are some tips for painting skin:

- Paint a little bit of red hue where we know there is more blood, such as the palm of the hand or the fingertips.

- Paint a dark tone where we know for sure there will be an occlusion shadow, such as between the fingers.

- Paint a yellow tone where we are sure there is less skin and the bone could be a little bit more visible, such as the knuckles.

It's a process of trial and error for this one: you paint, you look at the **Editing texture** window, and you modify what you have done:

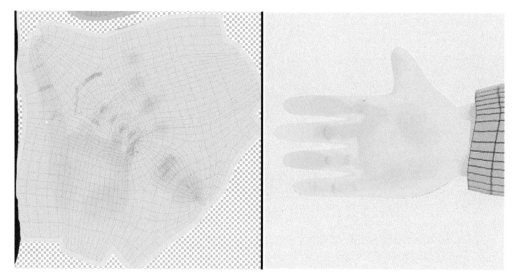

Figure 6.47 – My finished painted hand

> **Important note**
>
> A little bit of a warning before closing the instance of CSP. Sometimes when you close Modeler, don't ask me why, it will reset the textures. So, I would recommend that you save a duplicate of your finished texture just in case. Just go to **File | Save duplicate | .csp**. This is a "just in case" procedure.

After you're done, you just need to close the CSP file by pressing *Ctrl + W*, which will apply the texture. This shortcut works even to close a single internet page, or *Ctrl + Shift + W* to close all tabs in your browser in a fast way. You're welcome…

Now we can go on to paint the shoes, shirt, trousers, and hair.

We darken when we know there will surely be a shadow, such as where we put the cuts. Remember that we are not creating this 3D model to have a finished product, but to have a base to use, so don't go overboard with the texturing:

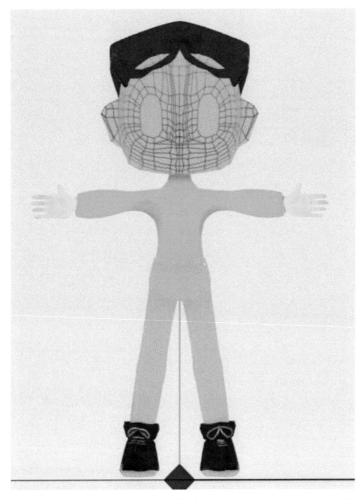

Figure 6.48 – My character with body and hair completely textured

As you can see, it is nothing fancy, as this is just a way to not lose time sketching your main character every time. It also provides you with ready-made flats for your colors.

Texturing the face

Now, take a deep breath, make a cup of tea, and relax a little bit, because this process is easy, but it's a really long one. This is because we will need to make a CSP file with a precise layer structure.

We will need to draw four expressions:

- Default
- Smile
- Anger
- Sad

For each of those expressions, we will need to draw the following:

- Eyes:

  a) Eye right

  b) Eye left

  c) Eye down

  d) Eye up

  e) Eye closed

  f) Eye open

- Mouth:

  a) O sound

  b) E sound

  c) U sound

  d) I sound

  e) A sound

  f) Closed

If you're better than me at math, without using a calculator you will know that you will need to create 48 different drawings.

In reality, it's 49, because every expression will use the same base, with the skin color and the eyebrows, and this takes us to the next step.

We will texture the face as we did with the rest of the body. But this time we will not apply the texture; we will save it as another file. Practically speaking, we will use the 3D preview to see what we are doing in real time, and after that, we will save the file. So, we will need to paint the head texture with the same layer structure for the expression.

Fortunately, it's pretty easy. You just need to name the folders and the layers the way I have done it. The black bullet points are folders and the white ones are layers:

- `exp_NAME_`
  - eyes
    - `eye_right`
    - `eye_left`
    - `eye_down`
    - `eye_up`
    - `eye_close`
    - `eye_open`
  - mouths
    - `mouth_o`
    - `mouth_e`
    - `mouth_u`
    - `mouth_i`
    - `mouth_a`
    - `mouth_close`
  - base

Figure 6.49 – Folder structure and layers for head texture

NAME after `exp_` is the name of the expression, which can be `default`, `smile`, `anger`, or `sad`. So, if we want to create a folder for the default expression, we will write the name as `exp_dcfault_`:

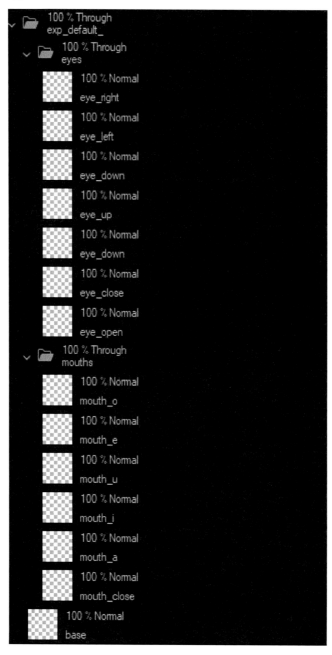

Figure 6.50 – Folder/layer order for the expression

As you can see, it's not difficult per se… it's just a little bit boring setting it up. Now we just copy and paste the exp_default_ folder and we rename the pasted folder with the right name for the expression:

Figure 6.51 – Final expression folders stack

After setting all this up, let's start painting a base that we can use in all the expressions. Remember—do not paint the eyes or the mouth!

Figure 6.52 – The face base

I swear it will always be creepy…

Figure 6.53 – The result in CSM; a little bit PS1 era… but I like it this way

Now we copy this face base to every **Base** layer in our expression folder stack. We can add the eyebrows for the various expressions:

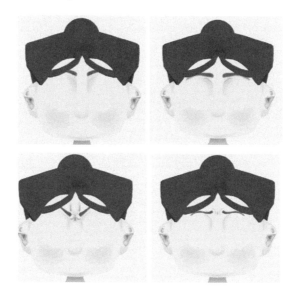

Figure 6.54 – The base face with eyebrows for the base of the expressions

Now let's continue with the eyes. I would recommend you take the default eyes, copy and paste them into the other expression folder, and change them. Why? Because when you look around it doesn't matter whether you're angry or happy; your eyes can still only rotate so much before you see the inside of your skull. So, because the limit of the movement of the eye is the same for every facial expression, we will change the position of the eyelids:

Figure 6.55 – Head with all the eye-open expressions

Now the mouth is practically the easiest one, because we only need to draw the default one and after that, we just straight up copy and paste it in every folder. We will only modify the closed mouth, which is practically a line:

Figure 6.56 – Faces completed with the basic expression

Now that we have done everything, we just need to go to **File | Save Duplicate | .psd (Photoshop document)** and save it. I don't know why, but it will recognize the expression file only if it is a .psd.

Now, once you're 100% sure, and I mean like completely sure, without an ounce of doubt, that you have saved the file, you can close the instance of CSP and return to Modeler. If you're not sure, don't do it—because it means you will need to do all the work again, OK?

Now we need to go to the **Character information** tab and select **Use facial expression texture**:

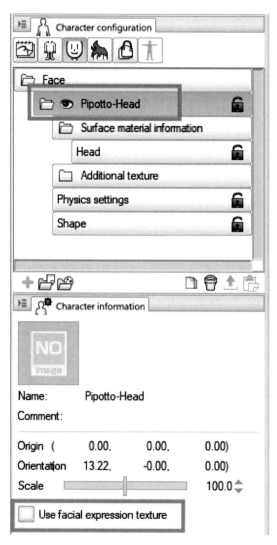

Figure 6.57 – Location of Use facial expression texture

Say OK to the warning. Now Modeler creates a new folder called **Facial Expressions**. The next step is the hardest thing we'll do in this chapter… or not! You need to press the **Import facial expressions** button:

Figure 6.58 – Location of the Import facial expressions option

Select the .psd you've created and wait a second. CSM will load up all the facial expressions:

Figure 6.59 – My finished character

Now, there is only one little thing to do before importing the finished character into CSP. You need to go through all the various folders in the various character tabs, and every time you see the blue icon saying **No Image**, you need to double-click on the blue icon so you start the capture thumbnail process:

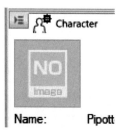

Figure 6.60 – Icon that says that there is no image for that material

For navigating in this screen, the **middle mouse button** (**MMB**) will pan the view and the **right mouse button** (**RMB**) will zoom in and zoom out. Just click on **Complete**.

When you arrive at the **Facial Expression** folder in the **Face** tab, you need to select an expression such as **Open**, **A**, or whatever you want, and click on the little camera in the bottom corner:

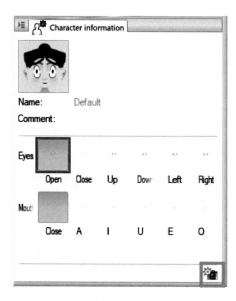

Figure 6.61 – Location of the capture component thumbnail

Now that you've done all of this tidying up, you can go to **File** and click on **Register as a new material**. That's it! We are done!

You just successfully created a 3D character in Modeler to use in CSP!

Figure 6.62 – Me shedding a tear for the sheer amount of pride I have in you for doing this

Summary

You've learned a lot of things in this chapter, but we have mainly covered how to unwrap a human character, how to rig it so that you can animate it, and how to then export all of that in to Modeler. You also learned how to add textures and expressions to your character, so you can modify them on the fly.

As a bonus extra, we learned a super-fast shortcut for closing internet tabs… but you didn't hear it from me!

In the next chapter, we will start doing some 2D cartoon and painting style illustrations. Remember, I will only give you the tools for expressing your imagination, not teach you basic stuff such as values, anatomy, and perspective.

7
Making Your Own Illustration

Now, before starting on what you will learn in this chapter, I need to say this one thing that might seem a little bit damaging to this book, at first glance:

Software doesn't matter.

This is my golden rule regarding everything I draw. What do I mean by this?

It means that I could make whatever I will show you in this chapter, *Chapter 8, Creating Your Own Comic*, and *Chapter 9, Building Your Own Concept Art,* in any other software, and so can you. So why should you keep reading? Because even if the software doesn't matter, the emotional response you have while producing your art is what really matters.

So yes, if you land an in-house job, you will probably need to use some specific software. But trust me, you just need to know where the brush tool, blur tool, and eraser are and that's it—you're good to go. But in day-to-day work, when no one is watching which software you're using, you should use what you enjoy.

When I first opened **Clip Studio Paint** (**CSP**) 7 years ago, it was like love at first sight. I loved the fact that I was in control of everything. I didn't need to learn the software—the software learned how to be used by me.

CSP was painterly software that could run on a potato PC. I'm talking about a used HP computer with an Intel Core i3 and 4 GB of RAM. I was using this with a Wacom Bamboo—to give you an idea of how limited my hardware was.

So, if you're here reading this chapter, it means that you have the same positive emotional response to creating art in CSP. It means you enjoy creating with the software and don't feel ashamed by it when searching for a job. Because in the illustration field, the software doesn't matter, because you will only send an image as a .jpg, .png, or .pdf. So, you can still land a job as a professional artist even without using so-called pro software. This quote is from Brent Patterson in the *Don't go pro* talk at BlendCon 2018:

> *"So, I'm gonna sum it up. I'd like to reconsider this term professional, or rather pro… when attached to any software, let's reconsider that word is not referring to professional, it's referring to proprietary."*

In short, enjoy creating.

In this chapter, we will learn about the following:

- Getting started with your illustration
- Creating a cartoon illustration
- Creating a painterly illustration

Now, let me help you enjoy this software even more!

Getting started with your illustration

I will create an illustration based on the next story of *Bunnyfable*, a personal comic project in which I tell modern dark fables, to show everything you need to know.

Creating an illustration, or whatever you're creating, is 99% of the time about preparation. So, it means that if you prepare a good workspace in advance, you find good references, and you have a pretty decent color palette, 99% of the time, your work is done even before starting. So, let's start with the first step.

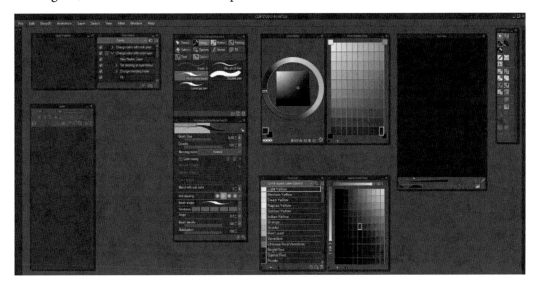

Figure 7.1 – Every window I use

Those are all the windows I use for every job. Every workspace is just an iteration of these windows.

Setting up the workspace

When you work with an illustration, the things you need to be most concerned about are the following two things: color and reference. If you're doing a cartoon illustration, you need to add layers, because you will need to do some layer management.

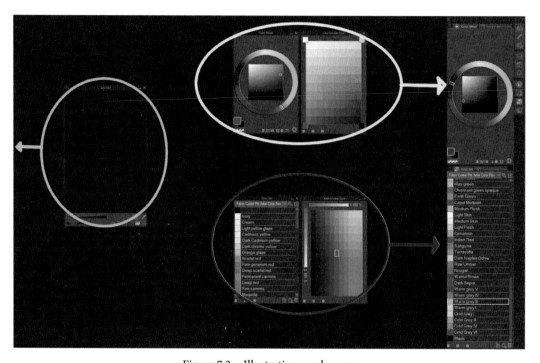

Figure 7.2 – Illustration workspace

These are my illustration settings: **Color Wheel** and **Intermediate Color** are nested together, and **Color Set** and **Approximate Color** make another group. **Sub View** is our references palette, and I will put it on the left because I find it comfortable putting it there.

Now, before going on, you need to remember our old friend **Quick Access**, in which you can put **Pop-up palettes** for easy access:

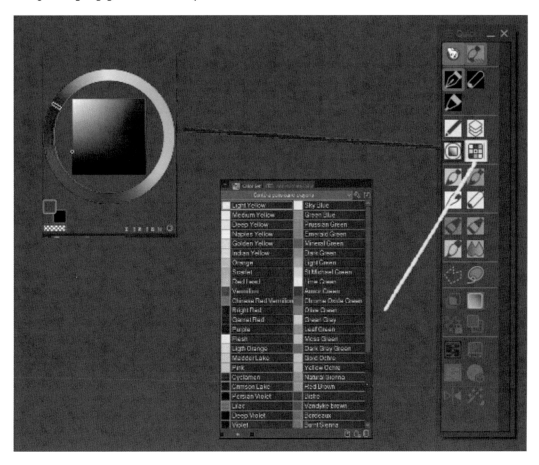

Figure 7.3 – Our old friend Quick Access

This means that you can have **Layer**, **Subtool Group**, **Color Wheel**, and **Color Set** hidden because those are options that you need to see only when you need to change them. As an example, once you select a layer, that layer will be the one selected until you select another one. So, do you really need to always have the layer list in your vision? It's the same for the **Color Wheel** and tool list.

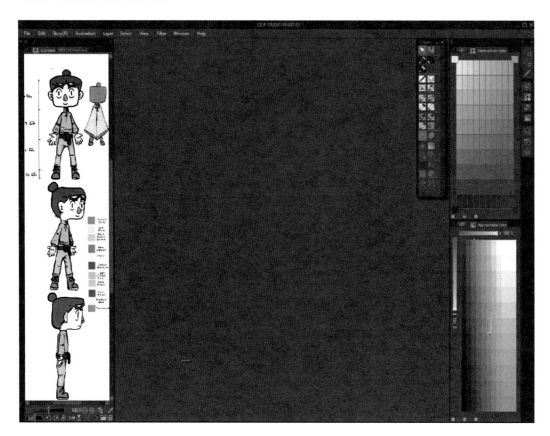

Figure 7.4 – Resulting workspace

As you can see, you have a lot of space for your drawing, meaning that you can be more immersed in your work.

Now let's analyze those three new windows. I will not explain the Color Wheel and Color Set because those are self-explanatory: one is a wheel that you use for selecting colors, and the other is a way to have a set of colors, similar to a watercolor palette with a precise color set.

Let's explore the three new windows:

- **Sub View**

- **Approximate Color**

- **Intermediate Color**

The first one is a pretty easy one—it's like a reference image folder that you can even use for color picking. I recommend you put your character design or mood boards in here so that you have a quick way to have references. The following screenshot shows how the **Sub View** window looks:

Figure 7.5 – Sub View window

The icons highlighted with a red square are for **To the previous image** and **To the next image**, meaning that you can cycle through a set of images.

The icon highlighted in blue is to **Import** the set of images you want, and the yellow one will **Clear** an image, meaning that you remove it from the **Sub View** window.

The icon highlighted in green is to **Switch to eyedropper automatically**, meaning that when you click on the image, you will sample the color. I recommend keeping it activated because you would usually use the Sub View for color sampling. If you need to **Pan** the image, you just need to press the spacebar. To **Zoom in**, press *Ctrl + LMB*, and **Zoom out** is *Ctrl + Alt + LMB*.

Approximate Color and **Intermediate Color** are pretty much hidden features of CSP if you are used to using other software, but once you have discovered them and learned how to use them, they are game changers. They can give you a lot of granularity in your color selection.

The first one we will analyze is **Intermediate Color**:

Figure 7.6 – Intermediate Color window

This window gives you intermediate color between a maximum of four colors. I used a CMYK color scheme to show you what I mean. In the top-left corner, we have the color cyan, in the bottom-left corner we have the color magenta, and between those two colors, we have the whole gradation between cyan and magenta.

To change a color, you just need to select a color on the color wheel and click on the big colored square in the corner:

Figure 7.7 – Big colored square location

Why do I say that this is a little bit of a game changer? Because you can have a precise color scheme, without it being linked to your color wheel.

If, for example, I'm making an illustration of a character with a precise palette and the background needs to have a precise color mood, I can select the character colors using the Color Set, Color Wheel, or Sub View, without the colors of the **Intermediate Color** window changing.

Plus, you can use it to have an analogous, tetradic, triadic—or whatever type you want—color scheme! As an example, if I use the color yellow twice and red and purple, I will have a triadic color scheme. If I use four different colors, I will have a tetradic color scheme. Easy, no?

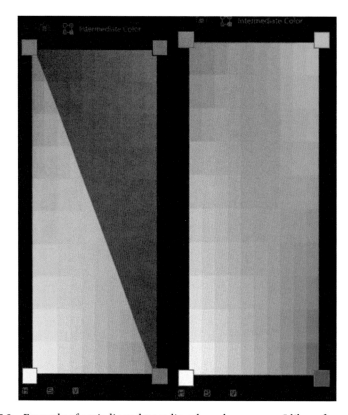

Figure 7.8 – Example of a triadic and tetradic color scheme—yes, I like soft pastel colors

And this brings us to the **Approximate Color** window, in which you have a percentual increment on the values of the color selected. In this case, the colors shown are linked to the color wheel. If you continue to select colors shown in the approximate color window, the base color will not change. If you select a new color from the **Color Wheel** or **Intermediate Color** window, it will change the base color in the **Approximate Color** window:

Figure 7.9 – Approximate Color window

Now, as you can see, we have two sliders: one for **Saturation** on the *y* axis and **Luminosity (V)** on the *x* axis. The selected color is your base color and is found at the center.

The percentual increments work in a really easy way. I use the following as a rule of thumb because I don't know the precise math.

In the middle, there is your color, which at 50% luminosity is your base value:

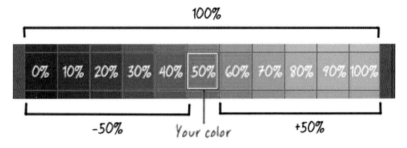

Figure 7.10 – Visual aid for Approximate Color

On the right, you have an increment of 50% of your value and on the left, you have a decrement of 50%, meaning that the total difference between the left side and the right side is 100%.

Figure 7.11 – Approximate Color window at 50%

In the case of 50%, I have an increment of 25% on the right, and on the left a reduction of 25%.

But the fun part is this: you can change more than just the luminosity and saturation. If you click on the percentage number, you will open a menu in which you can choose the parameter to change:

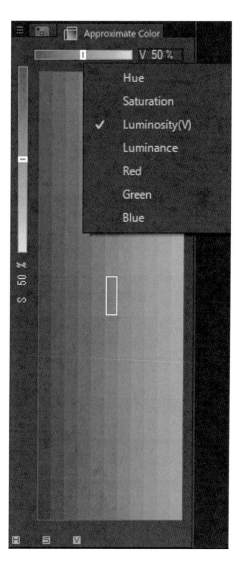

Figure 7.12 – Parameters for Approximate Color

You can choose between these parameters:

- **Hue** is the percentage of pure color (hue). On the right, you will have a clockwise movement on the Color Wheel, and on the left, a counterclockwise movement on the Color Wheel:

Figure 7.13 – Approximate Color with hue value

- **Saturation** is how much color there is. If the value is 0, you have gray.

- **Luminosity(V)**, in a really simplified way, is how much lighter the color is, based on the intensity of the light.

- **Luminance** is how much lighter the color is based on the area of the light. So, if the area of the light is smaller the color is lighter, and the larger the area, the darker the color.

- **R-G-B**: And finally, we have the possibility to change the percentage of **R-G-B**, as separate values. Just remember that RGB is an additive color scheme, meaning that if you put 100% of every color, you have pure white, and that color addition is a little bit counterintuitive. Here's a list on how RGB color addition works:

a) Red + Blue = Magenta

b) Red + Green = Yellow

c) Blue + Green = Cyan

If, for example, I need to shift the color red to a more yellowish hue, I will need to add some green.

In this tutorial, I will use luminance and saturation/hue based on the point I am at in the process. If I'm doing shading, I will use saturation. If I'm adding details such as reddish parts on the hands, I will use hue. You're free to change those values based on your needs. Regarding colors, there is no ready-made technique. For example, Takumi Wada, the illustrator of *Legend of Zelda: Skyward Sword*, used bright colors as shadows, and it was the amount of detail that told us what was in shadow and what wasn't.

If you want to learn more about colors in painting, there is *Color and Light: Illustrated edition, 2010, by James Gurney, Andrews McMeel Publishing.* Alternatively, you can check out the YouTube channel of Marco Bucci.

I use the two following general rules for color:

- Decide on a chromatic range for your base tones, a color for light and a color for shadow, and stick with it.

- The value of the color, if converted into gray, is more important than the hue of the color. As an example, if you choose to have light blue as the color for your light, all your other colors will need to be darker than that value.

As an example, see the following figure. The black background was made so you can see the light blue translated into a light gray:

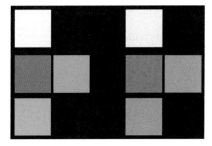

Figure 7.14 – A simple color palette translated into grayscale

As you can see, the color green is too similar to the color orange, so we darken it a little bit. By making it a little bit more blue and darkening it, we have a pretty usable color palette:

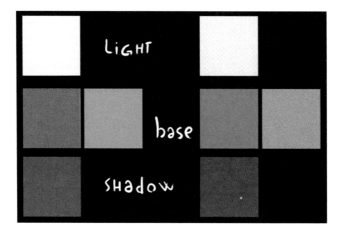

Figure 7.15 – A more usable color palette

With this, we have the color of the light, the color of the shadow, and two base hues as our main colors. Remember that those are our basic values, and we will refine them with the **Approximate Color** window.

If you're deciding on a color palette, always do this value checking—99% of the time, if the colors don't work, it is because the values are too similar to each other.

> **Important note**
>
> To perform good value checking of the colors in grayscale, there is this method—thanks to Marco Bucci for discovering it: you create a new layer, and you fill it completely with white or black and change the blending mode of the layer from **Normal** to **Color**.

Summing this up, we decide on a color palette, while value checking it, put our base values in the **Intermediate Color** window, and refine them in the **Approximate Color** window.

With this, we have a pretty clean workspace with all the information we need. We have the Sub View as a reference window, and the **Intermediate Color** and **Approximate Color** window, to have a controlled degree of granularity in our colors. We also have the possibility to recall, as a pop-up window, the **Color Wheel** and **Layer** windows, as well as having all our necessary tools thanks to the **Quick Access** palette.

Now, it's all well and good with regard to colors… but we still need an idea!

Coming up with an idea

Now we have set up the workspace, and we have a general idea of how to choose a color palette. Before starting, take a hot tea, coffee, chocolate, or whatever calms you and helps you focus. Take a bathroom break before starting, so you're not interrupted by your body saying: "Hey! We need to sit on the meditation throne."

Coming up with an idea is easy. You take random inputs that will spark your imagination and continue from there.

But, if you have artist's block, a serious one, one in which you feel nauseous whenever you take a pencil in your hand, or one in which you hate everything you do, it means that you are stressed from what you're doing. In that case, the problem is not coming up with an idea—that is easy, as we will see. The problem is the drawing/painting part itself. You probably think in the back of your mind that you will produce only bad pieces, and that's because you're comparing yourself with someone that has lived in different conditions, with a different education, and different values. So, simply put, draw for yourself and not to impress someone else.

I'm here to tell you that you will produce a good piece, not thanks to me, but thanks to yourself—I'm here just to give you the tools to do it.

Now, I mentioned taking random inputs to have an idea. How can you do this? It's pretty easy. First, you don't draw lines, but use blocks of shapes. The random relationship between those blocks will stimulate your imagination. This is a method that goes back as far as Leonardo da Vinci.

CSP can help you greatly in creating controlled chaos while working, and we can create a brush for that. Yes, we can create brushes for everything…

Creating an "idea" brush

This kind of brush is pretty straightforward and easy to create. We will need a brush that gives a random hue in a precise range every time we use it, meaning that we can't control the precise hue but only the range in which it works. This means that you will concern yourself only with finding some intriguing shape in the mess you will create. It's practically the equivalent of taking a couple of bottles of acrylic paint, strapping it to some gunpowder, and letting this color bomb explode near a canvas.

For this kind of brush, I like to use a square-shaped brush, but you can use whatever you want. In the example, I even used a unicorn-shaped brush tip, so do what you fancy!

Figure 7.16 – An idea brush

To create this brush, I glued some tissue paper onto printer paper, colored it with some black acrylics, scanned it, and created some squarish shapes for brush tips:

Figure 7.17 – Brush tips created from glued paper

For the rest, the method is the same one seen in *Chapter 2, Adding Brushes to CSP*. We go to the **Sub Tool Detail** palette and we add the brush tips by going to the **Brush Tip** section and clicking on **Material**.

Now, to create the random hue change, we need to go to the **Color Jitter** section:

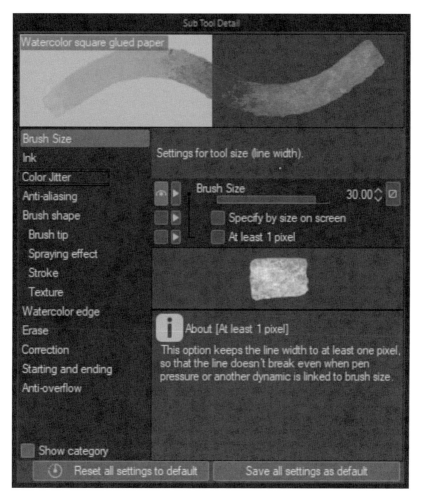

Figure 7.18 – Color Jitter location

In there, we will find a lot of options to change our color, from precise **Hue**, **Saturation**, and **Luminosity** changes linking all of those attributes to our pen modifiers. And if this isn't enough, we can have a random **Hue Saturation Luminosity** (**HSL**) variation per pen stroke, meaning that the HSL values will change with every different pen stroke:

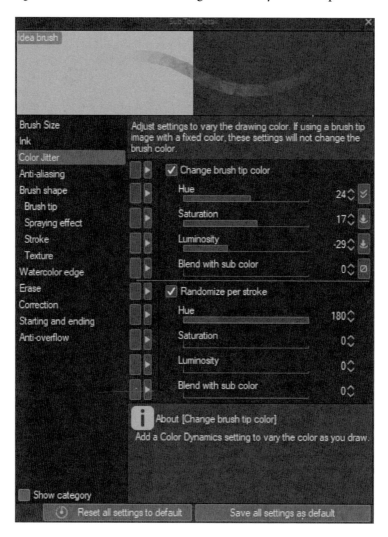

Figure 7.19 – Color Jitter options

The slider in **Change brush tip color** works in a really simple way. 0 is the default value, and the sliders will work like this:

- **Hue**: A positive value means movement in a clockwise direction on the color wheel. A negative value means the opposite.

- **Saturation**: A positive value means an increase in saturation, and a negative value means a decrease in saturation.

- **Luminosity**: This is the same as saturation, only a positive value means a tendency toward white, and a negative value means a tendency toward black.

The **Randomize per stroke** option is even more simple. The **Hue** slider changes the angle of the random value, based on the color wheel. If you set it at 45, it will mean a 45° distance between your base hue and the maximum random value you will have:

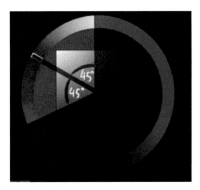

Figure 7.20 – Workings of the Hue option in Randomize per stroke

The other two options, **Saturation** and **Luminosity**, range from a value of 0 to a value of 100, which indicates the degree of randomness. 0 means that nothing will change, and if you set it at 100, it will mean that you will have 100% randomness—meaning that your brush shape could start to shift to the shape of a narwhal:

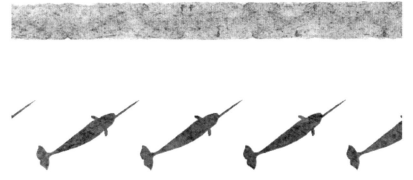

Figure 7.21 – As you can see, 100% saturation and luminosity randomness is a powerful tool for drawing narwhals

Now, on a serious note, 100% randomness for the **Saturation** and **Luminosity** values doesn't create a narwhal shape… Shocking, eh?

In reality, a 100% random value means that you can have a completely random value in the whole saturation and luminosity spectrum.

Now, to create an "idea" brush, you just need to activate **Change brush tip color** and slide the value to the right a little, to something such as 25-33. We don't want to go crazy here—the key is being subtle. Now, on the far right of the **Hue** slider, there are the **Hue Dynamics** settings. Click on the highlighted button in the following screenshot:

Figure 7.22 – Hue Dynamics settings location

When you open it, you need to check the box for the **Random** value and slide it a little bit to the right. Nothing crazy—15-20 will do the trick:

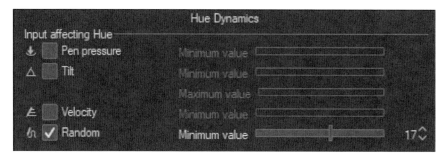

Figure 7.23 — Hue Dynamics | Random | Minimum value

Now, this creates a random value between your brush tips on the hue selected, while staying in the same hue range, meaning that if you've selected pure red as your color, your first applied brush tip will be pure red, your second will be slightly orange, the third a little bit yellow, and so on. If the value is 0 for the **Hue** value, you will not see any change. In the following figure, you can see the difference between activating the random value and not activating it:

Figure 7.24 – The difference between a) random and b) not random

In stroke A, we have hints of a bluish-purple mixed in the base purple of the brush. While in stroke B, we have only one hue value. This creates controlled chaos in the hue of your brush, creating a subtle vibration.

If you have a **badly baked potato computer** (**BBPC**), and using different brush tips slows down your BBPC too much, don't worry—this trick works even with a basic round brush.

Painting the idea

This part is the easy one. Creating a sketch to start your imagination is really easy—you just need to create a new canvas. Let's get started:

1. Create a new canvas on A4 at 72 dpi. We don't need a lot of resolution right now—we will change it later. We just need to be fast and use large brush sizes, and a high dpi will create problems:

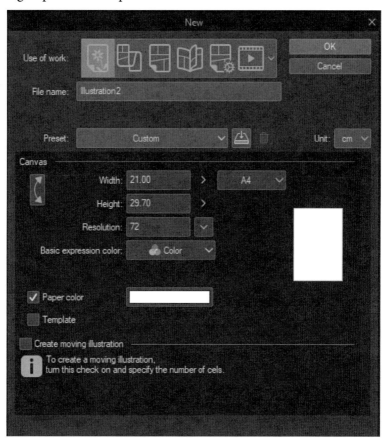

Figure 7.25 – New canvas dialog

7. Now, I do the same with the belt details, the turnaround of the character, and the material information. I then activate the grid, go to **View | Grid**, and start experimenting a little bit until I'm satisfied with the results. You can see the final version here:

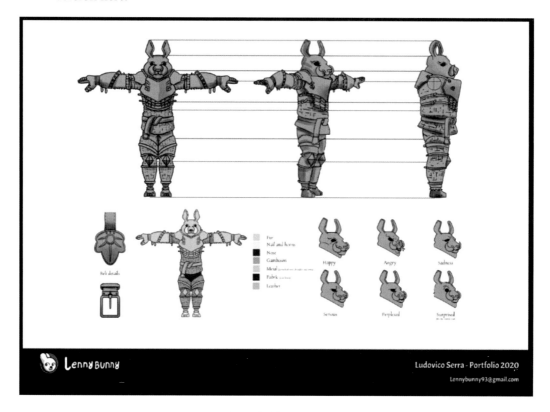

Figure 10.28 – Final Berthold: modeler information page

Now, remember your job as a concept artist is to put out ideas that can be used during the work pipeline, not to create a beautiful picture.

You have now learned how to create three different types of portfolio with CSP. Good work!

- An elf warrior fighting against a cyclops:

Figure 7.28 – Random drawing 2

- Two people dancing, and one of them is an Elvis impersonator:

Figure 7.29 – Random drawing 3

In a really short time, I have three different ideas. Are they all perfect ideas? No! No idea is perfect. Do I have something to work with? Absolutely, yes!

As you can see, finding a workable idea is pretty easy. Now we will start with a real drawing. I want to make the cover of *Pipotto Fattaposta and the Smith Pendant*.

Sketching

I will be honest, I don't know what I want to put on the cover. I know the story, but I have no idea how to put those elements onto the cover. But I know that I want to create good cover art.

I know I need these two things to be present on the cover:

- Main characters: Pipotto, Elka, and Mokopi
- A pendant, or something that suggests a pendant

An extra could be putting in the King of Ferrets. Why? Because I like ferrets, as they are overcooked noodles, and it's a central part of the story.

So, I just start using my idea brush on a small A4 canvas at 72 dpi and make 4-6 random-colored shapes:

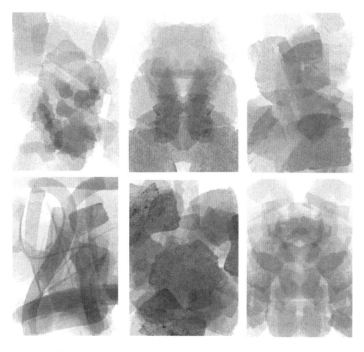

Figure 7.30 – A series of random shapes and colors

Now, looking at them, the ones that "inspire" me the most are the middle-top and right-bottom ones, but I'm also a fan of middle symmetric composition.

> **Middle symmetric composition**
> This kind of composition is based on having a symmetry line in the middle of your canvas. This creates an effect in which it's easier to create vertical movement.

Now I just need to find a composition with the characters and background that I like. Usually, I prefer to use some references. For example, I like the covers of *Hilda* by *Luke Pearson* and *Anya's Ghost* by *Vera Brosgol*.

I can't show you all the concept versions I've created, and how I decided on the final one, because it would spoil the story.

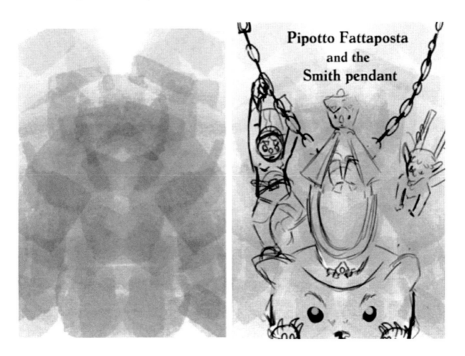

Figure 7.31 – Loose sketch of the cover

Remember that at this stage, it is not important to create a cool sketch that we can show on a social network. This stage is for finding a general direction for your illustration and seeing whether you like the general composition. In my case, I like the idea but I don't like the title in the position it is in, because it is a little bit too floaty. So, I will put it at the bottom:

Figure 7.32 – Final sketch version

Now we need to refine the loose pencil sketch: there is no particular brush that should be used—just use what you feel comfortable with. When refining your work, I really recommend you use references. For the characters, I have the 3D models to use as references, but I will need a reference for a medieval necklace, a ferret, and some fancy medieval codex decorations to put on the frame of the text. We don't want to be like a medieval miniature painter that paints an animal from memory.

For references, if you have a second monitor, I recommend you use **PureRef** on the second monitor and use the **Sub View** window for the color picking. If you only have one monitor, I recommend using the **Sub View** window alone.

Little pro's tip: Sub View

If you don't want to cycle between a lot of images in the **Sub View** window, I recommend creating a mood board with all the references and putting that in the **Sub View** window.

If you have a touch monitor, you can pan and zoom with two fingers.

Figure 7.33 – Loose pencils

I would like to have some decorations that give the feeling of a medieval book, and fortunately, I have some assets for that. And as you can see, the 3D characters are a little bit creepy. But we don't need to copy and paste them and be done with it—that's laziness. It's smart to use them as a tracing base. Never be lazy, be smart!

Figure 7.34 – Loose pencil with decorations and pencils for the characters

Now we have finished our loose pencil sketch, the next step is the tight pencil work. For this, I really recommend using a **vector layer**, which is a layer that will let you have lines that will work as a vector. You can find this in software such as **Illustrator/Affinity Designer/Inkscape**.

To add a **vector layer**, just go to **Layer | New Layer | Vector Layer**. Or, click on the highlighted button in the **Layer** window:

Figure 7.35 – Vector Layer location

This layer lets you move and rotate lines using the **Object** tool. You can also unify, increase, or reduce the size of the line using the **Connect vector line** and **Correct line width** tools. In addition, if we use **Vector eraser**, we can erase the whole line we made, or erase the line up until an intersection with another line:

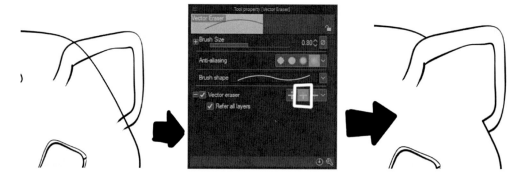

Figure 7.36 – Vector eraser with the Erase up to intersection option activated

This allows us to have a little bit of leeway when creating the pencil sketch. There is no precise brush for this stage, so use whatever you want. Just don't go wild with the size linked to pen pressure brushes:

Figure 7.37 – Our tight pencils

Now we have our vector tight pencil lines that we can use to create a cartoon illustration or a painting illustration, based on our preference.

If you're a beginner, there is no difference between a cartoon or a painting illustration, because the steps are the same:

1. To come up with an idea, just use an idea brush or just doodle something.

2. Loose sketching—now we just need to refine our scribbles into a more coherent shape.

3. Tight pencils—now we refine those loose pencils so we can have a better understanding of what's happening.

I recommend sticking to these steps if you have trouble with your final artwork. Sometimes our perceived level is different from our actual level, so we skip some steps. There is no shame in taking your time to create your work; professionals with 10 years experience or more, such as the ones responsible for the illustrations of *Magic: The Gathering* or the inkers of *Marvel/DC,* require more time than you think to create their pieces. For a *Magic* card, they require approximately 3 weeks, and for a full-inked page of your *Batman* issue, they require approximately 10 hours. Don't worry about speed; worry about quality. After spending a number of years focusing on quality, you can think about speed. How do I know that this works? If you listen to interviews with Kim Jung Gi, you'll learn that that's what he did. So, if you want to be Kim Jung Gi, take your time, think about quality first, then speed can come later.

Just a little advice: don't try to work for 10 hours a day on your drawing if you're a beginner—that's the easiest way to lose motivation and have burnout/artist's block. If you can do half an hour, use that half an hour for sharp-pointed focused training. The next day, try 35 minutes, and the next day 40 minutes, and so on. Focused training over time beats straining through long sessions of training.

Now, before continuing with everything, it's time to increase the resolution of your canvas. To do so, you just need to go to **Edit | Canvas Properties** and just increase **Resolution** from **72** to **300**.

We will start with the cartoony version of this cover, which we will be covering in the next section.

Creating a cartoon illustration

By "cartoon" illustration, I'm not just referring to comics such as *Mickey Mouse*, *Erma*, or *One Piece*, but more of a type of style in which the heavy lifting is done in the inking stage. In the cartoon style, things such as brushstrokes or color variations come second.

The steps for cartoon illustrations are simple:

1. Inking
2. Flatting
3. Coloring

We will start with the inking part. As you will see, it will be pretty easy once you have created the tight pencil work. Inking purists may disagree with me.

For the cartoon illustration, I recommend using this setup:

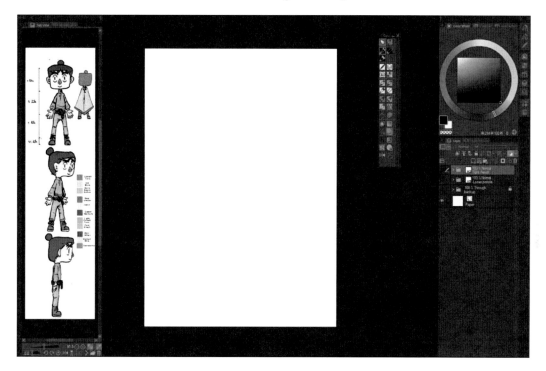

Figure 7.38 – Workspace for cartoon illustration

Color Set is nested inside **Color Wheel**, and the **Layer Property** palette is nested inside the **Layer** palette. In this way, you can do most of the operations we will do within a really compact space.

Inking

Inking in CSP is a pleasure because you can set the pressure with curves, giving you the ability to customize the pressure level based on how heavy-handed or light-handed you are.

To change the pressure curve of a tool, you know the procedure:

1. Go to the **Sub Tool Detail** window.

2. Click on **Brush Size**.

3. Click on the **Brush Size Dynamics** button:

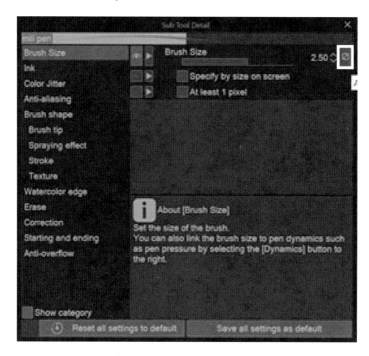

Figure 7.39 – Brush Size Dynamics location

4. Check the **Pen pressure** box.

5. Tweak the curves by clicking and dragging them.

6. Enjoy!

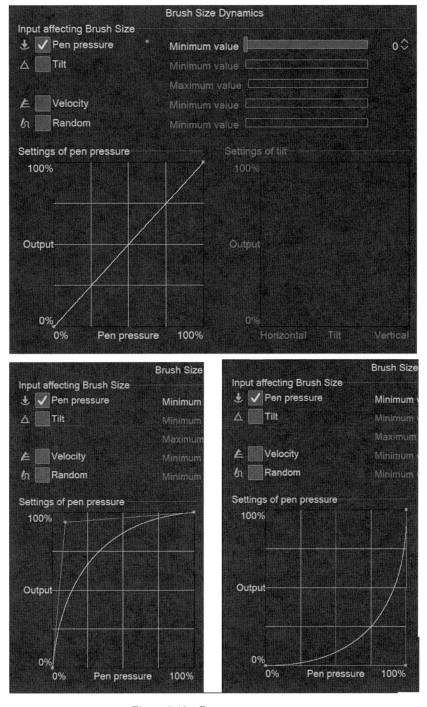

Figure 7.40 – Pen pressure curves

The standard pen pressure curve is the top one, and it is pretty standard. It will have a smooth transition between big wide lines and smaller narrow lines.

The curve on the bottom left is for achieving big strokes with a very small amount of pressure, and the curve on the bottom right is the complete opposite: you will have really thin lines, even if you press hard.

Before inking, we need a good inking brush, and the standard selection available in CSP is pretty good. But let's say you want something with a rougher flavor.

This is pretty easy to do. Simply take some circles, and create an effect that looks like a mouse ate through them.

Go to **Sub Tool Detail | Stroke** and set **Repeat method** to **Random**. And there you have it:

Figure 7.41 – Brush tip for rough inking pen

If you want a brushstroke that is similar to a fast stroke with some bristles that go outside of the central path, just take the cheese wheels you created before and add some little circles near them at more or less the same height. This has the same options as the rough inking pen from before and you get a rougher feeling, with which you don't have the perfect circle of a digital inking pen, while still being able to create smooth lines:

Figure 7.42 – Brush tip for texture – rough inking pen

Now we have a couple of brushes to use for our inking. Thanks to our pencil lines, we don't need to worry about where to put our baseline art. Why? Because we can transform the pencils we have done in the **vector layer** to a ruler that we can use to retrace our pencils by using a simple option:

1. Duplicate your pencils.

2. Go to **Layer**.

3. Go to **Ruler/Frame**:

Figure 7.43 – Ruler/Frame location

4. After this, select **Ruler from vector**:

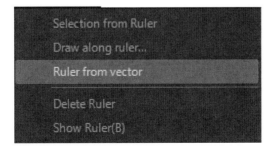

Figure 7.44 – Ruler from vector location

5. Now you just need to empty your layer by pressing *Delete* on your keyboard or going to **Edit** and clicking on **Delete**.

This will create an empty vector layer with a ruler that you can use to trace your inks. That's why I've said that some inking purists will hate me because it means that your inks will be a perfect tracing of the pencil lines and not the free expression of the inker's hand:

Figure 7.45 – Pencils converted in a vector ruler

But this in turn means that you will only need to worry about the line pressure of your inking.

If you want a less pencil-tracing approach, but you have a shaky hand, don't worry! There is a built-in **Stabilization** option. It's located in the **Sub Tool Detail** window under the **Correction** section:

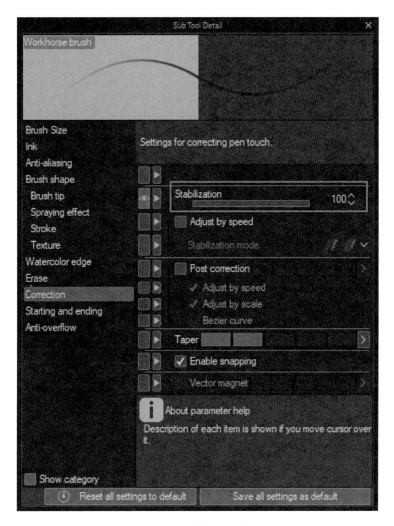

Figure 7.46 – Stabilization location

Now you have two different approaches for how to ink your pencil lines.

Figure 7.47 – Finished inked cover

Little pro's tip: Cross-hatching

It can be effective to do line art without cross-hatching on a layer and do the cross-hatching on a new layer. This is so that when you need to select inside the inks layer, you will not need to worry about filling inside the cross-hatching.

The next stage, that is, flatting the illustration, is a little bit tedious, at least for me.

Flatting

This process is creating a flat color that you can easily pick with the color wand. There are two ways of doing it in CSP:

- Doing flat colors in one single layer, with colors based on different hues. With this method, you're not worrying about the realism of the scene. It's a pretty fast method, but it's less precise by default.

- Doing flat colors in multiple layers. This means that the flats for the skin (for example) will be in a different layer to those in the shirt layer. This gives you complete control over what you can select, but it will be more work on your part. So, remember to charge a little extra if you do it in this way!

Now before doing anything else, we need to talk about **Reference Layer**. This is a setting that enables you to reference a layer for color picking or filling a shape:

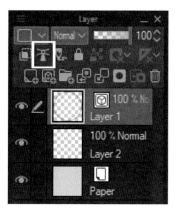

Figure 7.48 – Reference Layer option location

Before showing you what I mean, you need to be sure that the **Fill** tool has the **Refer multiple** option checked. To check it, just go to the **Tool property** palette:

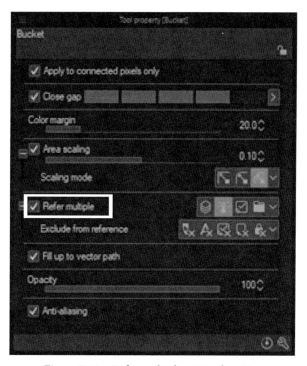

Figure 7.49 – Refer multiple setting location

Now, for the example, draw a circle, a pure line circle, on a layer. Set that layer as a **reference layer**. After this, just create a new layer. Now go to the **Fill** tool, with the **Refer multiple** option checked, and fill in the circle:

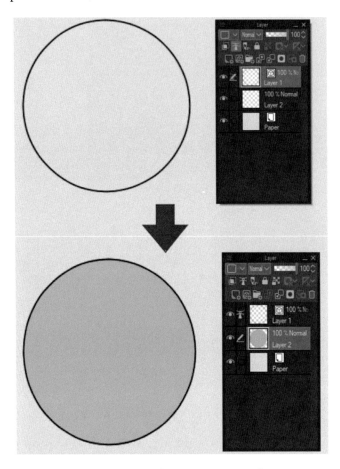

Figure 7.50 – Reference Layer example

As you will see, even if you didn't select the layer with the circle, you were able to fill inside the layer. I think you're smart enough to guess where we're going with this.

We will put our ink layer as a reference layer, we will create a folder called `Flat color`, and we will decide which method of creating flats we will use.

I prefer to use a mixed method if it's for a personal project. If you work for someone and they give you a precise way of doing it, guess what? You will do it the way you're paid to do it.

My way is to create a folder for each character, plus one folder for the objects. Every folder for the characters will have a layer for the skin, a layer for the clothing, and a layer for the miscellaneous stuff.

In the case of this illustration, the folders would be the following:

- Pipotto

  a. Clothing

  b. Skin

  c. Miscellaneous

- Elka

  a. Clothing

  b. Skin

  c. Miscellaneous

- Mokopi

  a. Clothing

  b. Skin

  c. Miscellaneous

- Ferret

- Objects

In this way, I'm organized but I don't need to create an infinite number of layers for everything.

When I have created all the required folders, I set the inks layer as a reference layer and I start to fill the inside of the character with random colors in the right folders. A good tool for this part is the **Close and Fill** tool. You can find this tool under the **Fill sub tool**.

A little word of warning: there will be bright and saturated colors in the next image, and it's probable that they wouldn't even be printed correctly. Do you know the story *The Color Out of Space* by *H. P. Lovecraft*?

The Color Out of Space

A color from space crashed in to the well of a farm, influencing and transforming the family that lived on the farm. The book inspired the film *Annihilation*.

Doing flats is practically being exposed to this kind of maddening extra-terrestrial color. I always find that I have a headache after doing flats:

Figure 7.51 – Finished flat colors – welcome to the 60s

Now, if you want to keep your sanity and avoid a huge headache, trust me on this one… I really recommend you keep a **Hue/Saturation/Luminosity** correction layer above the flats folder, in which you reduce the saturation:

Figure 7.52 – How to prevent a headache while doing the flats

This will help us in the next step, which is coloring.

Coloring

This part is probably the easiest to do because we've created the flat colors. We just need to switch the reference layer based on the things we are coloring. If I add colors to the ferret, I will put the flat of the ferret as the reference layer.

So, now our only job is adding our colors... That's it! We take our **Intermediate Color** window with our color palette and we just color pick and fill.

Yep, coloring is pretty straightforward, but shading is another topic. There are a lot of ways to do shading, but let's say for the sake of argument that you're shading for a cartoon illustration using cel shading, meaning you will use flat tones without blending.

The rule of thumb, if we want to simplify it, is this:

"For everything that is inorganic, you use the **Multiply** blending mode; for everything organic you use the **Overlay** blending mode."

Why? Because light works differently depending on whether it travels through an inorganic or organic surface. Simplifying this greatly, if it is inorganic, it will just shift toward black, but if it is organic, it will be darker and more saturated:

Figure 7.53 – The Blending mode of layer location

The **Blending mode** of a layer is practically a way to draw on a layer while automatically applying hue/saturation/luminosity changes based on the layers below. The **Multiply** mode will decrease the **Luminosity** of the below layer based on the **Luminosity** value of your color.

If, for example, you use pure white, you will not see anything. This is because you will not apply any changes to the color below. It means that with this blending mode, you can only darken a color by shifting it near black. A good way of using it, if you're a beginner, is by color picking your base color and using it to draw the shadow:

Figure 7.54 – Pipotto's cape with Multiply shading

As you can see, I used the cape base color, *Ice blue*, from the *Faber-Castell Pitt Artist Pen*, and drew the shadow while staying in the **Multiply** layer.

The **Overlay** blending mode is a mode in which the color will be darker and more saturated if you use black, and it will be more desaturated and near white if you use white or a whitish color.

For this mode, I recommend using straight-up black for the shadows:

Figure 7.55 – Pipotto's skin and hair with Overlay shading

Just to recap the difference between the **Multiply** and **Overlay** modes, here's a little reference figure:

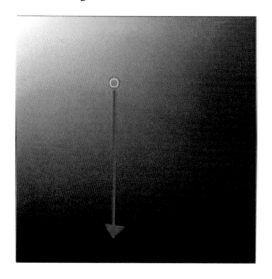 

Figure 7.56 – The difference between Multiply (left) and Overlay (right)

For doing the light, I recommend using a separate layer in **Overlay** mode using the color of light you've chosen:

Figure 7.57 – Pipotto with shadow and light

Now you just need to color pick, put the shadows and light onto all of the characters, and you're done!

Figure 7.58 – Final cartoon illustration

Little pro's tip: Layer organization

In total, I had approximately 80 layers. Now, we don't want to select a layer in error and modify its contents when we just finished working on it, do we? A good way to stay organized is to lock a layer after we have finished working with it. And after we have finished in a folder, we lock that folder, too.

With this, we have finished our cartoon illustration. What you've read are not set-in-stone rules; they are more general rules of thumb that you can use to start drawing and creating something. Down the line, you will find something that will work better for you.

In the next section, we will see how to create an illustration in a painterly style.

Creating a painterly illustration

In this section, we will see how to create a basic paintbrush, or a more textured one, and how to use them. Plus, I will show you your greatest ally, the gradient map.

Creating a paintbrush

Creating a painterly illustration is half taking precise steps and half intuition that is based on training regarding which color to choose or the type of brushwork style to use.

For a painterly style, you don't need a fancy brush if you're a beginner; you can use your workhorse brush with the **Color mixing** settings on. This is because, in painting, the most important part is not the texture but the color and shape of the strokes in relationship to each other. A good video talking about this is *The best brush for digital painting* by *Sinix Design*, which can be found on YouTube.

There are three color mixing options: **Amount of paint**, **Density of paint**, and **Color stretch**:

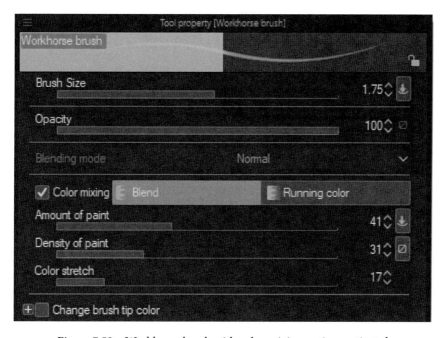

Figure 7.59 – Workhorse brush with color mixing options activated

What do these three options do? It's pretty simple in reality:

- **Amount of paint** is practically the "opacity" of the color. The less you have, the more transparent your brush will be.

- **Density of paint** is the resistance to mixing between your color and the color you're putting it on. At 0 it will mix easily, and at 100 it will practically not mix.

- **Color stretch** is how much your color will stretch. At 0 it will practically not move, and at 100 it's practically a penguin sliding on ice—it goes wherever it wants.

Usually, I prefer to have those settings with a low value, but you need to find your sweet spots regarding those three values. My only advice is to never go fully to 100 because it will mean you will have a normal round brush.

Before continuing, I need to talk about the **Change brush tip color** options in a little more depth:

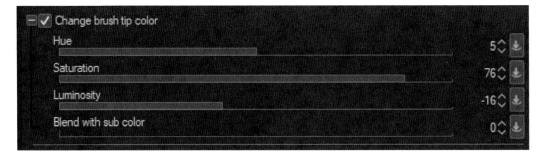

Figure 7.60 – Change brush tip color options

Why? Because in the real world, paint is a "liquid." To be more precise, it is a dense liquid. This means that the light inside the paint will bounce inside before going out, so when it hits your eyes it will be more saturated, and darker. It's the same reason why it is better to use an **Overlay** layer for the shadows on organic material.

But what does it mean for us? It means that, thanks to this option, we can set the color we put to be more saturated and darker with pressure. This means we can have a truly realistic effect when we paint, and if we want to have an even more realistic feeling, we can let it have a slight hue change because some pigments have hue changes in real life. An example of this would be the *Phthalo Turquoise* of *Winsor & Newton*, which is a deep bluish-green when you use a lot of paint, but becomes more of an azure green when you use less of it:

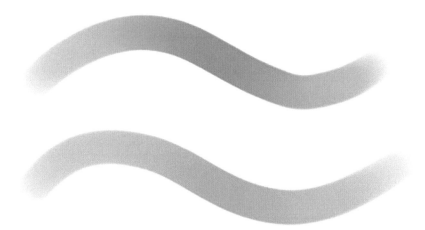

Figure 7.61 – Difference between using Change brush tip color (top) and not using it (bottom)

With this, we have a pretty realistic brush, regarding the colors, and with this basic brush, you can tackle practically anything.

But let's say you want a more textured, grainy brush—something like the one in the following figure:

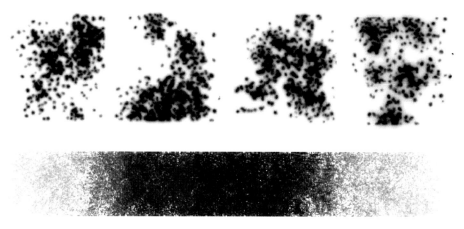

Figure 7.62 – Example of a textured painterly brush

It's pretty simple to do. You just need to think about the stroke **Gap** value between the brush tips. In layman's terms, it means that when we press less or use a fast stroke, we will need to see the single brush tip. When we do the opposite, we will need to have a solid color. This method is pretty useful because it means (if you consider **Repeat Method** is set to **Random**) we can have a different brushstroke every time we draw with our pen.

To create a textured brush based on the stroke **Gap** value, we repeat the usual steps for creating a brush:

1. Go to **Sub Tool Detail** and go to the **Stroke** section.

2. There, click on the **Fixed** settings in the **Gap** section:

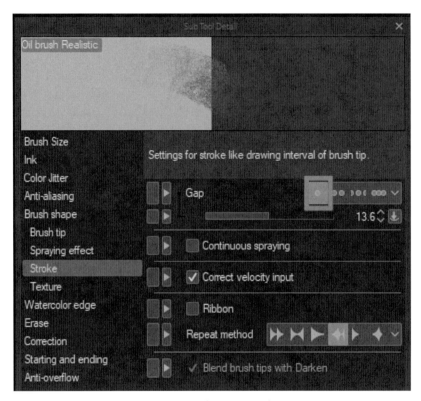

Figure 7.63 – Fixed gap setting location

This will unlock the **Fixed value Dynamics** settings.

3. In the **Pen Dynamics** settings, check the **Pen pressure** option.

4. Now we just need to revert the pen pressure curve as in the following screenshot. This will reduce the gap when you press harder, and vice versa when you press lightly:

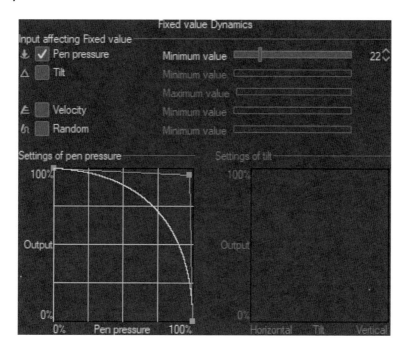

Figure 7.64 – Reverted pen pressure curve

If you want a rougher feeling to your painting experience, you can use the **Dual Brush** option in CSP. This was introduced in the May 2021 update. At the time of writing this book, you can't use **Watercolor edge** and **Color mixing** while using **Dual Brush**, but you can still use **Color Jitter**.

How does it work? It imposes a second brush on your brush. The key difference from Photoshop's dual brush is that you don't impose a pre-existent brush, but you create a new brush that will be applied to your selected brush, meaning you don't need to worry about changing the settings of other brushes; it will not be reflected in your **Dual brush** option.

To activate this option, you just need to go to the **Sub Tool Detail** palette. If you can't remember, you can access it by clicking on that little wrench bar in the **Tool Property** palette:

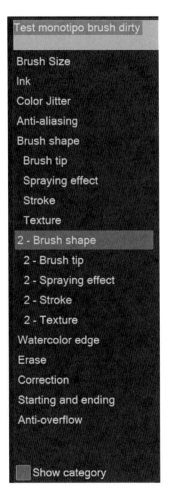

Figure 7.65 – Dual Brush location

You will see that some options have a **2** on the left. Those are the **Dual brush** options. Only **2 - Brush shape** is a new option altogether from the May 2021 update. The following screenshot shows the settings of the **Dual brush** option:

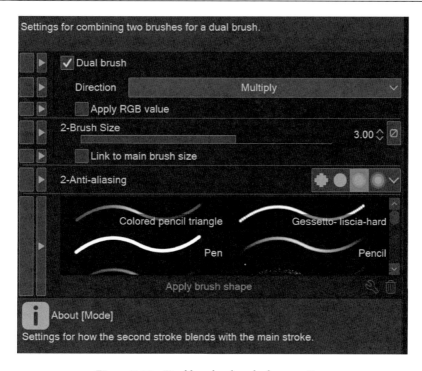

Figure 7.66 – Dual brush – brush shape options

Let's explore the options in this window in detail:

- The first option, **Dual brush**, lets you activate the dual brush feature. **Direction** is how the second brush will be applied to your selected brush; this option work as a layer blending mode. I will be honest, I don't know the exact math regarding the **Direction** setting, so I strongly recommend you experiment a little bit. My favorites are **Overlay** and **Hard mix**.

- **Apply RGB value** is an option in which your dual brush will modify the color of your brush based on the **Direction** settings. For example, if **Direction** is set to **Multiply**, your dual brush will move your colors toward black.

- **2-Brush Size** is the brush size of your dual brush and, by default, it is not linked to your normal brush size. If my main brush size is 10 px and my dual brush is 3 px, and if I increase my main brush size to 20 px, my dual brush will stay at 3 px. To link them, you just need to check the next option, that is, **Link to main brush size**.

- **2-Anti-aliasing** is the anti-aliasing of your dual brush. This last option lets you apply a saved brush shape as your dual brush. To create a brush shape, just go to *Chapter 2, Adding Brushes to CSP*, under the *Workhorse brush* section.

But why is this option useful for realistic brushes? This is because we can add a "seamless" random texture over the brush using different brush tips. But now you will ask "Why is applying a texture using the **Texture** option not enough?"

The answer is simple: avoiding pattern repetition. A texture is a static image. Once applied, it stays like that, and you will reveal the texture image while you paint. Using multiple brush tips means that we will never have the same brush strokes twice. Sure, using a texture is fast and reliable, and you will have a less heavy brush, but it lacks a little bit of subtlety.

So how can we create a brush using the dual brush feature?

It's a lot easier than you expect. We take, for example, our previous brush—the one we created in the *Creating an "idea" brush* section. Let's get started:

1. We will take a nice-looking paper that we like. In my case, it's the brown *Kraft* paper of *Clairefontaine*.

2. We will set **Expression color**, on the **Layer Property** palette, to **Monochrome** and we will click on that little black square. This will automatically hide every white pixel:

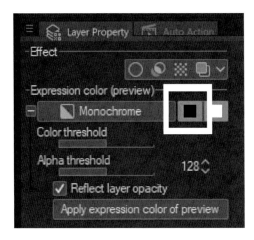

Figure 7.67 – Only black location in the Layer Property palette

3. Now we just need to play around with the **Color threshold** and **Alpha threshold** values until we like the results.

    Once you are satisfied, remember to click on **Apply expression color of preview**. This will apply the expression color. This is how my paper looks:

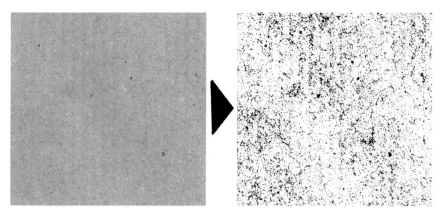

Figure 7.68 – My paper after using the Monochrome expression color

4. Next, we just need to take our **Rectangle** selection and create a square selection. To do so, just press *Shift* while creating the selection.

5. Now, cut and paste some squares from the paper. Four squares is a good amount:

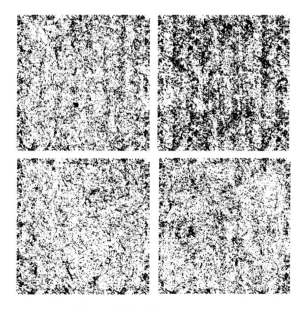

Figure 7.69 – My paper squares

6. Add them to your materials and slap them in your brush under **2-Brush tip**. This will give you a combination of your base brush and a paper texture.

7. Now go to **2-Brush shape** and change **Direction** from **Normal** to something that you like. I used **Overlay** and this is how it looks:

Figure 7.70 – My result

But we can go a little bit further with the realism, because a texture is more visible the less you press, and we can pretty much copy this behavior for our brush using the **2-Brush density** option if we go to **2-Brush tip** and go to **2-Brush density** and we link **2-Brush density Dynamics** to **Pen pressure**. Now, we need to create a reverted curve, as we did with the **Stroke** option. If you don't remember, just look at the screenshot. This will increase the density of the **dual brush** the less pressure you apply:

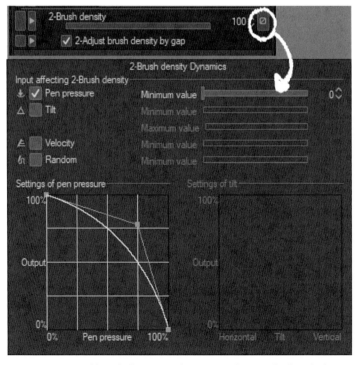

Figure 7.71 – Dual brush density with a reverted curve for brush density

This will create an effect in which the less you press, the more visible the paper texture will be. Here's a sample gradient of this brush:

Figure 7.72 – Sample gradient of the newly created brush

Now just go to **2-Stroke** and set **2-Repeat method** to **Random**, and you're done. In this way, by using the dual brush feature, you can create a random non-repeatable paper texture that will be applied to your brush.

Now you're fully equipped to create a simple painting and textured brush and are ready to make a little painterly cover.

Grayscale, or grisaille for the cultured

Creating a grisaille is pretty simple. You create a base painting without worrying about colors, but only about the basic values between the objects. And after that, you put colors over the grayscale using a color layer or a gradient map. I prefer a gradient map because it's a little bit easier to use.

For this kind of technique, there is no special method, but there are a few things we can do to help ourselves in our job.

The first thing is to create light-grayish silhouettes of our subjects so that we can use a **clipping mask** above them. What is a clipping mask? A clipping mask is a layer option that lets you draw only over whatever layer there is below the layer with the clipping mask applied. We covered this in the first chapter, and I think it is one of the most important features for increasing your speed while working:

Figure 7.73 – Clipping mask location in the layer window

So, we create a folder for every major subject we have, we select the **Pencil** layer as a reference layer, and we start creating our gray silhouettes:

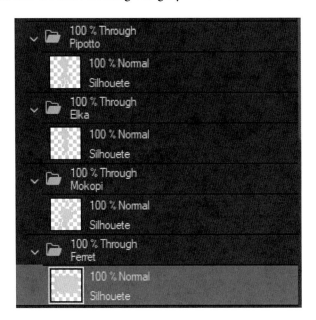

Figure 7.74 – Layer folders with the silhouettes

Now maybe I'm a little bit fixated on layer organization, but I create a folder for every main character and main object. The only necessary thing is to create a new layer for every silhouette we need.

Now we just start shading. For this part, I recommend not using a textured brush, but a basic circle brush with only **Color mixing** activated. This is because having a change in the saturation or hue can be detrimental, and for the luminosity of your color, it's better to use **Amount of paint** combined with **Brush density**.

Little pro's tip: Invisible selectable line art

To be honest, I just discovered this trick 2 months ago, but it's a complete lifesaver.

If you set your line art as white, just select **Object tool**, go to **Tool property**, and change the color from there to white. Set the blending mode of **Layer** to **Multiply**. The line art is invisible because a pure white value can't darken the layers underneath it so it doesn't show. CSP still recognizes it if you select this layer as a reference layer, meaning that the lines you create will be recognized by CSP for selection by the **Auto select** tool and now the **Fill** tool will fill with the selected color with the **Refer multiple** layers option checked.

For shading, I recommend you start by locating the terminator of your shadow—and no, you don't need to find a little robot in your painting!

The terminator, in really simple terms, is the darkest part of your object. In *Figure 7.75*, it is the red dotted line. Just remember that this is applied only while considering the object without considering the cast shadow. If you want to see a more in-depth analysis regarding this, there is the video by Proko, *Shading Light and Form*, or the video by Dorian Iten *Mind-Blowing realistic shading trick*. I would love to go into detail here, but learning drawing is not within the scope of this book as its purpose is to be a manual on how to use CSP:

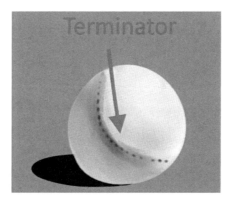

Figure 7.75 – Terminator location

So, locating your terminator means that you know where your darkest value will be, meaning that half of the first part of the job is done:

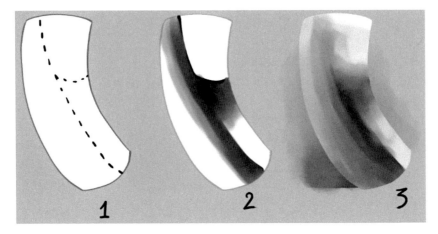

Figure 7.76 – Process for doing a grisaille

All I will do now is follow the process shown in the figure:

1. Locating the terminator
2. Blending a little bit on the shadow side, hiding the pencils lines a little bit
3. Continuing to blend…
4. Having fun, possibly

For deciding where to soft blend and hard blend, there is a simple rule:

"How intense and how big is the light?"

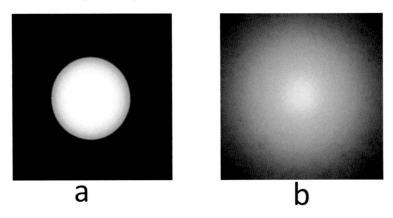

Figure 7.77 – Light demonstration

If the light is sharply focused and small, you will have a really hard edge. If you have a big, soft light (like a fluffy white cat with long fur), well, you will have a soft shadow.

So, remember:

"Fluffy white cat = soft shadow; little white mouse = hard edge."

Figure 7.78 – Finished grisaille

My last piece of advice for the grisaille is don't go full black or full white, because we will do the darkest and lightest part during the color phase—or, in other words, the next section, *Color mapping*. The advice is the same for details such as eyebrows: we will do them later. What we need is a base of values that we can paint over. This grisaille took me approximately 2 hours. As we will see in the next section, there is a reason for the side decorations looking as they are.

Color mapping

Now, this is a little bit of a cheat method, but you could say that using acrylics is cheating in the perspective of a Renaissance painter, so…

Practically speaking, a gradient map is a gradient that will substitute all your gray tones with a gradient. Shocking, eh?

You can use this to create a base mood for your work, or to create your final colors.

To use it, you just need to go to **Layer | New correction layer | Gradient Map**. Let's try an example using the side decorations:

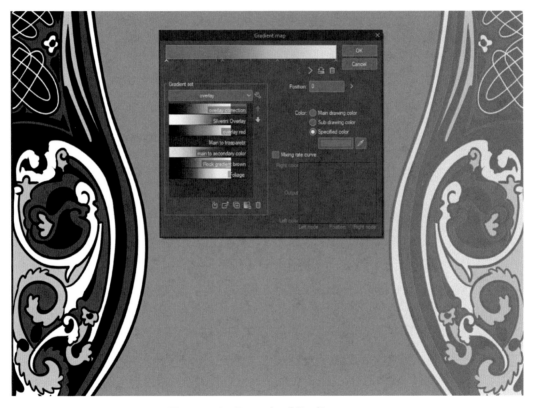

Figure 7.79 – Example of Gradient map

As you can see, everything that is toward black will be that shade of blue, dark indigo, and everything that is toward white will have that yellow color. You just need to click those little arrows below the gradient to modify the placement of the color. If you click somewhere on the gradient, it will create a division in the gradient, and you can add another color. For example, I added green for everything that has roughly 75% luminosity and red for anything that has roughly 25% luminosity.

Now, what interests us the most is how do we change a color? On the middle-right side, there are three settings:

- **Main drawing color**: Will use your selected main color.

- **Sub drawing color**: Will use your sub drawing color.

- **Specified color**: Guess what? It uses a specified color:

Figure 7.80 – Color settings location in Gradient map

With this, we create the first layer of colors in our piece. We use our line art as a reference layer, and with the magic wand, we select and create a gradient map. With this technique, we have created all our base colors:

Figure 7.81 – The illustration with all the base colors

Remember that those are not the final colors, they're a base that you can use for the final colors. If you've enough patience, you can create your final colors with this method, but I don't have that kind of patience. This is why this heading is called *Color mapping* and not *Coloring your grayscale*.

Final colors

To be honest, this is my favorite part. This step is all about you and your artistic expression. You can still get pretty good results with the previous steps, and this is an extra step, in a way, if you have used the gradient map trick to create your final colors.

We have all we need—the base value and the base color. Now create a new layer, above the gradient map, take your color palette (the one in **Intermediate Color**), and start painting little imperfections, and little variations in the colors based on your preference. This is the time to use a textured brush and your realistic painting brushes:

Figure 7.82 – Pipotto with new colors painted

Just to help you understand, the previous step took 1-2 hours at most, but this stage required a whole day of work for me. Why? Because I fine-tuned everything.

Now, the trick here is not to go overboard. You need subtlety here, and you need to play with the transparency of your color to give your illustration a personal flavor: your flavor.

Here's the finished illustration. Am I a good painter? Absolutely not. Do I need to learn a lot more about painting? Yes. Did this stop me from having a blast while painting it? Absolutely not!

Figure 7.83 – Finished painterly illustration

I wish there were a trick in CSP that would help you paint better, but there isn't. It's just you and your canvas, and hopefully, you're having fun.

Summary

You probably wanted a chapter in which I would teach you about anatomy, composition, or color theory and all that stuff, but the purpose of this book is to teach you how to use a tool. And in that regard, I think I have taught you a little bit in this chapter.

In this chapter, you've learned how to create a proper workspace, for all your needs. Next, you learned how to stimulate your imagination using an "idea" brush, how to refine it with a sketch, and even how to use the new update to create realistic brushes for your paintings.

After this, we branched out. You learned how to create a cartoon illustration with all the necessary steps: inking, flatting, and applying colors. Finally, we learned how to use CSP in our steps to create a painterly illustration.

In the next chapter, we will learn about the main use of CSP, making comics.

8
Creating Your Own Comic

Now, when I said in *Chapter 7*, *Making Your Own Illustration*, that "Software doesn't matter," there is a tiny caveat in there, and that is this:

"Every software has its unique perks."

For example, if I wanted to edit a photo using CSP, it is a little bit of a pain … it can't even open RAW files, which are the native files of the camera. So, what I do? I use Photoshop or Affinity Photo, which both have more features for photo editing.

Why am I saying this? Because one of the main features of CSP is a comic page management system, but this is only for the **EX version** of the software. Wanting to use CSP as comic software and not use the EX version is, well, a nonsensical choice. CSP's EX version has a page management system, with batch export, and batch text edit, but the pro version of CSP doesn't have these things. Plus, with the December 10, 2020 update, you even have options for webtoons.

If you don't have the money for the EX version, you can use Krita as page management software, but you need to export all the files in `.PSD` and refresh them manually. It is an alternative, not a comfortable one, but still an option. Remember that Celsys offers a 50% discount on CSP's EX version roughly every 6 months. Hence, you don't need to pay the entire amount, just half the price.

In this chapter, everything you will see is only for the EX version of CSP.

My advice is this: if you want to make comics with CSP, you should buy the EX version. It's a one-time payment and you have it for life; it's an investment.

In this chapter, you will learn the following:

- A brief introduction to comics
- Setting up the workspace (yes, again)
- Creating a story and a storyboard
- Finishing a page
- Exporting for print

Introduction to comics

Making comics is a really hard job, and completely different from making illustrations. Why?

I can quote Scott McCloud in his *Understanding Comics* book, which is a book that every serious comic artist needs to read. McCloud defines comics as:

> *"Juxtaposed pictorial and other images in deliberate sequence, intended to convey information and/or to produce an aesthetic response in the viewer."*

This quote means that you create two or more images that are in a sequence, but not entirely for narrating a story. For example, the artist *Moebius* sometimes doesn't narrate a story, strictly speaking, but still makes comics. To help you understand this concept a little better, **silent books** are not regarded as comics, but we can all agree that we read the book by looking at images juxtaposed in a deliberate order. If you put multiple images on a single page, it's definitely a comic, and I'm certain of that, but if it's only one image per page, it's more of a picture book. In short, speech balloons and the story are not what make something a comic.

This means that you need to create more images per page, and you need to create a lot more pages than when you make a simple illustration. What does this translate to? If I make a story that is 10 pages long, and I spend 6 hours creating every page (meaning that I'm pretty fast), then I will need 60 hours in total to complete the comic. Let's say I can only work for five hours a day. This would mean less than a page a day, meaning 12 days of work. However, if I have a lesson at university, or I need to go to the doctor's, or my computer crashes because my cat decided that it needed to stay on the floor and it pushes it from my desk, and I spend a whole day hoping to fix everything … accidents happen, as you know … then this translates to more like 13-15 days of work.

This means that I will need 2 weeks of work for a 10-page comic. And what if I need to make a short story of 50 pages? The result is 300 hours of drawing, plus all the time you need to do the lettering, laying out the pages, and so on. This would result in 60-65 days of work.

Do you see why I say doing comics is a pretty hard job? Drawing comics is not a short burst of energy, like an illustration; it's more like a marathon.

The first thing you need to understand is that making comics requires a lot of energy and time. Why do you think a lot of webcomics only create 1 page/week? For the reason that humans cannot possibly work for 10 hours a day without some side effects, for example, burnout. So, think of the long run when it comes to comics. It's better to have a consistent page a week instead of producing 4-5 pages/week and burning yourself out.

However, you could say: "Japanese comic artists (mangaka) produce 25 pages a week." Well, they have assistants, meaning that while I spend 2-3 hours on the pencils of the next page, someone else spends 2-3 hours on inking the previous page, which means we can produce 2 pages in approximately 9 hours. If you consider that sometimes you have different people for backgrounds, tone work, layouts, lettering, and so on, manga artists can complete 5 pages a day. This is likely accompanied by a lot of stress and difficulty, but it can be done.

Before starting, I'd like to offer a little explanation regarding the term **comic**. When I say *comic*, I mean the narrative medium, not a precise narrative style such as Manga, Manhwa, or Marvel/DC comic style. I am referring to the melting pot that is the medium of comics.

So, let's take a look at all the tricks you can do to save your time. It's not cheating— plainly put, it's for your own survival. When it comes to saving time, CSP can help you a lot. Let's start with the basics: the workspace.

Setting up your workspace

In general, you are expected to do the following things when creating a comic:

- Change brushes on the fly, moving between decoration brushes, inking brushes, and coloring brushes

- Change layers on the fly

- Change layer properties easily

- Select colors from a color palette

You can also expect to do the following things that are unique to CSP:

- Use the **Sub View** palette to have the references you need, and for picking colors for your characters.

- Use your material folders in case you need to add textures, 3D models, layer structures, and in the event that you create materials and use them. Every decoration you see of my work is 50% material and 50% a decoration brush:

  a. Trees = materials

  b. Textures = materials

  c. Buildings? Guess what: Also materials, and you know how to make them thanks to *Chapter 3*, *Creating 3D Backgrounds in CSP*, and *Chapter 4*, *Using Your 3D Props to Create a Scene.*

  d. Main characters? Well, just go to *Chapter 5*, *Implementing 3D Characters in CSP*, and *Chapter 6*, *Importing 3D Characters in CSP*, and you can see that even those are materials.

  e. CSP itself? Yes, even that is materials.

- Use the **Quick access** palette to quickly select effects, such as Gaussian blur, and also for corrections, such as gradient maps. In addition, **Quick Access** is for switching between sub tools – I can switch between my drawing tools and decoration tools.

This will be your final workspace:

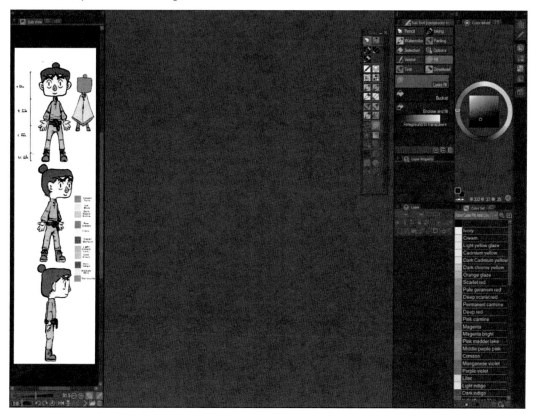

Figure 8.1 – Comic workspace

If you have a small monitor, the next workspace is a little better because you can use more vertical space for the layer frame.

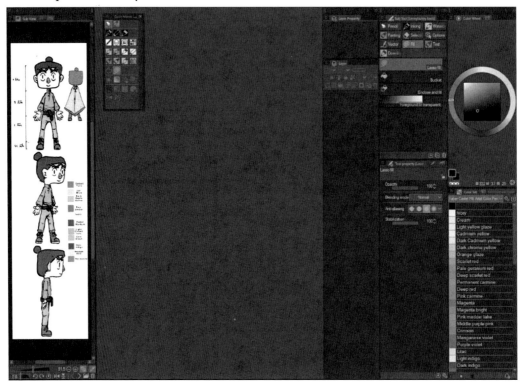

Figure 8.2 – Comic workspace for small monitors

You will need to zoom in and out a lot, but if you use a 13" or 16" monitor, you will need to do it by default for good inking and coloring. If you use a cellphone, well… this section doesn't matter, because you don't have the screen space. It would be better to buy a tablet that you can attach to your phone, because trust me, to manage 8 hours of drawing on your phone, you would need the spine of an air dancer: non-existent.

Now, remember that this is a workspace where I feel at home. If you are left-handed, you can invert this workspace. If you prefer to have the **Layer** window next to the **Sub view** window, you can do it.

Now, let's start the creative process of making a comic.

Creating a story and a storyboard

Every comic starts somewhere, and that start is the creation of a story. Every story starts with a concept: an idea, or something along those lines. Now, there is no failsafe method when it comes to the concept. The only thing I can say is this: the concept is not important, what is important is the execution. What do I mean by this? Let's see some examples:

- Batman? A rich orphan who fights crime

- Sonic? A blue hedgehog that runs really fast

- Castlevania? A guy who needs to whip Dracula to death, and sometimes Dracula's son helps too

So, even if you have a high concept, it doesn't mean you will succeed. I think you can name at least 10 stories with high concepts that failed miserably.

So, the question you should be asking is not "How do I come up with a good concept?"

Instead, you should be asking: "How can I execute my idea well?"

For that, there is some general advice that could be useful.

General writing advice

When it comes to the question of good writing, the answer is (in a way) to train and study. There is no short road for this: you study storytelling, look at the stories you like, analyze why you like them, write a story, rinse and repeat, and you will start to have a feeling as to whether something works.

Some good books are *Story* by *Robert McKee*, *Hero's Journey* by *Joseph Campbell*, *Making Comics* by *Scott McCloud*, and *Manga in Theory and Practice* by *Hirohiko Araki*. Those are not storytelling books in themselves, but they can give you a good insight. The first book is a more traditional analysis of stories, whereas the second book analyzes a basic structure found in myths: a structure wherein a hero who has a normal human status enters the magic world, returning into our world as a hero. The book by McCloud is the most important book you can buy for understanding comics. The fourth book is a book on making comics, made by the author of *Jojo*.

My take on reading those books, plus all the other books, comics, games, and films I've seen, read, and played, plus what I like to do, is this: it is not a perfect formula, but it's like a compass.

The predominant structure used in storytelling is one of three acts:

1. The introduction, in which you introduce the concept and provide the main problem of the story.

2. The confrontation, in which the protagonists arm themselves to resolve the main problem.

3. The ending, when we see the resolution of the main problem in which the protagonist a use what they obtained and learned in the confrontation phase.

This is a "fine" structure, but it's a little bit dry and it feels like a set of rules. Therefore, I modified it to my needs and narrative beliefs:

1. **Rulebook**: The first part of the story is the part in which I explain the ground *rules* that I will use for the rest of the story. Because it's a story, by default, you will have a "beginning," or something that will set everything in motion. My main job in this part is telling the reader that the information they will read is laws that can't be broken.

2. In *Little Sophia Escaping World*, my first *Bunnyfable*, those rules are as follows:

    a. The main character is weak.

    b. The monster is stronger than her.

    c. She can't win in a direct fight.

    d. The door lets her travel from world A to world B, and vice versa.

3. **Performance**: This is the tricky part. In the previous step, I set the rules for me, the reader, and the character. Now I need to outline a performance that can be played out by my character that fits within these rules.

4. A good trick to remember this: "You can't decide why character A wants to shoot character B, but you can decide where the projectile hits."

5. In short, you can't decide the motivation for a character, because if you make a good character, they will start to think for themselves, but you can decide the outcome of their decisions.

6. **Catharsis**: This is the most important thing, and it's the first thing I decide. What kind of emotional payoff will the reader have from reading my story? Will they feel empowered, as in *DOOM* games, or feel depressed, like the ending of *The Mist*? I always decide which kind of catharsis I want to create, and after that, I make a casting for the characters. I create one character after another and I fire them until I've found "the one." Only after all of this can I decide everything else.

Remember that a **story** and the **setting** are two distinct things. For the setting, I advise you to follow these suggestions:

*   The history of your setting. For a single story, this shouldn't take you more than a Word page in font 12 in Times New Roman (or similar font).

*   Create a set of rules and abide by them always. If your protagonist is in a bind, you can't subvert them. An example is the Kryptonite in the *Superman* stories. Superman will always be weak to that glowing rock, no matter what. I believe that in the long history of *DC*, no one has tried to make Superman invulnerable to Kryptonite, though it's a little bit difficult to know everything that happened in 90 years of a comic.

These are simply some basic tips on how to start with your writing process. Now, we can move on to creating a new comic folder.

Creating a new comic

To create a new file, you just need to press *Ctrl/Cmd + N*; it's a pretty standard shortcut. All the settings you need are located from the second icon to the fifth icon:

Figure 8.3 – Comic settings option location

The first option is for **Webtoon** settings, and those are the most basic settings. The first options you will have are in common with all the other settings, and also with every kind of software. These are the **Width** and **Height** options for your canvas as well as **Resolution**.

Basic expression color is a setting more unique to CSP because it tells the software whether you want your basic layer to be in **Color Mode**, **Gray Mode**, or **Monochrome**. Which mode you need to use is a pretty easy choice:

- **Color**: If you need to use colors

- **Gray**: If you need or want to use screen tones, and you can choose the frequency at which it will be printed

- **Monochrome**: If you need a bitmap image, an example is the comic *Fables*, by *Bill Willingham*, in the black and white edition.

> **Important note**
>
> The DPI is a pretty easy setting to understand. It's how many pixels per inch you want, so 300 dpi means that in A4 format, you will have 300 pixels in an inch. So, if you have 1 in = 300 px, 8.27 in = 2,480 px. So, an A4 at 300 dpi is equivalent to an A5 at 600 dpi. Easy, no?

The **Paper color** setting is your **Paper layer** color. It's the base color of your canvas.

The **Template** setting is for adding a frame base or a layer folder structure to your canvas across all the pages. If you need to create a series of 4koma or a cartoon strip, this could be a useful setting.

The rest of the settings are more specific to webtoons:

- **Number of page divisions** is a setting in which CSP will divide your entire page by that number, so as an example, if we were to select 100 px divided by 10, every page will be 10 px of height.

- **Number of pages** lets you choose how many pages you want. So, if your base page is a 10 x 10 px and you include 10 pages, you will have a total of 100 px of height:

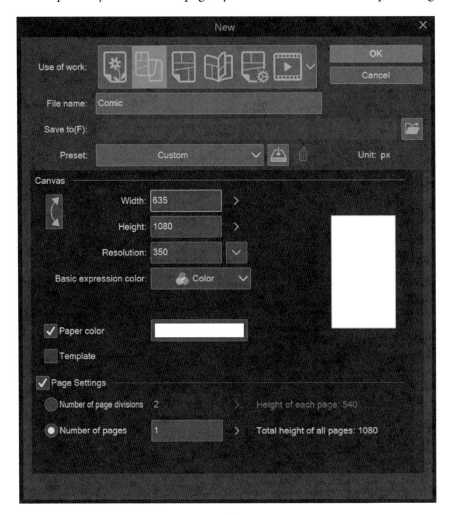

Figure 8.4 – Webtoon settings

Regarding the size of a single page, every website has different requirements. *Tapas* comics don't enforce any limitation in that regard, *Line Webtoons* requires `800x1280px`. Generally, try to have a 1:1.7 ratio between width and height, because these are the common proportions for the width and height of monitors.

Webtoon

Those settings are for vertical scrolling webtoons, but if you know for sure that you will not print your work, those settings are good for page reading comics, too. You just need to put the px dimensions as a printed page comic and export your story as single files.

The following diagram shows the page manager when a webtoon has been created:

Figure 8.5 – Webtoon page manager

One last setting regarding webtoon creation that is useful to know is a view option that will let you see how the webtoon will be seen on a cellphone.

To activate it, you just need to open a page and go to **View | On-screen area (webtoon)**. Right below there are the options for this view mask. The grayed out area marks what will not be shown:

> **Onscreen area**
>
> This option is more useful than you think. Let's say you want to publish an illustration or a comic online. You can use this feature to see what the viewer will see on different displays.

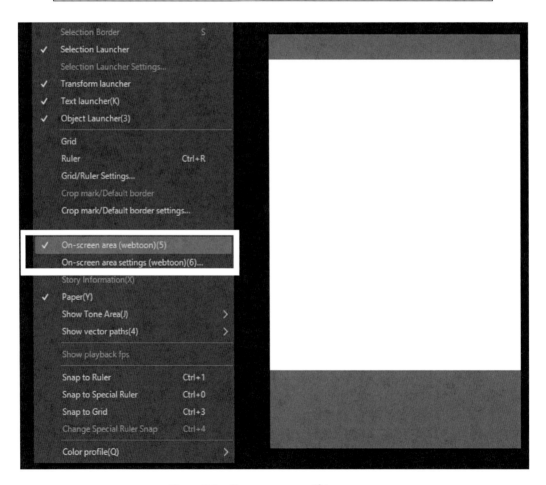

Figure 8.6 – Onscreen area within a canvas

The next setting in line for comics is the well-named **Comic settings** option. Here, you can find all the settings you need for printing your comic. Now, before starting to explain the settings, a little word of advice: Call your printer shop first. You don't know which printer shop you will go to? Go to Google and search for printer shops, or ask friends. Just have a general idea, call them and ask them how they want the file, in what format (jpg, png, tiff, pdf), which color profile (CMYK or RGB), whether they need the blind folio, whether they need the margins, and so on. Just ask away! This will resolve a lot of potential issues further down the line:

Figure 8.7 – Comic settings Binding (finish) size

The **Binding (finish) size** is the size of the page that will be trimmed. So, if you set it as an A4, your canvas will be larger than an A4, and this is not something you want. Usually, printer shops can only print an A3 as the maximum format, meaning that your page can't be more than an A4 in dimension. Why? Because when you print a comic, you print two pages together, fold this huge page, and bind it with the other pages. So, if you print your single page larger than A4, they can't possibly bind the comic. So, your **Binding (finish) size** needs to be less than an A4, or at least smaller than the maximum format of your printer shop's maximum printable format. So, that's another question you need to ask. If you are dealing with a publishing house, they will give you precise measurements, so you will use those measurements.

The **Bleed width** is a counter-intuitive setting until you see how they print a comic in front of you. The bleed is outside the trim zone, your final size, meaning that everything in the bleed zone will not be shown. So, why should you put something in there? Because if you don't, you will probably have a white border along your page. For example, consider a cover. If you don't put anything in the bleed area, there will be a certain amount of white border near the edges of the cover.

The bleed is something you need to set so that your full pages or your overboard frames will look good.

The option immediately underneath is **Check whether to export fanzine printing data**. This is simply an option that will check whether every setting is good for fanzine printing.

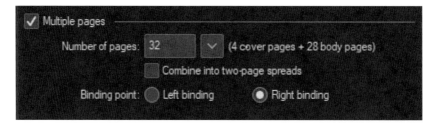

Figure 8.8 – Comic settings Multiple pages

The options below are **Multiple pages** settings:

- **Number of pages**: This number needs to be a multiple of four. Why? Take a sheet of paper, fold it in two. Congratulations, you created the simplest book in history. Your total page number is four. That's why, when you set your page number, it should always be a multiple of four.

- **Combine into two-page spreads**: This is an option in which all the pages, except the cover pages, will be glued together to form a double page (also known as a spread).

- **Binding point**: This is how you decide whether you're creating a comic with a left-to-right or right-to-left reading sense. Western books have **Left binding**, whereas some areas of Asia use **Right binding**.

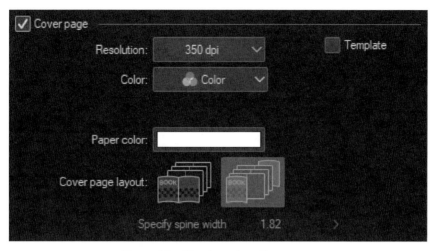

Figure 8.9 – Comic settings Cover page

Next in line are the **Cover page** settings. The only two new options are as follows:

- **Cover page layout**: Here, you can decide whether you want a stitched cover, in other words, a cover that has the front and back cover as a single image, or a cover that is only one image, or a cover that is two distinct images. If it is your first time printing a comic or you're self-publishing, I recommend using the second option, because with a stitched cover, you will need to specify the spine width, something that is a little bit tricky.

- **Specify spine width**: This option is the height of the comic, the spine. This measurement can vary based on paper, the number of pages, and the paper of the cover. It's a little bit tricky being precise with this when you're starting out.

The last two option groups are **Story Information** and **Folio**. The first one comprehends all the settings for your metadata, but before continuing, I need to show you what you will see once you have created a comic:

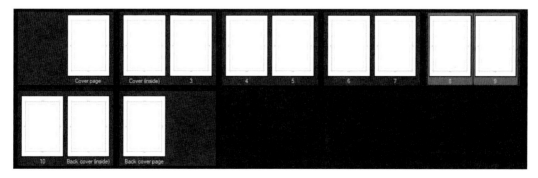

Figure 8.10 – Page manager layout, following comic creation

Now we need to observe one striking thing about our page numbers. The page after the cover page is not 1 but 3, because page 1 in CSP is the cover page:

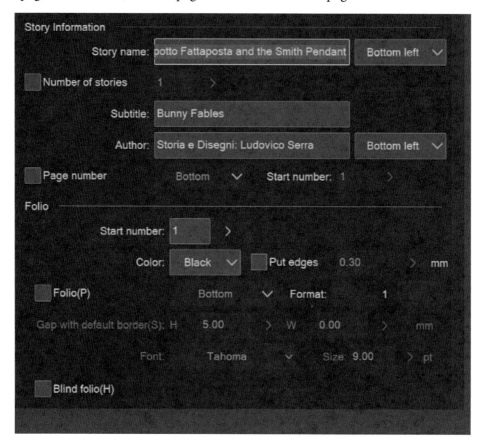

Figure 8.11 – Comic settings – story information details

This little piece of information is a pretty important one regarding page counting. The following points detail everything that we can see in the preceding screenshot:

- **Story name**: This is where you insert the name of your story.

- **Number of stories**: This setting was the bane of my existence in terms of trying to understand what it meant. It's practically a chapter count. Story number 1 is practically issue/ch. 1.

- **Subtitle**: This setting is for additional information. Usually, I put the name of the series in there. In this case, it is *Bunnyfables*.

- **Author**: You just insert your name there. If you are part of a collaborative effort, specify who did what. If, for example, I alone did the story, I would write "Story: Ludovico."

- **Page number**: As you can see, you have two values for the page number, one in **Folio**, and this one. This setting creates a page number that will not be seen by the reader, so this really is information for you instead of for the printer or the reader. Remember that in CSP, pg. 1 is considered the cover. In this case, the **Start number** option is related to the number that will be shown on the cover page, just to make it more compressible… If you need to make a comic for a collection, or a publisher like *Jump*, they put more than one comic story in one volume. So, your comic can be on page 250 or pg.120 or pg.10… So, **Start number** is for this kind of purpose.

The **folio** options, the ones under **Story Information**, are all related to page numbers for the reader and the printer. Various options let you decide the look of your page number:

- **Start number**: This start number references which page you want your page numbers to start at. However, this is a little bit counter-intuitive because it is based on the cover page. If you set it at 3, for example, the cover page will be Pg.3. So, if we want pg.3 of our example to be counted as pg.1, we will need to set this value at -1:

Figure 8.12 – Start number explanation

- **Color**: You can choose to have the page number, also known as the folio, in black or white, and whether to add an edge to your page number. If you have set the color as black, the edge will be white, and vice versa:

Figure 8.13 – Example of folio. Black (left) and white with borders (right)

- **Gap with default border** is just a setting where you can choose the distance of your folio from the border of your page.

- **Font** is an obvious one. This is where you decide the font of your page number. **Size** is where (you guessed it) you choose the size.

- **Blind folio** is a setting that is a little bit tricky. If you check this option, you will add your folio to the inside of your pages. This number will be hidden during the binding of the book. In the case of a standard issue in the style of DC or Marvel, you don't need to add it. However, in the case of a graphic novel format, you perhaps will need to add it, because it's information that the printer may need. How do you know whether you need to add it or not? Ask your printer:

Figure 8.14 – The printer every time you call it

The third setting for comics we will encounter is the one related to fanzines. As you can see, it's a lot less cluttered. Because a lot of the information required is already filled in as standard, we can't change options such as the **Binding (finish) size**. My advice would be to stick with the B5 size that is preset:

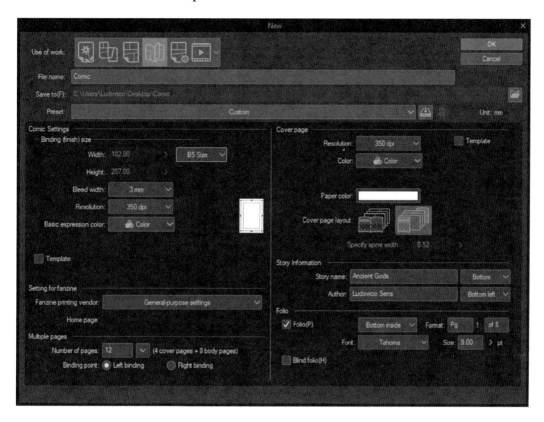

Figure 8.15 – Fanzine settings

Now, take a deep breath, because the final setting presets are a lot to take in. This is because it will release all the eldritch knowledge of comic settings. The fourth and final comic option preset is **Show all comic settings**:

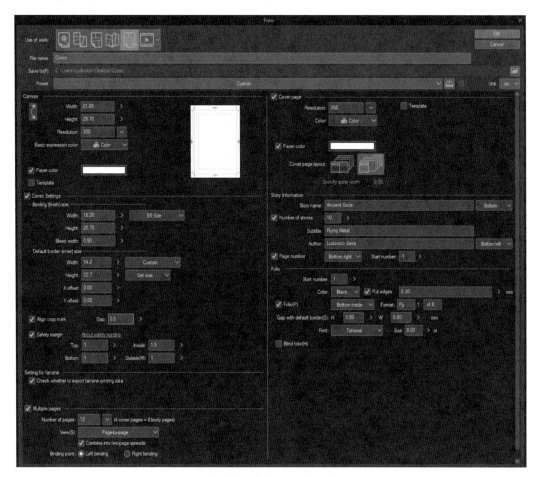

Figure 8.16 – The eldritch knowledge of comic settings

Now, let's start with the first setting group – **Canvas**. This refers to the printed final page, so you can't go over the A4 format or the ½ of the maximum printable page of your printer shop.

The rest of the setting groups are the same as the **Comic** setting presets. The only new one is the one under **Canvas**, the **Comic Settings** group.

Now, before moving on, I need to let you see a "finished" page with all the settings applied:

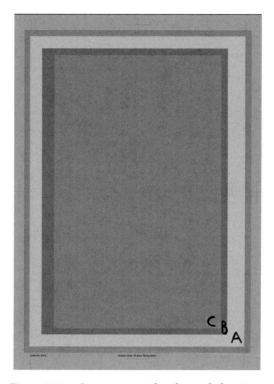

Figure 8.17 – Comic page with color-coded settings

Here follows an explanation of *Figure 8.17*:

- Everything in the red-orange part will be trimmed by the printer shop:

    a. The orange part will be the complete page, **Canvas**, printed by the printer shop. Once all the pages have been printed, they will be stacked together and trimmed.

    b. The red part is **Bleed**. You need to draw in this part for the splash pages or for full-page frames. Don't include important details here.

- Everything in blue color will be seen by the reader:

    a. The furthermost part (A zone) is the final page, **Binding (finish) size**, meaning that everything in this part will be seen by the reader, but with a caveat.

b. The B zone, the blue one, is **Safety margin**. Safety margins are for the printing size. It's easier to understand this by using an example. CSP is originally a Japanese software, so some options don't make sense at first glance. But, if you reframe it for a Japanese environment, it makes sense. This is one of those options. In Japan, you have a weekly or monthly magazine with various comics, an example of which would be *Shonen Jump*. Their weekly magazine has a single page of B5 size, but the published volumes/tankobon editions are in a different proportion. So, **Safety margin** creates a box in which you're completely sure (irrespective of the proportion of the paper) that your drawing will be visible. This is the caveat I was referring to in the explanation of the Binding (finish) size. If you're a Western comic artist, you don't usually need to think about this, but if the use of safety margins is required, your printer will tell you. For a self-published comic, this is a useless option.

c. The C zone is **Default border (inner) size**. This is where you want to put all your balloons and frames. Remember that if you want to draw splash pages or a page with a full-page illustration, you need to draw over this section. Practically speaking, it's the area where you will place your story, so everything important needs to stay inside this box. If you're self-publishing, you can put whatever you want, but if you're working for a publisher, they will give you exact measurements.

All the options in **Comic Settings** are for setting those values. Now follows a little word of advice regarding **Default border (inner) size**. I highly recommend changing the setting from **Set size** to **Set margin**, as this means the margin will be calculated based on border distance and not measurements. In this way, you don't need to do any math:

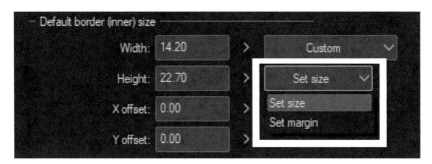

Figure 8.18 – Setting the size/margin location

And now you have a complete understanding of how to set up your comic in CSP. In the next section, I will show you how to use **Story Editor** to start defining your story in CSP.

How to use the story editor

Now I will start showing you the features while I'm drawing one page of my new Bunnyfable so that you can see the practical application of what I'm talking about at each step.

Let's start with the story editor. But before continuing, I need to clarify that using *Scrivener* (a writing software that I recommend), I have drawn up a rough synopsis of the plot, detailing how many scenes there will be, and so on. The scene for the first page is like this:

- Scene 1:

    a. Action 1: Pipotto wakes up.

    b. Action 2: Pipotto's father tells him to go to Albrecht.

    c. Action 3: Pipotto goes out of the house.

All the various scenes are written in this way in a comfortable *Scrivener* folder. That said, let's start! To find the story editor, just go to **Story | Edit text | Open story editor**:

Figure 8.19 – Story editor location

This will open a window that lets you batch process and insert the text on the specified pages without opening the file. Just a little word of warning: opening the story editor will delete the history, so you can no longer use "undo" on any of your open pages. Because of this, if you know that you need to use undo, open Story Editor first and then open the pages later. The story editor will appear as a full-screen canvas. Just click and drag that little icon at the top with *"Name of your story"* + *story editor* and put it on the left or right:

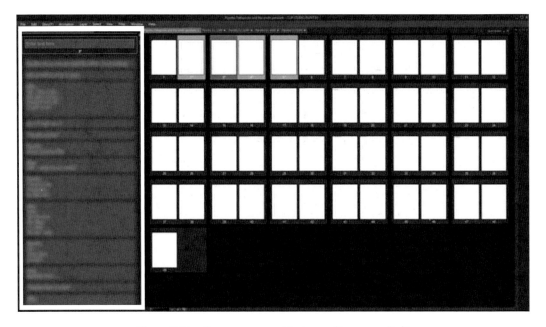

Figure 8.20 – Page manager with story editor open (left)

During this stage, we will only use the **Story editor**, **Sub tool palette**, and **Tool property** palettes.

But what does the story editor do on a practical level? Let's open a page. Now we take the text tool. I will copy and paste all the actions I've written in *Scrivener*:

Figure 8.21 – Story editor phase workspace

Now, I select the **Text** tool, then I go to **Tool properties**, and then I select a light font with a green earth background color. You can find all of these options in the **Sub Tool Detail** palette, the extended tool option, in the **Font** and **Text** categories:

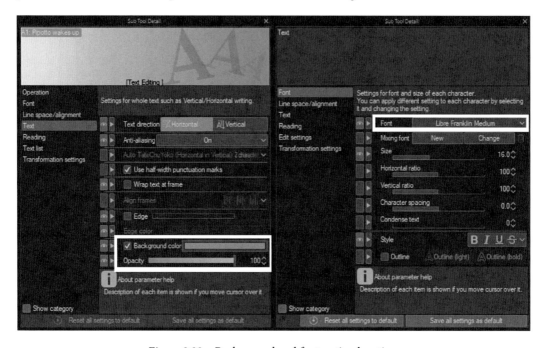

Figure 8.22 – Background and font option location

I like to use **Libre Franklin Medium** because it's a free Google font and comes with a lot of weights. For **Actions**, I will use **Libre Franklin Light**. Now I will write directly on the page, and it will appear in the story editor:

Figure 8.23 – Story editor – the page text relationship

Now I will go to **Story editor** and create a text style of some sort inside CSP:

1.   We select the page we want to edit, in my case, page 2:

Figure 8.24 – Balloon number 1 at pg.2

2. Now we press the *Enter* key twice, or *Shift + Enter*. This will create a new balloon:

Figure 8.25 – New balloon created in the story editor

3. Now we type `Action 2: Pipotto's father tells him to go to Albrecht`.

This adds text to the page... but how will the story editor add it?

A1: Pipotto wakes up
A2:Pipotto father tell him to go to Albrecht

Figure 8.26 – Text added via the story editor

As you can see, the A2 action will have the same text style as the A1 action, giving us a way to have text styles in CSP. Now I will add a new text with a dark chrome yellow background color and a Libre Franklin Medium font, and I will write `Scene description`. Now I create a new text, with no background and with the font *Inkslinger BB*. This will be my base style for dialogs, so I will use the font that I will use for my dialogs.

Now I create an **Actions** text style, and organize them at the top of my page like this:

Figure 8.27 – Text styles in CSP

Now we will need to go to the **Page Manager** tab. To open it, just go to **Story | Page Manager**.

What we will do now is batch paste the text styles we just created on every page we created, so we will have the same text styles on every page. Perform the following steps to achieve this:

1. We need to close the story editor. I don't know why, but the **Batch process** option can't be used when the story editor is open.

2. Now, with the **Object** tool, we select the *Dialogues* text style and we press *cmd*/**Ctrl** + **C**.

3. Now we go to **Page Manager**, right-click and scroll down until you find **Batch process | Batch process**:

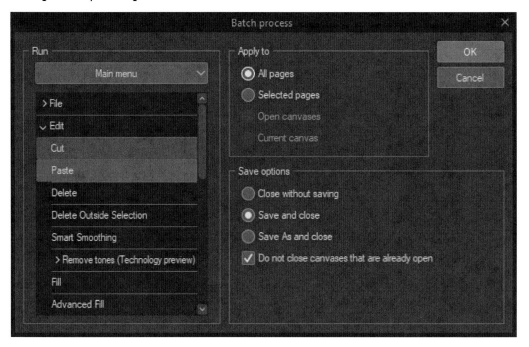

Figure 8.28 – The Batch process tab

4. Now you just need to select **Edit | Paste**, **All Pages**, and **Save and close**.

This will copy our *Dialogues* text style onto all the pages, and we need to do the same thing with the *Scene Description* and *Actions* text styles.

> **Batch process**
>
> Every time you need to make a batch operation for something that can be found in the main menu, or for an auto action, I strongly recommend using the **Batch process** feature.

Now the steps are pretty easy. We open the story editor and we start to think about the scenes based on the action we decided. Here is an example:

- A1: Pipotto wakes up.

    a. The scene is in the morning; could a sunrise shot be useful?

    b. I need a shot of Pipotto in bed.

    c. Maybe even his morning preparation?

After this, we refine the scene description until we have something like the following:

- A1: Pipotto wakes up.

    a. A wide shot of the city from sunrise.

    b. Pipotto wakes up.

    c. Pipotto puts his belt on while standing in front of a mirror.

This translates into three frames. Now I do the same with *Action 2* and I will have the following:

Figure 8.29 – First page of the comic with scenes and dialogs

In general, I take approximately 5-10 minutes for each page in choosing scenes and creating dialogs, so all of the pages will take roughly 4-6 hours.

Now that I've finished the general outline of page 2 of my comic, I will show you how you can use the story editor to create a storyboard. But before doing that, I prefer to create the frames, so I can draw inside a mask and have a more organized layer stack.

Creating frames

Now, the powerful thing about what we did before is that every single piece of text is a separate object that you can move within your canvas. So, we can use this to experiment with frame composition without spending too much time.

> **Frame composition**
>
> You have two options in terms of saving your frame composition at this stage. The first one is by copying the text layer and merging it with a layer and putting the obtained layer at the bottom of your layer stack. Another is just by duplicating your frame composition and activating/hiding your text layer.

With the method I've shown you, I can create 3 frame compositions in roughly 1 minute. My workflow is usually formed of small, fast, and changeable steps, done in rapid succession. As a result, if I make an error somewhere, I can correct it easily:

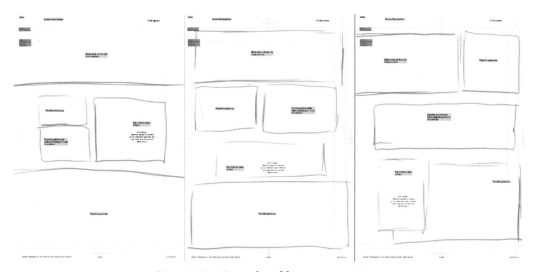

Figure 8.30 – Examples of frame compositions

I decided to go with the middle composition, as I think it's balanced and easily readable. Now it's time for me to create a more common acceptable storyboard, with all the drawings, perspective, and so on.

But before drawing, I make the frames. You can make them later, but I prefer to do them now. I make the frames first so that I can draw my storyboard inside the frames:

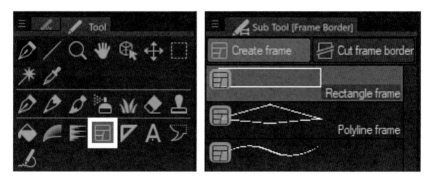

Figure 8.31 – Creating a Rectangle frame tool location

Remember that you can change the **Brush tip** option of the edge of the frames by going into **Sub Tool Detail**.

Creating frames is easy and fast in CSP; you don't need to create rulers, or draw the frames using brushes. You just take the **Rectangle frame** tool, click and drag, and you have a frame!

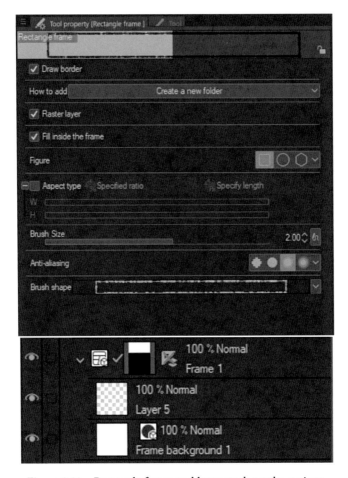

Figure 8.32 – Rectangle frame and layer stack results options

The options we need to interest ourselves in are the following:

- **Draw border**: If we check this option, the frame will be drawn with a border; unchecked, there will be no border.

- **How to add**: This is important for organizing your layer stack. You can select the **Create a new folder** option, meaning that every frame will be in its own frame folder, or the **Add to selected folder** option, meaning that all the frames will be in the same folder. There is no right way of doing this; you simply need to find your own preference.

- **Raster layer**: This setting is for creating a raster layer inside the frame.

- **Fill inside the frame**: This will create a fill layer inside the frame folder.

- **Brush Size**: This is the size of the edge of the frame. Easy, no?

The result will automatically create a folder in which, based on your settings, there will be a raster layer and a fill layer, plus a mask applied to the folder that will mask everything outside the frame:

Figure 8.33 – The page with all the frames

Now we just need to create a layer folder called `storyboard` inside every frame folder.

Drawing the storyboard

Now it's time to take your tablet pen and start drawing.

There are two main ways of drawing storyboards. The first one is to draw using quick lines, and the second is to use shapes:

Figure 8.34 – Example of a line storyboard type (left) and a shape storyboard type (right) for the second frame

Personally, I prefer to use the shape one, as it is faster for me due to my training in woodcut printing (xylography). However, you can use whichever option you prefer.

Storyboard character brushes

If your storyboard requires a less refined approach, such as the one used in manga creation, you can create a brush that has your character stickman as a tip. You just need to go to the **Sub Tool Detail** palette and go to **Stroke | Repeat method | One time only**. This will let you apply your character stickman every time you click. If your story is especially long, you can even create a frontal, profile, and 3/4 character storyboard brush.

I really recommend using assets at this stage, such as a foliage brush, tree brush, and brick texture.

A good place to find assets that are in *Clip Studio Assets* is *Nomad Photo Reference* (`https://www.artstation.com/nomad-photo-reference`) by *Ibrahim Lancoln*, which sells cutout `.png` files of clouds, trees, and people at a reasonable price.

To create backgrounds in a storyboard, I really recommend using a **perspective ruler frame layer**. To use it, just go to **Layer | Ruler/Frame | Create Perspective Ruler…**:

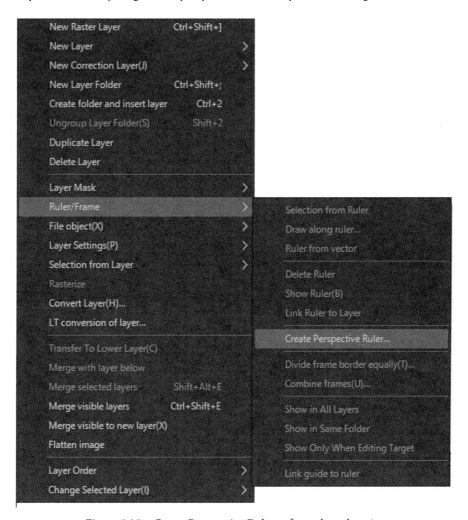

Figure 8.35 – Create Perspective Ruler… frame layer location

This will prompt a window in which you can choose the kind of perspective you want, from 1-point to 3-point perspective. This will result in perspective ruler being applied to the layer, with all the settings you've chosen:

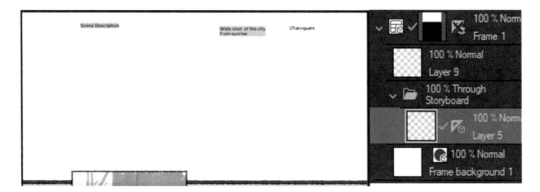

Figure 8.36 – Ruler frame on a layer and results

The perspective ruler will snap every line you make to the vanishing point. This can be useful or not based on what you're doing. In this case, it is not so useful because you only require a general direction rather than needing to be completely precise.

To remove the snapping of the perspective ruler, just go to **View** and deselect **Snap to Special Ruler**. I recommend putting this option in your shortcuts or **Quick Access** because this option activates and deactivates **Symmetrical ruler** and generally activates/deactivates every ruler tool.

Now for something approaching an advanced trick. If you select **Object Tool**, select **Perspective ruler**, and then go to the **Tool property** palette where you will find an option called **Grid**:

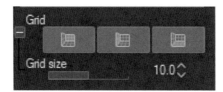

Figure 8.37 – Grid settings

This will activate a set of grids that will follow your vanishing points:

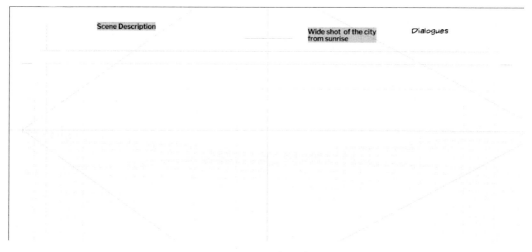

Figure 8.38 – Grid on the layer

You can modify the transparency of the ruler by going to **File | Preferences | Ruler/Unit**:

Figure 8.39 – Final storyboard for the comic

At this stage, don't worry about scribbling over the page for annotation: I need to remind myself to add a mask to frame 4 so that I can see the underlying head of the character. So, I scribbled a little annotation to remember this when I come to do the pencils.

You could say that this method for creating storyboards is only useful if you auto-produce a comic, but it can be useful according to the type of work you're doing. And what if you're creating a graphic novel? Absolutely.

Creating Marvel-style comics? I guess. Setting all the pages with the text styles and deciding the scenes and dialogs took me roughly 4 and a half hours of work while storyboarding a page takes me 10-15 minutes based on assets and the complexity of the scenes… This adds up to 10-13 hours, so do your math and see whether it can help you.

What if you're making a Japanese-style comic in which there are a lot of people working on the same page? Absolutely, and if we add to the equation the **Group work** feature, well, it's a pretty nifty trick.

Now we just need to finish the page, and CSP gives us a lot of different options. One of the main options is the group feature and the balloons.

Finishing a page

Now I will talk about group work data, and I think that this aspect doesn't receive enough love here in western countries.

There may be two reasons for this:

- You need two people with an EX license. This translates into two comic artists with an EX license who wish to collaborate. In places such as Marvel and DC, some passages of the comics are done with other people and usually using Adobe software, such as *Illustrator* for the lettering, meaning that your files will need to be in .psd format. Hence, it removes any kind of convenience associated with using the group work feature.

- Usually, when you're working on a webcomic or a self-published graphic novel, it's not economically reasonable to collaborate. If you're earning around €400 per month from your webcomic, and you collaborate with someone who isn't your partner (meaning that the money doesn't come back into the household), you need to pay for the help. So, you're no longer earning €400.

However, if there are cases in which it's not a good choice to use the group work feature, there are cases where having group work data can be highly beneficial. For example, you are working with a publisher such as Marvel. They put you, a pencil artist with CSP EX, together with an inker who has an EX version. In that case, it's beneficial to collaborate. I'm here to explain to you how to use **Group work** in CSP in those cases where it may be beneficial to you.

Another option, as of the May 2021 update, is the **Team work** feature. I will start with the **Group work** feature because it will take a little longer to explain.

Group work

You need two things in order to use the **Group work data** feature:

- A service such as OneDrive, Google Drive, Dropbox, or anything that creates a shareable folder between different computers. Do not use the website of your sharing folder service for sharing the data because it will not work.

- Have the same OS as your collaborator, whether that's Windows, iOS, Android, or Chrome OS.

The first thing we need to do is open **Page Manager** and go to **Story>Group Work**. Now we have two options that we can use:

- **Prepare group work data**, which will open the tab with all the settings for data creation.

- **Obtain group work data**, which will let you import the group data. This will practically copy the comic to your PC and create a live link between the folder on your computer and the online folder.

Selecting **Prepare group work data** will prompt this window:

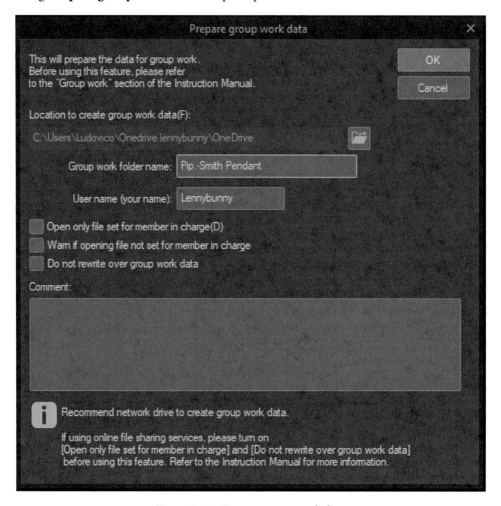

Figure 8.40 – Prepare group work data

The **Location to create group work data** part is easy. You just select your online folder and that's it. The **Group work folder name** field is the name of the folder that will be created in the online folder. The **User name (your name)** field is your username, and usually it's auto-filled.

Open only file set for member in charge and **Warn if opening file not set for member in charge** are two options I have never used because I have only ever worked with one person and those options are used when you need to manage a large group of people. So, we won't be covering how to use them at an advanced level. The general gist of them is that the first option only permits allowed users to open the pages. This means that the pages and files will not be openable except for you and your collaborators. This can be used as a way to organize the work and prevent unwanted changes.

To only provide selected people with access to the page, just select the page you want to add a member to, right-click on it, and go to **Group work | Set member for work**. This will prompt the following window to open:

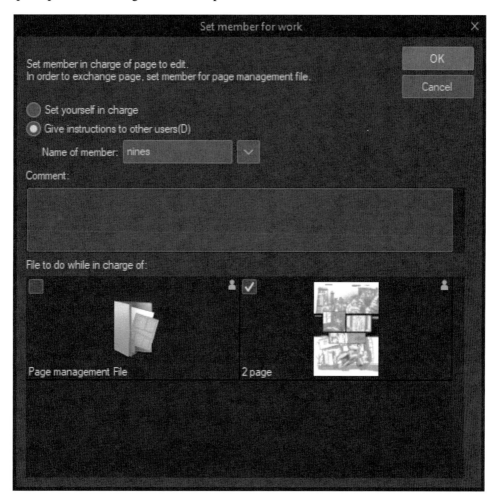

Figure 8.41 – Set member for work page tab

Now you just need to click on **Give instructions to other users** and then, in the **Name of member** field, type the nickname of your collaborator. The name will be created when your collaborator obtains the group data.

To remove a member, just select the pages you want, right-click, and go to **Group work >** **Cancel setting for member of work**. This will prompt the following window:

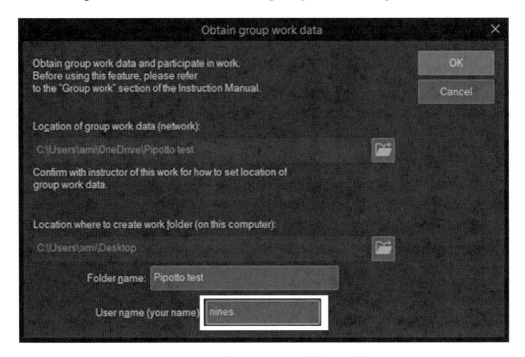

Figure 8.42 – Obtain group work data window

Remember that **User name** will be used by the administrator, the creator of the comic, to permit you to edit the page and that it's case-sensitive. So, don't choose anything that is difficult to remember, OK?

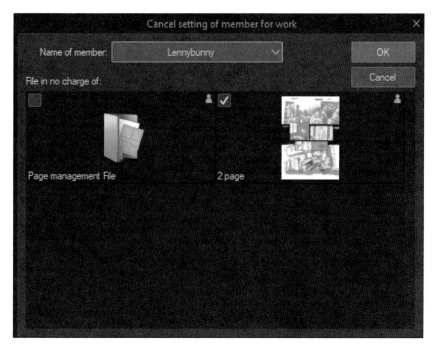

Figure 8.43 – Cancel setting of member for work window

Now, just select the user and check the page to which you want to cancel access, and then click **OK**.

The **Do not rewrite over group work data** field means that when a person uploads their changes in the group work data, the file will be temporally copied to a folder inside your **Group Work** folder. Only the administrator of the work, in other words, the author (you) can synchronize the data. If person A and B work at the same time on pg. 2, only I, the author, can decide which change, the one made by A or B, will be applied.

But this means that apparently, we can't work on the same page at the same time, meaning that a background artist can't work on the same page at the same time as the character inker. Why do I say *apparently*?

Because when you copy and paste between canvases in CSP, every pixel will remain as metadata.

Let's say that your background artist, let's call him Bob, like the planet in Titan A.E, needs more time to finish his work, but the inker has just finished theirs:

Figure 8.44 – Bob needing more time to texture that room

Bob will lose all his work! Well, not if the following steps are taken:

1.   Let's start by making a little sign in the top-left corner of your canvas:

Figure 8.45 – Location of the size mark

2. Now, just select your background folder.

3. Now, press *Ctrl/Cmd + C* to copy everything that you selected.

4. Then, go to **File | Create New from Clipboard**:

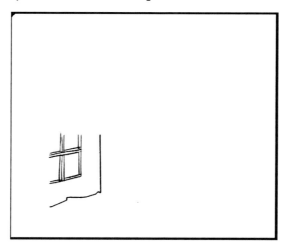

Figure 8.46 – Copy of your background layer stack

Now, the character inker can upload their work to the **Group Work data** just by saving the page, right-clicking on the page in **Page Manager**, going to **Group Work**, and then clicking on **Reflect change on group work data**. Now Bob can reopen the page, and just needs to copy and paste his work back onto the page, save it, and then click on **Reflect change on group work data**:

Figure 8.47 – Frame with the character inking and the amazing background of Bob

In this way, everyone can work on the same file and have a good time. Bob is a happy background artist because he can work at the speed he likes: be like Bob.

If you found the **Group work** feature slightly too complicated, don't worry. There is another option called the **Team work** feature.

Team work

For the May 2021 update, Celsys added a new feature where you can create teams using your Celsys account, which you can use to store backups of your work and materials. This feature is only for people who have a Celsys account, something that I highly recommend.

To see your account, just go to **Clip Studio** and click on your little avatar icon:

Figure 8.48 – Clip Studio account location

Once you do that, a little drop-down menu will appear. Just click on **Account**. This will open your browser. You will probably need to log in. After this, you will find an option called **Manage Teams** at the bottom of your options in the left corner:

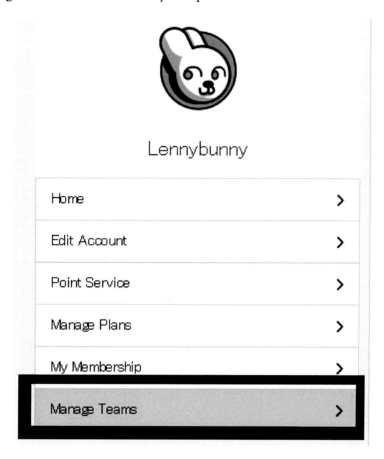

Figure 8.49 – Manage Teams location

Once you click on **Manage Teams**, you will have two options – **Create team** and **Join team**. The first one is the one that interests us. If we click on **Create team**, it will prompt the process of creating a new team:

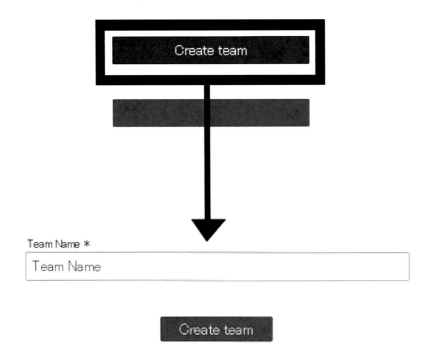

Figure 8.50 – Create team options

Give it a name and once you have done that, add an avatar image to distinguish it a little bit from other possible teams by clicking on **Change team icon** and you're done:

Figure 8.51 – Say hello to the newly formed Team – Smug-face Loki

Once this is done, we can invite other CSP users who have a Celsys account by clicking on the **Invite to team** option:

Figure 8.52 – Team work invite options

You can choose to invite someone using an email or a direct link, which you can send to your co-worker using a direct message through a social media service such as Facebook, Twitter, or pixiv.

With this, you're all set up. Easy, no?

Now you just need to tell CSP which work you want to share with your co-workers and friends.

> **Important note**
>
> Please note that as of the May 2021 update, you can only share a comic file (.cmc) with your teams.

To share a comic file, you need to open the **Clip Studio** software and go to your **Manage work** section. In the upper-left corner, there is a **This device** section, and just to the right to it, there is your **Cloud** work section. Click on **Cloud** and you will see every piece of work that you have synced with your cloud:

Figure 8.53 – Cloud works location

Now you just need to follow these simple steps to share your work:

1. You can see two little guys under your work. Just click on them:

Figure 8.54 – Teamwork button location

2. This will take you to the **Set up team for this project** screen. Just select the team and then press **Confirm**:

Figure 8.55 – Set up team for this project screen

3. Now you are done and have successfully shared your work with your co-workers.

Now… if you're Bob, and you need to download the team file, what will you do? It's easy. Go to the **Cloud** district part of **Manage works** in CSP. In the top-right corner, you will see the same two guys that you found under your synced file:

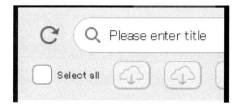 

Figure 8.56 – Team work cloud file location

Click on them and then click on **View my teamwork work**. Now you can find the work you need to download by clicking on that little cloud icon:

Figure 8.57 – Download cloud work location

And you're done. You've just downloaded the **Team work** file. Just remember that if the icon is orange, this means that it will replace your computer file, and if it's blue, it will download as a new file.

Cloud file locations and changing them

Your cloud files will be automatically downloaded to the ClipstudioCommon file folder on your computer. If you don't know where it is, you just need to right-click on your work in the **Manage works** section inside CSP and select **Open Save Folder**. If you want to change the location, you just need to cut and paste those files, and to relink them to your **Team work** feature in the cloud. You just need to open the file using CSP in the **Manage works** section. This will start the procedure of relinking the files to the cloud.

Now a brief word regarding syncing files … the process is completely painless. Just bear in mind that two people cannot work on the same page. If the second person opens the file, it will be opened in read-only mode and you will not be able to change anything.

So, how does syncing work? It's pretty easy. You just close your page. This will send the updated version to the cloud and it will be automatically downloaded by your co-workers. In case you still need to work on the file, but you prefer to send the updated version, for backup reasons or showing how work is going or something like that, just click on that blue cloud called **Sync all pages now** in the **Page Manager** window:

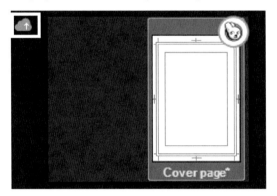

Figure 8.58 – Location of the Sync all pages now button

Just a little bit of extra information before finishing. You can also see, in the top-right corner of the page, who is working on what from their little avatar. Nice isn't it?

Those are the two ways in which you can work with other people using **CSP EX**.

Let's now have a quick recap.

The **Group work** feature is a feature where you use a file-sharing service such as OneDrive or Dropbox by creating a shared folder. It can only be used by the same OS Clip Studio Paint users. The page manager administrator adds people sharing the folder with other people. Once the co-worker receives the **Group Work** folder, they will set up a nickname. This will be used by the administrator to grant access to the single pages. Updating the pages work in this way:

1. You modify the file and then you save it.

2. You click on **Reflect change on group work data**.

3. This will update the **Group work** folder

4. The other co-workers will need to update their pages manually.

This feature is pretty useful if you're in a closed environment, such as a studio or something like this where everyone will probably have the same OS and you can probably have a shared folder by default. Plus, you can still use it even if you're offline or if your computers are connected using an offline method, such as Ethernet cables.

The **Team work** feature is an online feature where you need a Celsys account. It can be used by different OS Clip Studio Paint users. The project administrator will add people using an invitation, sent via email or a direct link. The syncing is practically automatic.

Just note that the speed of your syncing for the **Team work** feature will be based on the Celsys servers, while for the **Group work** feature, it will be based on your internet connection.

Now, having said all of that, it has probably become clear that for this kind of operation, having a precise layer structure helps a lot. So, how do you structure a layer stack for comics? Let's look at that in the next section.

Layer structure

The answer to the question is a question in itself because it's subjective:

"What steps will I need to perform?"

If, for example, you do not use flats, because you are making a painterly coloration that doesn't require the use of flats, like the one made by *Minna Sundberg* in *Stand Still Stay Silent*, you will not create a flat folder.

So, you create a folder for every step you undertake and you put them inside your frame folder.

My layer stack is organized in the following way:

- Frame folder
  - Text: This depends on the project. Sometimes it's more useful to create a single text layer folder outside the frames folders.
  - Inking
    - Character
      - Lineart (vector layer)
      - Invisible lineart (vector layer)
      - Cross-hatching (vector layer)
    - Background
      - Lineart (vector layer)
      - Invisible lineart (vector layer)
      - Cross-hatching (vector layer)
  - Colors
    - Character
    - Background
    - Flats
      - Character (draft layer)
      - Background (draft layer)
  - Pencils
    - Tight pencils
      - Character (draft layer)
      - Background (draft layer)
    - Loose pencils
      - Character (draft layer)
      - Background (draft layer)
  - Storyboard (draft layer)

Figure 8.59 – Layer stack

As you can see, it's organized in such a way that it doesn't matter who my collaborator is; they will be able to find whatever they need.

An item on the list that will be new to you is **Draft layer**. This is a type of layer that you can hide during the final export, meaning that you don't need to worry about hiding your layers before the final export. The button to toggle this setting on/off for a layer is on the right of the **Reference layer** button:

Figure 8.60 – Draft layer icon location

This will create a little cyan line on the left of the layer and a little pencil icon to the right of the name of the layer:

Figure 8.61 – Draft layer option activated

The downside is that this creates a lot of layers. It would take 10-15 minutes to make this layer stack. So, how do I resolve this? Simply put, I select all those layers and then go to **Edit | Register Material | Image**. I then put the layer stack somewhere in my materials folder and every time I need it, I just go to my materials, click and drag it to my layer panel, and I have my layer stack when I need in less than 1 second. So, even if you have a complex layer stack, you don't need to remake it every time for every page:

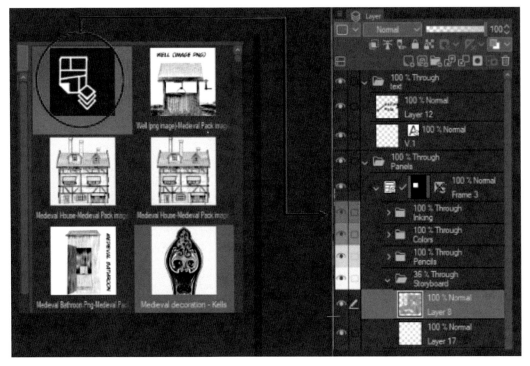

Figure 8.62 – Example of comic layer material applied

Now, as you can see, some of my layers have a color code that is pretty simple to implement. To the left of the layer blending mode, the default blending mode is "normal." There you'll find a little square, click on it, and this will reveal a menu in which you can choose a series of colors. In this way, you can see right away where your Inking folder is (it's the red one in my example), so it's easier for you to find it while scrolling through your layers:

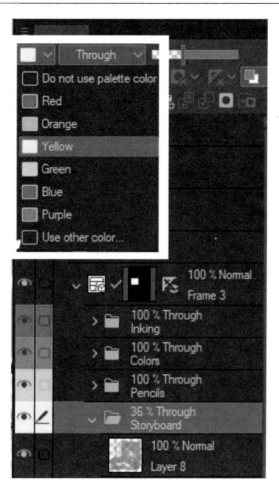

Figure 8.63 – Layer color code location

And that's more or less it. Usually, you don't need anything fancy for a layer structure. You just need to be able to select everything you need without having to ask yourself, "Where on earth is the layer for this thing?"

And that's it for this section. The rest of the procedure is just the same as the one for the cartoon illustration that we made in the previous chapter.

However, there is a little trick up my sleeve that I can teach you regarding colors.

Automatic colors for your character

Now, this is one of those things that you will need a little bit of preparation for, but after that, it will speed up your workflow significantly.

There is a caveat for this procedure: you will need flats with precise colors. I will show you an example, isolating Pipotto in the last panel:

Figure 8.64 – Pipotto with the flats

As you can see, my flats follow a precise color. Why?

I went ahead and created a silhouette, created a new layer above it, activated the **Clip to Layer Below** option so that I can color only where is the silhouette. I then put my character flats as a reference layer, like this:

Figure 8.65 – My character prepared for the automatic colors

All the preparations for the automatic colors are ready. Now, all you will see is recorded in a comfortable auto action, this auto action, to be precise:

Figure 8.66 – Pipotto automatic colors auto action

Here are the steps to create an automatic color system:

1. Select the layer clipped to the silhouette.

2. Go to **Select | Select Color Gamut**.

3. This will prompt this window:

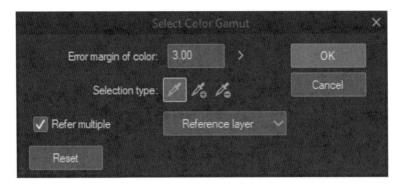

Figure 8.67 – Select Color Gamut window

4. Put the settings as you see them in *Figure 8.67*. In this way, the selection will only take from the reference layer.

5. Select a part of your character; in my case, it's the skin. This will be recorded by the auto action.

6. Select the color of your choice. As I'm coloring the skin, I choose the medium skin color from my color palette.

7. Click on the bucket icon:

Figure 8.68 – Fill option location

8. Deselect by going to **Selection | Deselect**.

9. Repeat for every part of your character from *step 2* onward until you're done.

The final result for me will look like this:

Figure 8.69 – Final result of the automatic colors

Now we have a character ready to be rendered. This auto action trick is pretty useful when used to meet the following conditions:

- You have precise colors that you need to use.
- It's something/someone that recurs so many times in your comic that it justifies the creation of this auto action.

Now, the last thing we need to learn about is lettering.

How balloons work

The rules for lettering your comics change based on where you live. But if you want some general rules, you can read the articles entitled *Comic Book Grammar & Tradition* and *Lettering Tips*, by *Blambot*, which is the pen name of *Nate Piekos*. Everything I could say would merely be a copy and paste of that article, and I respect the only rule there is in our field:

"Never plagiarize content."

Taking inspiration from different people to create your own mix, however? This is generally acceptable.

Copying someone's work to train yourself without monetizing the work is also acceptable.

Plagiarizing work? That is absolutely unacceptable.

So, do yourself a favor and read those articles, plus, on Blambot's website, there are a lot of good fonts. The one I used for *Little Sophia Escaping the World*, is *Inkslinger BB*, and it's from Blambot's website. He also has some free fonts such as *Ashcan* and *Anime Ace*.

Regarding fonts, I will give you the same advice given by Bringhurst in his book *The Elements of Typographic Face, Hartley & Marks Publishers; 4th edition, 2013.*

> *"It's better to buy one good typeface than a lot of mediocre ones."*

So, find a good typeface for your comic. In my case, I chose *Inkslinger BB*, which I would recommend buying and learning how to use it if you have the money.

In CSP, you have a tool called the Balloon tool:

Figure 8.70 – Balloon Tool property palette

As a tool, this will create well… a *balloon*. If you go to the tool properties, we have all our usual settings: **Line color**, in which we choose the color of the edge of the balloon; and **Fill color**, in which we decide the color of the balloon:

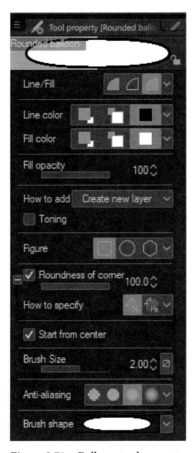

Figure 8.71 – Balloon tool property

Out of these two settings, the former is perhaps the less important one. It will allow us to decide whether we want a balloon that has a fill only, a line only, or a line with a fill:

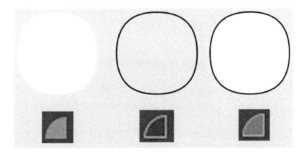

Figure 8.72 – Balloons with create fill, create line, and create line and fill options

The third icon is unaligned with the rest, which is just for my own amusement in making artists angry. I just love my readers…

When you select the balloon with the object tool, you will have two types of handle, a blue one and a red one:

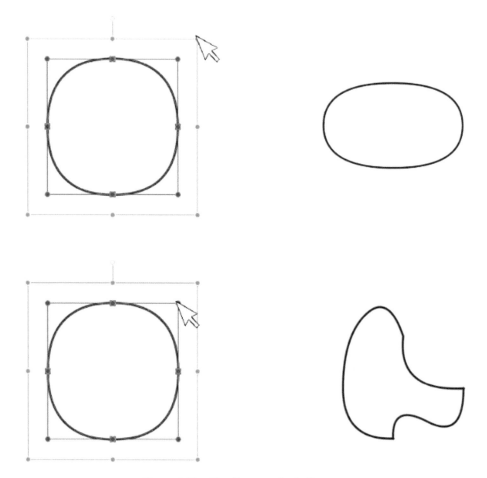

Figure 8.73 – Handle types for balloons

The blue handle changes the proportions of the balloon, and the red handle lets you create eldritch horrors, changing the shape of the balloon.

Another feature of the balloons in CSP is that if they're in the same layer, they will connect automatically, as shown in the following image:

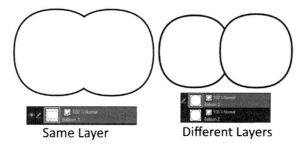

Figure 8.74 – Difference between adding a balloon in the same layer and two different layers

My recommendation would be to create a balloon layer for characters, plus a layer for special balloons such as screaming.

Where you should place your lettering is all dependent on your preferences. Just remember that if you used **Story Editor**, all your text is in a single layer, so if you want to do the lettering inside the frame, you will need to cut and paste the text into a folder called *Lettering* inside your frame. You just need to click on the text and right-click and cut and paste it wherever you need.

There is one final behavior of the balloons that you need to know about. It is that the text will link to the balloon:

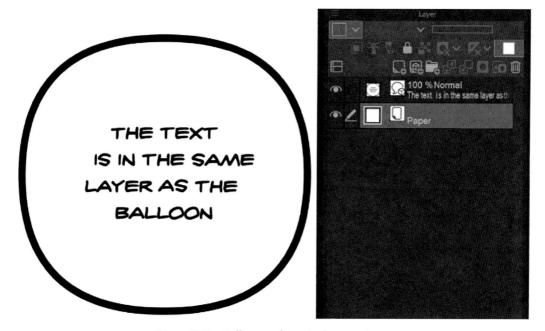

Figure 8.75 – Balloon and text in the same layer

In the preceding image, the balloons are in the same layer as the text, and the text will snap to the balloon. So, every time you move the balloon, the text will move with the balloon. If you want to move the text, you need to select the text itself and not the balloon. If you move the text out of the balloon, it will no longer snap to the balloon.

The last option that we need to consider is the **Balloon tail** tool. This is in the same **Sub Tool** group as the **Balloon** tool. It's just what the name implies: you click and drag and you create a balloon tail:

Figure 8.76 – Balloon with a balloon tail

It will insert itself in the balloon, while being a separate object. In this way, you can modify it without issues and without needing to worry about erasing the balloon line where the tail is inserted.

I have now explained everything I know about lettering. I will be honest. I am not much of a lettering artist, so I don't have much advice about it. And, being double honest, I download the balloons from *Clip Studio Assets*, so I don't even have any advice on how to create balloon shapes:

Figure 8.77 – Here's a pretty balloon as an excuse

The only advice I can give you is regarding the font size. If you're working on A3 page size and you're printing on A4 page size, remember that your fonts will be half of their original size. If you want the font size to be 16 pt, you need to insert a 32 pt font size. So, keep your final print size in relationship to your page size in mind.

We have arrived at the last step of our little comic journey: it's time to talk about printing.

Exporting for printing

Now take a deep breath because at this stage, if something goes wrong, sometimes it's not your fault, nor is it the fault of the guy who prints your file. It's just the printer that is smelling your fear and decides that everything needs to go wrong one day before an exam. 99% of the time, however, it's a problem created by you or your printer. A lot of the time, errors occur because you've sent a file with the wrong color profile, values that can't be printed correctly, or the wrong file type. So, before anything else, you need to call the printer and ask the following questions:

- Do they print comics?

- Which color profile do they use? Usually, it's the last FOGRA color profile (at least here in Italy).

- Which type of file do they want? Do they want a JPG, PNG, Tiff, or PDF?

- How much bleed do they want? Do they want a 0.3 mm or a 0.5 mm bleed? Or do they use a different one altogether?

- Which kind of paper do they have and what is the cost? Usually, you will print on uncoated paper.

- What is their maximum printable format for book pages? Usually, it's A4, because they can print a maximum of A3, and folded A3 creates an A4. Maybe you're in luck and they can even print B3, so your maximum print size is B4, giving you a little bit more leeway in terms of the size.

More or less, those are the most relevant questions you should ask (in my experience).

The first thing you need to know is whether your values are print-friendly. Tell me if this has happened to you: you go to the printer; you have an awesome illustration with lots of colors and values. You print it, and everything is wrong. That deep dark magenta you used is now a mushy blueish black, and all those values are practically gone.

This can happen for two reasons:

- The CMYK color gamut is smaller than the RGB color gamut. So, it's physically impossible to replicate all the colors you see on the monitor. To be honest, you can do it, but let's just say you probably don't have the money for it, or it's just not worth it.

- You selected the wrong color profile, or you didn't preview your work.

As regards the first point, there is nothing we can do. But for the second point, we can do a lot of things, and the first thing we need to do is set our CMYK profile.

To do so, just go to **File | Preference | Color conversion**. This will let you decide the RGB and CMYK color profiles while exporting. This doesn't change how your color will be displayed, just the output information:

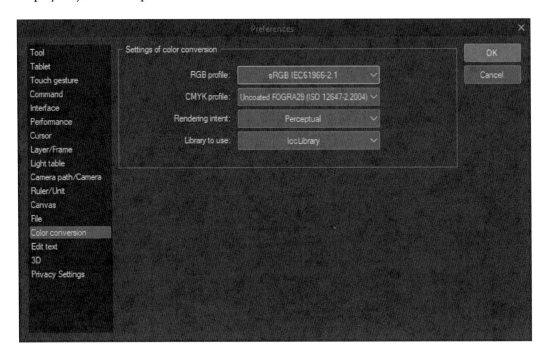

Figure 8.78 – Color conversion tab

Now, for the **RGB profile**, you just need to put **sRGB**, which is the one that will give you less of a headache. If you think you will work with someone who uses Photoshop or Adobe in general, you will need to select **AdobeRGB**.

> **Exporting for Photoshop**
>
> If you need to convert your CSP file to a .psd file, don't, and I repeat, *don't* convert it by going to **File | Save as**. This is the fastest way to have problems. What you need to do is go to **File | Save Duplicate | .psd (Photoshop Document)**. This will open a tab with the PSD export settings. Now, you just need to check the **Embed ICC profile** option and you're good to go.

Correction layers

A little word of advice. There is no way of exporting correction layers between CSP and Photoshop correctly, or at least there isn't a way that I'm aware of. So, even if you export with the correct RGB color profile, if your file has different values and there is something strange, it's because of a correction layer. Apply every correction layer before exporting, or don't use them at all if you know you will need to change between Photoshop and CSP.

For the CMYK profile, **call your printer**. There are a lot of different CMYK color profiles, and trust me when I say that there isn't any right answer:

Figure 8.79 – All CMYK color profiles

I use **Uncoated FOGRA29** because it's the one that gives me the least trouble. So, I repeat, *call your printer*.

Regarding **Rendering intent**, just put **Perceptual**, and for **Color Library**, put **IccLibrary** and forget that those settings exist.

The last thing we can do for color-checking our pages is to use **Color Preview**. That's how we color proof here in CSP. It will show you how your image will probably be printed, and based on that, you can make adjustments.

To activate your color preview, just go to **View | Color profile | Preview**. After doing so, you will need to set your color profile for your color preview. To do so, click on **Preview Settings**, which is always to be found inside **View | Color profile**.

Don't expect it to change too much. The changes you will need to do will be in the order of creating some tendency to the cyan, magenta, or yellow colors using a **Color Balance** correction layer. You can find **Color balance** under **Layer | New Correction Layer | Color balance**. For comics, you don't need anything fancy, the same for illustrations. Photographers, on the other hand, have a pretty difficult job regarding color correction.

Now, to do a batch export of all your pages, you just need to go **File | Export multiple pages | Batch export**.

3D preview

In **Export multiple pages**, there is the **3D preview for binding** option. This will create a 3D preview of your work. This is handy for having a general idea of what your final product will be, but it's a little bit heavy on the PC and it can take a while. So, I recommend doing this while doing something else, such as cleaning the dishes, making lunch, or taking a little nap… because we are human beings, and we need rest too.

This will open a menu where you can choose **File format** and **Page range**:

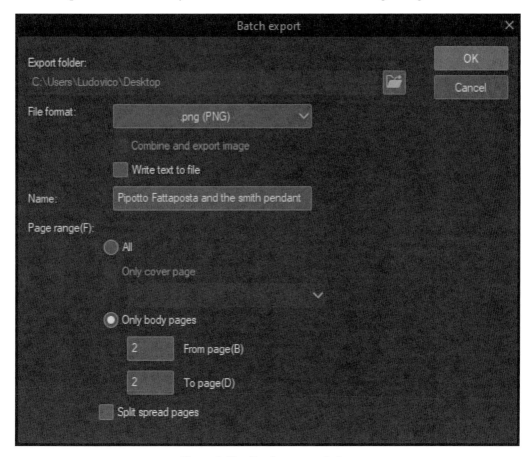

Figure 8.80 – Batch export window

The only counterintuitive option is to **Write text to file**. This refers to the text in **Story Editor**. It means that every text you've created will be exported as a .txt file.

If you check the **All** option in **Page range**, this will export all the pages. If you select **Only body pages**, this will export only the selected pages.

After you click **OK**, you will open the **export settings** page:

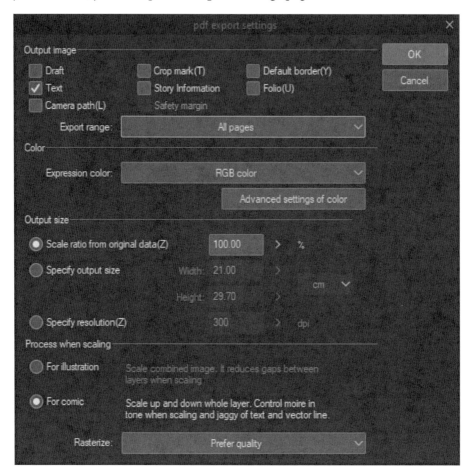

Figure 8.81 – pdf export settings window

Now, let's analyze all the options here:

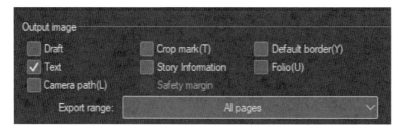

Figure 8.82 – Export settings window output image section

The first one is **Output image**. Everything checked will be exported. If we deselect **Draft**, all the draft layers will not be exported. **Crop mark(T)**, **Default border(Y)**, **Story Information**, and **Folio(U)** are all things that you should ask your printer in terms of whether you need to export them. **Text** needs to always be selected for a comic unless you're making a silent book/comic. **Camera path(L)** is for animators.

The export range is pretty easy:

- **All pages** means you will export all pages.

- **To offset of crop mark** means you will export your page plus the bleed. If the printer asks you to give the pages with the bleed, you need to select this.

- **To inside of crop mark** means your page will be exported as if it were trimmed and bound in a book. If you're printing your book, don't select this option. If you're making a webcomic, this is the setting you need to choose.

The next one is an expression of color:

Figure 8.83 – Expression of color section

This is simple. You're choosing the expression of color based on what you need to do. Is it for the web? Then select **RGB color**. Is it for print? Then select **CMYK**. Is it a grayscale project? Guess what? You choose **Gray**…

The **Advanced settings of color** options are not so complicated. They just let you choose the colors for **Crop marks/Default border/Safety margins**.

The output size section is pretty intuitive:

Figure 8.84 – Output size section

You can scale the resulting image based on a percentage, width/height, or resolution.

Webtoon exporting

As you can see in figure 8.81, in the output size section, an A4 set at 300 dpi translates to a size of 2,480 x 3,508 px. Let me just say that if it's too big, it will be heavy and your readers will need at least a couple of minutes to download the image, which is really bad. Generally, for the web, an HD image is something in the region of 1,500 px as regards height, so the Line Webtoon standard of 1,280 px for height is a pretty good compromise.

The last section is **Process when scaling**. If you're exporting at 100% of the scale, this setting is useless because you will not scale anything:

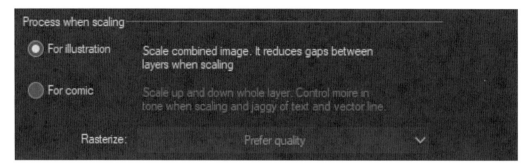

Figure 8.85 – Process when scaling section

The choice here is easy. If you're exporting the cover, select **For illustration**, while if you're exporting the pages, select **For comic** and then select **Rasterize: Prefer quality**.

If you use screen tones, you must use the **For comic** option, because if you don't, there is a high chance that you will have a Moiré pattern. In layman's terms, your screen tones will overlap.

And that's it… you now have everything you need.

Summary

Now you should know pretty much everything regarding comic creation here in CSP. You probably wanted to see how I created a comic page from scratch, which is something I like to see when I'm learning from another artist, but everything I have gone into (such as inking, coloring, and flatting) has already been covered in the cartoon illustration chapter. Just multiply this by 50 and you have it for comics. Here's what I did after the *Drawing the storyboard* heading:

1. Loose pencils. I wanted to experiment a little bit at this stage, so they're more elaborate than they should be:

Figure 8.86 – Loose pencils

2. Tight pencils. To be honest here, I worked too much on the loose pencils and I realized it would be a waste of time doing tight pencils. This can happen sometimes.

3. Inking:

Figure 8.87 – Inked page

4. Flats. I will not show these to you to prevent you from developing a headache!

5. Base colors:

Figure 8.88 – Flat colors

6.　Shading:

Figure 8.89 – Page with shading

7.   Lettering:

Figure 8.90 – Finished page

As you can see, telling you what I did would only be a repetition of the previous chapter.

But in this chapter, you learned a couple of new things. The first thing is absolutely how to set up your workspace because you will stay on the monitor for a lot of time with this kind of job. You also gained a general understanding of how to write a story, with some book recommendations, and how to use the story editor and the frame tool to translate this into a comic format. You then learned how to use that base to create a storyboard. Together with this, you've learned how to use the Group Work feature to collaborate with other people, and how to have a functional layer structure that you can use. We concluded with how to finish your comics with the lettering and how to export them for print.

As a bonus, you learned how to automatically color your characters.

In the next chapter, we will talk about concept art.

9
Building Your Own Concept Art

When you hear the term **concept art**, the first thing you will think of is probably not **Clip Studio Paint** (**CSP**), but Photoshop. That's for one simple reason: concept art is usually associated with the concept of photobashing, a practice in which you combine (bash) photos together. Here, you can see an example of an image in which I used that technique because I needed to create a concept to show to one of my teachers for an exam in 10 minutes flat:

Figure 9.1 – Photobashing example

So, obviously, you would think that Photoshop is the ruler of concept art, and Affinity Photo is the second in command. You're theoretically right—but technically wrong. The technique of photobashing is pretty useful for creating fast ideas that don't look like some scrambled lines, but being honest here, it's just one facet of the different approaches that you can have for doing concept art. If you're working for *Blizzard* in the *Warcraft* department, is creating an ultra-realistic photobashed illustration really needed? Or, if you're working for *Activision* for the *Spyro Reignited* trilogy, or for *Atlus* for *Persona 5*, is it really useful? No…

The technique and your portfolio are related to the studio you want to be hired in. And even if you need to do photobashing, CSP has some tricks up its sleeve, even in its Pro version, without going for the EX version.

This chapter will cover the following topics:

- Concept art introduction
- Setting up the workspace
- Making concept art for props
- Creating concept art of your environment
- Creating character concept art

To give a more interactive guide, I will show you the process for creating a forge of Albrecht, Elka's father, and his character.

Now, let's see what we can do with CSP.

Concept art introduction

Concept art is a pretty easy and straightforward job for when you need to put a concept given to you into a visual form. In that definition, there is no limitation in technique or software. So, sometimes you need a high-rendered concept, and other times you can use a simple dual-tone drawing. A good example of this is the *Doom Hunter* concept seen in the *The Art of DOOM: Eternal* by Dark Horse Books (2020). Another example is the *Early Development* section of *The Art of The Dragon Prince* by Dark Horse Books (2020).

You'll notice that the drawings are a completely different style from the final product, but you can see and read that the main point of those drawings was to put out ideas. This happens because there are various steps in the production stage, with different degrees of visualization of the final rendering. If you're at the early stages of production, some scribbling lines that give a general feeling will do the job. If you're making concepts for the modeler, you will need the drawing with a flat value—in this way, the modeler will have an easier job. If you've done a **three-dimensional** (**3D**) character or a 3D environment following the guide from *Chapter 3, Creating 3D Backgrounds in CSP, Chapter 4, Using Your 3D Props to Create a Scene, Chapter 5, Implementing 3D Characters in CSP, and Chapter 6, Importing 3D Characters in CSP,* you will understand why that is, because having a complex rendering can slow down your perception regarding vertex placement.

A lot of times, what we perceive as concept art is, in reality, an illustration, and usually a polished illustration that took from 1 to 3 weeks. For example, have you seen illustrations of Rell from *League of Legends*? That's not concept art—that's an illustration done for marketing purposes. It means the artist had all the assets of production as a reference to work with. A good example of how a marketing artist works can be seen in the article *Made You Look: How Marketing Artists Get Games to Grab You* by Sierra Mon. Another good video that explains this distinction between an illustrator and a concept artist is *Illustration VS Concept* by Trent Kaniuga.

Now, I'm using video games as an example because it's easier to find the concepts used for the production of the game, but there are also jobs for concept artists in films and animation studios.

The main job of a concept artist is creating and pumping out new ideas in a fast and reliable way. The job is more about problem-solving than about creating an illustration that is pleasing to the eye.

This translates into a simple question if you want to be a concept artist:

Where do I want to be hired?

Every studio has its own style, its own little flavor. You need to find a studio that has the same flavor as you.

CSP can help us a lot in conceptualizing ideas, but before that, we need to do some cleaning in the workspace, as usual.

The first thing we need to do, as always, is set up our workspace.

Setting up the workspace

Now, the most important windows, for concept art, are these ones:

- **Material**
- **Layer**
- **Layer Property**
- **Sub Tool**
- **Tool**

The color wheel is something you can use with shortcuts because you will not change colors very much.

In the **Quick Access** window, I recommend adding the following:

- **HSL correction layer**, which you can find under **Layer | New Correction Layer | Hue/Saturation/Luminosity**
- **HSL tonal correction**, which you can find under **Edit | Tonal Correction | Hue/Saturation/Luminosity**
- **Tool property**
- **Gradient map**
- **Gradient** tool

This will give you all the tools you need to work with.

You can see an overview of the workspace here:

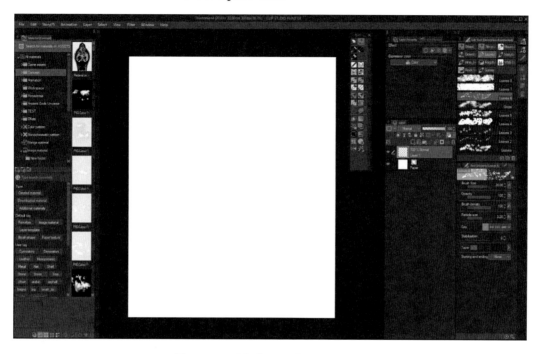

Figure 9.2 – Workspace for concept art

Before going any further, I need to help you understand how useful the **Material** palette is for concept art.

Material folder – your greatest ally

In a way, concept art is 99% preparation, and pay to win. Why do I say pay to win? Online, especially on the *ArtStation* marketplace, there are **Portable Network Graphics (PNG)** cutouts of lots of things. My favorite seller is Nomad Photo Reference. But what's a PNG cutout? It's an image in which the background is transparent. You can see an example here:

Figure 9.3 – PNG cutout example of a tree

As you can see from my **Layer** palette, the tree is in its own separate layer and the background is another layer altogether. This helps you save time if you don't have the time to clean the backgrounds of your images yourself and translates into having a good base for your concepts with only copy and pasting elements.

A type of material you can use for adding textures is a **Physically Based Rendering (PBR)** material for 3D, a type of material created by using different image textures, or in general for 3D texturing.

> **Tip**
> **PBR materials**: This is a simple definition of what they are—they are 3D materials that let you have the color of the texture, the tridimensional shape of the texture, the roughness, and in which part it's shiny and where it's not shiny. To give all the necessary information to the 3D software, the PBR material uses different image textures, all of which can be used—if needed—by a **two-dimensional (2D)** artist.

All those textures operate using different images with specific grayscale or **black-and-white (BW)** values that send all the information needed to the 3D software. In simple terms, it's a free real estate of textures.

Here's an example of a vertical brick texture:

Figure 9.4 – Example of a vertical brick texture; it can't be used for horizontal brick textures

The cool part is that generally, a **high-definition (HD)** texture in 3D is a 4K texture. So, you can find repeatable textures in a pretty high resolution (consider that 4,000x4,000 is the equivalent of a A4 at approximately 350 **dots per inch (dpi)**) for dirt-cheap prices. As an example, this texture was downloaded for free from **CC0 Textures** (https://cc0textures.com/). I recommend supporting CC0Patreon because he deserves it.

Another thing from the 3D world that can help us is the concept of alpha brushes. Alpha brushes are used to add decorations to your 3D shapes easily. You can see an example of their use here:

Figure 9.5 – Example of alpha brushes

The image in *Figure 9.5* was taken from the *CG Sphere* store on *ArtStation*, for the article *Ornament Alpha 200*—I didn't create that image.

Now, the cool part about this kind of brush, for 3D modeling, is that the brush tips they use are practically BW images, as we can see here:

Figure 9.6 – An image used for an alpha brush

I don't even need to tell you that you just need to import them to CSP, invert the colors by going to **Edit | Tonal Correction | Reverse Gradient**, remove the whites using the **Expression color: Gray** setting with only black pixels… And you have a high-resolution decoration that you can use as a brush tip or a general texture.

If you consider that you can use tree assets, PNG cutouts, PBR materials, and alpha brushes, it is likely that you have the tools to create concept art for any genre. But wait—there is more. The main advantage of those assets is that you can save them in your material folder.

The material folder is structured into three main parts, as illustrated in the following screenshot:

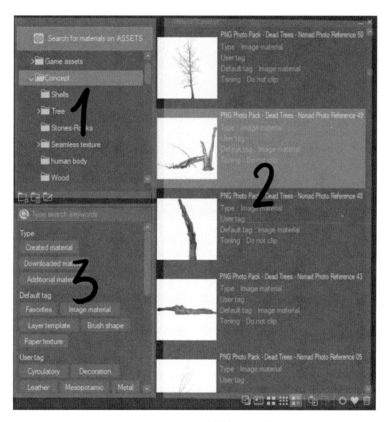

Figure 9.7 – Material folder window

The section labeled **1** is the **folder** section, in which you can organize your materials. To add, change, or delete the folders, you just need to right-click on this section.

The section labeled **2** is where your materials are located. You just need to click and drag the selected material onto the canvas or the layer palette.

The section labeled **3** is where you can see the tags used on the materials. During the creation of a material, you can add tags. Here, you can select one or more of those tags to refine the search of your materials. If you double-click on a material, you can open the **Material property**, which are the same options you see when registering the material.

There are two reasons why I state that the material folder is your best friend, as follows:

- You can organize your assets with folders and tags, without opening the **Finder** or **File Explorer**. This means that you don't risk losing your materials in some obscure folder that you created one time on your computer 10 years ago.

- You can upload your materials in your cloud, meaning that even if you change your computer you don't need to worry about backing up your assets. You will just need to wait a couple of hours for everything to download, which is still better than losing everything.

As you can see, the material folder is what lets you create a true little war machine from within CSP.

> **Tip**
>
> **Working from home**: Every time you buy a license, you can install CSP on two computers. This means that if your little indie development team of five people buys five licenses, everyone can install CSP on their computer from home and have a perfect copy of all the assets and work done in the office. Just remember that you need to buy one license for one person—it's illegal to let a third party use your license.

Now, let's start with the "easiest" (and less glorious) work in concept art, which is making concept art for props.

Making concept art for props

What is a prop? When I tried to search for the English translation of *oggetti di scena*, the Italian equivalent, I was surprised to find that prop is not an industry term such as rendering, but a term with synonyms and meanings in the normal English language. A definition that lets us understand what a prop is in concept art is provided here:

"Verb: (of a horse) come to a dead stop with the forelegs rigid."

No, wait…. Wrong one… Here's another definition:

"Verb: Support or keep in position"

OK—that's the right one... Props concept art is something that supports the rest of the production. It's the design of those little lamps in Kratos's home in *God of War*, the design of the swords of the Sun elves in *The Dragon Prince*, the shotgun in *DOOM*... Imagine *DOOM* without a shotgun!

Props concept art is about creating all those little things that give a flavor of your production. It's not the most glorious work, but it's the one with the most amount of work—depending on the production, obviously.

To start, we just need to create a canvas. The size is not so important, because we will probably not print these pre-production concepts. Maybe we will put it on a Patreon/Ko-fi reward or something like that, but it is unlikely that we will print it.

I usually go with 2,480x3,508 **pixels (px)** because it's the equivalent of A4 format, and I feel extremely comfortable with this size.

> **Tip**
> If you have the CSP EX version, you can easily create a digital sketchbook. To do so, just create a webtoon with the desired page size. Now, every time you open CSP and go to **Manage works**, you will find your digital sketchbook looking all nice and tidy.

Now, we take our canvas and we start drawing. Usually, it's better to have a little list of the main features of our environment. In my case, I have this:

Smith workshop—This smith workshop creates swords, armor, and miscellaneous stuff (such as locks). It used to work on jewelry. On a side note, the setting is an early Renaissance period, so we can have some refined metallurgy technology. If you don't believe me, search for **punchcutting**, the technology used by Gutenberg in 1455 for his bible, or search for Aldus Manutius' *Hypnerotomachia Poliphili* from 1499. Those are not books that you can make without precise crafting techniques.

I now have a broad understanding of what I need to do. So, I will just need to search *Medieval blacksmith* or *Renaissance blacksmith* or *List of medieval blacksmith tools* on Google to have a broad understanding of which tools a blacksmith uses in general.

> **Tip**
>
> **Searching for tools**: As an example, I'm pretty sure an anvil is a blacksmith tool. If I need to search for a reference, it's better to not search for *Medieval anvil* but *Which anvil to buy*. Usually, for this kind of artisan tool, you will find an in-depth review and understand how something works. Doing this will give me a rough idea of how a blacksmith searching for a good anvil would think in less than 5 minutes or so. In this way, I discovered that an anvil for horseshoes is different from a normal anvil.

Now, let's go to work. I will use my workhorse brush (the one I taught you to make in *Chapter 2, Adding Brushes to CSP*) with a triangle tip, because it gives me much-needed edge control.

Plus, I will use three other tools, as follows:

- **Polyline selection**, as illustrated here:

Figure 9.8 – Polyline selection icon

- **Lasso fill**, as illustrated here:

Figure 9.9 – Lasso fill icon

- **Gradient tool**, as illustrated here:

Figure 9.10 – Gradient icon

How I will use them? In a really simple and fast way, as follows:

1. I use my workhorse brush to create a silhouette, like this:

Figure 9.11 – Basic blob

2. If it is an object with hard edges, I will use the **Polyline selection** tool. If it's a rounded object, I will use the **Lasso fill** tool to refine the silhouette. Both types are illustrated here:

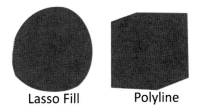

Figure 9.12 – Two types of edge refinement

3. I will use the **Polyline selection** tool to create a selection, as follows:

Figure 9.13 – Polyline selection

4. I will use the **Gradient** tool, with the **Where to create** option set to **Create a Gradient Layer** and not to **Draw on editing layer**. I will clip the gradient layer to the silhouette layer.

The following screenshot illustrates the process:

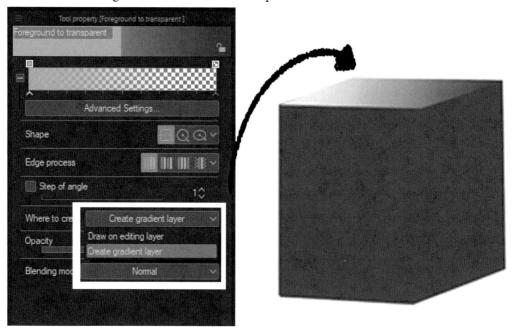

Figure 9.14 – Cube with one side shaded and Create gradient layer location

With this, we can create a finished object pretty quickly, as follows:

Figure 9.15 – Finished cube with all the gradients applied

When you create a gradient in this way, it will appear as a separate layer that you can modify using the **object tool** and give you the selection as a mask on the right of the layer, as illustrated in the following screenshot:

Figure 9.16 – Mask seen in the layer stack

The mask seen on the right in *Figure 9.16* can be used for a lot of things.

> **Tip**
>
> If you move your layer while pressing *Alt* you will duplicate that layer, and this applies to the mask too. If you move a mask while pressing *Alt*, the mask will be copied to the layer of your choosing.
>
> Another useful option is that if you click on the mask or layer while pressing *Ctrl/Cmd*, it will give the unmasked part as a selection.

This gives you the option to have a selection based on the tone you created with the gradient that you need to edit. Afterward, I just refine what I've created and I'm good to go.

You can see a representation of the Layer window here:

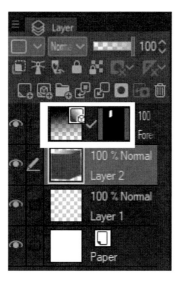

Figure 9.17 – Layer window with gradient map and mask

Another useful option for this is that you have a ready-made selection in case you need to add textures, decorations, or gradient maps to your drawing. All my prop concepts are made in this way. No other tricks!

Now, I will make the concept for the following:

- The forge
- The anvil
- A goldsmith workspace

Because it's not a *Warcraft*-style fantasy but is more similar to *Lord of the Rings,* I don't need to design the swords, locks, and so on. I just need to see what we have in our reality, and I'm done.

The following screenshot is an example of a props concept sheet:

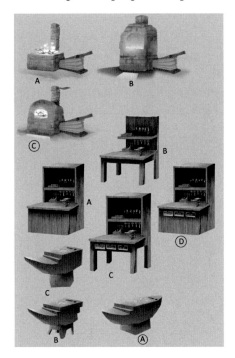

Figure 9.18 – Props concept sheet

With this, we've done a props concept sheet. Now, I will do the same for a lot of other things, such as Pipotto's room, the School of Flying Metal, and so on. Remember—I'm doing this because I know I will reuse the settings from *Pipotto* for other stories, so it's better for me to be completely sure of some of the details because later, I will use Blender to create those recurring backgrounds in 3D.

The next part is creating the room itself.

Creating concept art of your environment

Now, in theory, you should create the environment before the props because the props refine the concept of the environment you've created, but it was much easier to show you the basic techniques by looking at the props first.

Environment concepts work more in the mood department of the design: they are for conceptualizing the different moods and subtleties of a room, a city, or a forest. What you need to sell is that the environment fits the production—nothing more, nothing less.

CSP can help us speed up a lot of our processes, mainly for the following three reasons:

- We have an integrated perspective ruler.

- We can use different brush tips for a single brush.

- We can import different 3D assets, meaning that if we need a hard-surface object such as a bookshelf, we just need to copy and paste it from our materials.

The first point—the perspective ruler—was explained in the previous chapter. The second point is pretty much intuitive, if you think about it—you can add different natural shapes to a brush, giving you the possibility to create organic shapes without any problems. There are two ways you can achieve this, as follows:

- Using the **Ribbon** option, meaning that the brush tips will be connected with each other

- Using the **Spraying Effect** option, meaning that we will put particles in random places

We will analyze the first type of brush.

Ribbon brushes

Now, remember: if you want to create a new brush, the easiest way is just to select a brush that you like, right-click on the brush, and select **Duplicate sub tool**. This will create a copy of your brush, and you can modify it as per your liking.

Ribbon brushes are a type of brush with which we will connect various shapes and randomize their order and direction. A good example for this is using the branches of a tree.

I've started by downloading some leaf png cutouts from *CC0 Textures*, as illustrated in the following screenshot. I will firstly record it alone so that I can use it later for the **Spraying effect** brush, and after that, I will record it with a drawn branch:

Figure 9.19 – Leaf png cutout

Before recording it as a material, I prefer to reduce the **opacity** of the leaves to approximately 90%. In this way, if they overlay each other, they automatically create a shadow, as illustrated in the following screenshot:

Figure 9.20 – Leaves with an automatic shadow

Now, we just need to create some branches. The most important part is that they finish at the same height as where you started. A good trick is to use the **Parallel line ruler** to be sure of it, as illustrated in the following screenshot:

Figure 9.21 – A straight line made with the ruler

Now, we need to create some real branches and modify the silhouette of the main branch as follows, because I've never seen a straight branch:

Figure 9.22 – Our branch shapes

Now, we just need to add some wood texture to it, as follows:

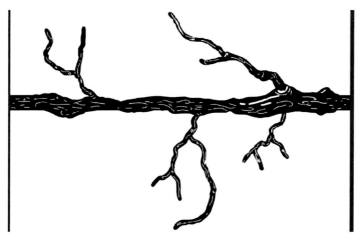

Figure 9.23 – Branch with some textures

Now, we add the leaves (being careful that all of the layers are in **Gray color** mode), as follows:

Figure 9.24 – Our final branch

Now, we record all of this as a brush tip, and we are done. We create a brush with this tip, we go to **Stroke** in the **Sub Tool Detail** section, and we check **Ribbon**, as illustrated in the following screenshot:

Figure 9.25 – Ribbon option

Now, here's an example with one single brush tip:

Figure 9.26 – Tree branch with one tip

Now, we add two more tips… and here are the results:

Figure 9.27 – Branch tree with three tips

Now, you can record the trees you create with a branch brush as brush tips and create a forest brush.

With a ribbon brush, you can create anything that can be stuck together. You can create some crazy stuff, such as an Egyptian hieroglyphics brush! You can see an example of this here:

Figure 9.28 – Egyptian Hieroglyphics brush

Or, you could create a simple stone decoration brush, as follows:

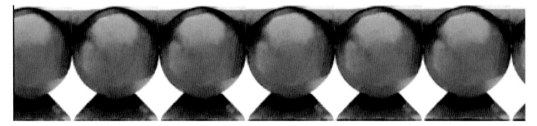

Figure 9.29 – Stone decoration brush

The second type of brush we will cover is the **Spraying effect** brush in which your brush tip will be scattered around, useful for creating textures or organic shapes with random variation.

Spraying effect brush

Creating a spraying effect brush is pretty easy—you just need to take the single elements you want to draw, add them to your brush, and check the **Spraying effect** option inside the **Sub Tool Detail**, as follows:

Figure 9.30 – Spraying effect location

Let's take as an example a foliage brush. I add a couple of leaves, and after that, I activate the spraying effect. You can see the before-and-after results here:

Figure 9.31 – Without spraying effect (left); with spraying effect (right)

I prefer to use a scanned leaf because I can always transform it in grayscale using the **Layer Properties expression color Gray** setting.

The main characteristic of this option is that the bigger the brush size, the bigger the scattering will be. You need to think of the brush size as being like a nozzle when using the **Spraying effect** option, meaning that the **Brush Size** option doesn't change the size of the brush tips but the scattering of the tips.

We have various options for the spraying effect that we can use to modify our nozzle and brush tips, all linkable to the **Dynamics settings**, as illustrated in the following screenshot:

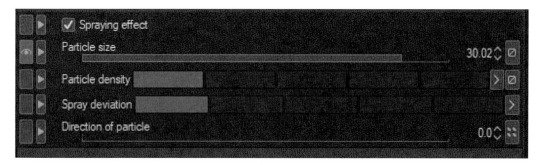

Figure 9.32 – Spraying effect options

There are four options, or five if we consider the first option that lets you activate/deactivate the **Spraying effect** option. These are outlined here:

- **Particle size**: A little bit self-explanatory. This lets you decide the size of the particles/brush tips. I usually activate **random** in the **pen dynamics** setting with a value of approximately 80-90 so that I can have some organic variation without being too extreme.

- **Particle density**: This is the density of the particles—the higher the number, the greater the number of particles emitted by a single tap of your pen.

- **Spray deviation**: This is the scattering of the particles. The higher the value, the less scattering you will have.

- **Direction of particles**: This is the angle of the particles. The pen dynamics for these settings are outlined as follows:

a) **None**: Nothing is applied. Easy, no?

b) **Direction of the line**: The angle will be based on the direction of the line. Here is an example of this:

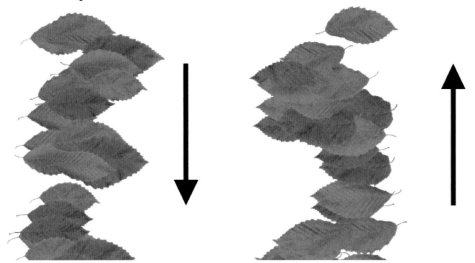

Figure 9.33 – Direction-of-the-line example

c) **Direction of the whole spray**: Changes the angle based on the **Angle** settings in the **Brush Tip** section.

d) **Spray toward center**: This means that every particle will point to the center.

e) **Random**: I refer you back to the narwhals.

You need to experiment a little bit with this brush to find your sweet spot.

Now, I will create a tree to show you how to implement what we have learned here, as follows:

1. I use a ribbon tree trunk brush to create a base to work on, as follows:

Figure 9.34 – Tree bark brush

2. After this, I add some branches with the ribbon brush we created before, as follows:

Figure 9.35 – Tree with branches brush

3. Now, I just add some foliage using the **Spraying effect** brush, and I set the **Expression color** setting to **Gray**. You can see the effect here:

Figure 9.36 – Tree after foliage brush

4. Now, I add a gradient map on top of it. After this stage, it's ready to be used as a forest brush. You can see the effect here:

Figure 9.37 – Tree plus foliage

5. Now, I just need to add some details, such as darker foliage under the main foliage, a shadow layer, a light layer, and a gradient layer on the overlay with the shadow and light color. All these are things you do even after using a forest brush. You can see the result here:

Figure 9.38 – Our final happy little tree

Now, returning to our main topic: how can we use this to create an environment concept? Well, if you need to create a forest, I just taught you how to create a forest brush, so...

But what about the blacksmith's workshop? We have all the tools we need. I will use my assets, ribbon brushes, spraying effect brushes, a gradient layer, and maps to create a workshop easily and quickly. My first step is surely creating a perspective grid. For this, I will use a material I've downloaded from Clip Studio Assets. It's the *Perspective Box Object*, content ID *1806972*, by the user *Pharan* (if you're reading this, know that you made a cool material). You can see the result here:

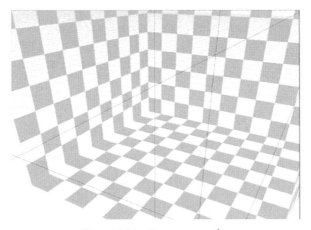

Figure 9.39 – Base room cube

6.   Now, I adjust the box, and I will copy and paste from the previous props concept sheet, plus some other materials I've downloaded from the Clip Studio Assets. All of the materials were free. You can see the result here:

Figure 9.40 – Room with assets

7. Now, I will create some shapes to decide where to put the rest of the room and make some quick notes. Plus, at this stage, I prefer to put a little human silhouette into the room to see if everything is in proportion. You can see the result here:

Figure 9.41 – Room with base shapes

8. Now, I will add textures by using brushes or materials, and refining the shapes, as follows:

Figure 9.42 – Room with added texture

9. After this, I will start shading, using the **Gradient** sub tool, with the **Where to create** option set to **Create gradient layer**. For having a base to refine for the shading, use multiply and overlay layers, as follows:

Figure 9.43 – Finished room

The wood texture is all ribbon brush, while some effects on the furnace and all the rock texture have been created with the spraying effect brush, and the walls and ground are directly a texture-brush effect.

> **Tip**
> When applying texture using brushes in CSP, a good strategy is doing it while using a vector brush. In doing so, you can rescale your canvas without worrying about having pixelated textures.

We have now done props and environment, but we still need to make the characters—we don't want to make a lifeless world, do we?

Creating character concept art

Creating a character is more about the emotional response that the character gives than the skill of the rendering used. A good example of this is Sans of *Undertale* by Toby Fox, which is practically a couple of pixels... But we can all agree it had a more emotional response out of the fandom than some other AAA games.

So, what creates a good character design? It's how much the concept behind the character aligns with the drawing you make.

Usually, a concept is a couple of lines of text. For example, here's the concept of the Doomguy of the *Doom* series:

"A man who is literally too angry to die"

It's not the real concept, but we can all agree it's spot on. In the case of my smith, his concept is this:

"A smith in his 40s, widower, and with a daughter"

So, translated into some key points and made into a checklist, it's something like this:

- Dad (single dad)
- Some emotional baggage
- Not in the prime of his life
- Smith

I now have something to work on, but I need to work out how all of these points can be reflected in the character's physique, his clothing, his general posture, and so on.

When it comes to this problem, CSP can help us a lot. The most obvious technique would be to use the 3D character. But there is a little bit of setup required before using it.....

Here's a basic 3D male model:

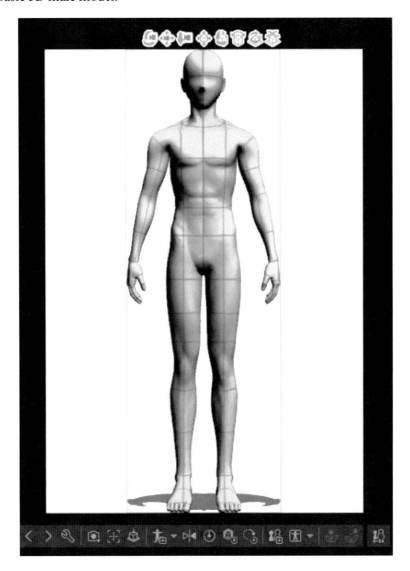

Figure 9.44 – Basic 3D male model

10. Under the character you can see a little bar—this contains options for changing the character. You can see this more closely here:

Figure 9.45 – All 3D characters' options

11. But the one we need to look at is the last one on the right. Clicking on that will open a menu in which you can change the body type of your character, as illustrated here:

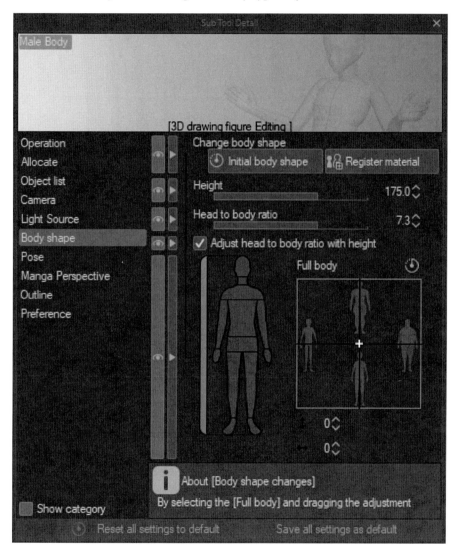

Figure 9.46 – Body-shape menu

12. To do so, you just need to move around the little white cross in that little graph, as illustrated here:

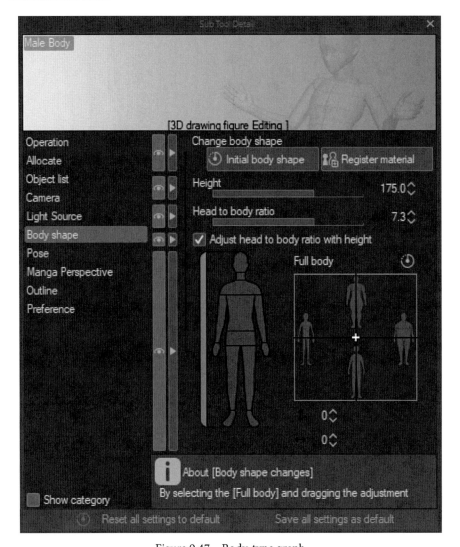

Figure 9.47 – Body-type graph

13. The vertical line is for the muscle percentage, while the horizontal line is for the fat percentage.

14. Using this option, I can decide which body type could be most appropriate for the character. For a smith of 40 years, a really skinny frame without muscle seems unrealistic. So, surely, I need to increase the percentage of muscle/fat. This means that I will lean more on the top-right area of the graph, as illustrated here:

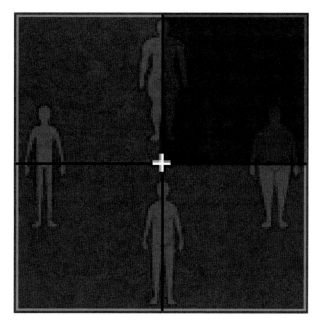

Figure 9.48 – Body type I will use

15. Now, I will start to experiment a little bit with how much muscle-fat proportion I want, as follows:

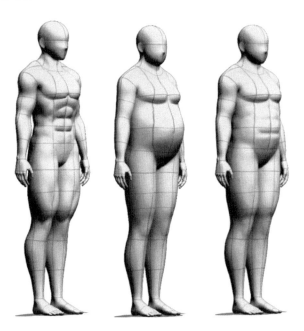

Figure 9.49 – Three body types

The left one is a little bit too muscular—it doesn't give you the right *daddy* feeling. The middle one doesn't have enough muscle mass—as a smith, my character swings a hammer every day, so he needs to have some muscles. I think that the right one is a good balance. It gives a good *daddy* feeling but with enough muscles for his job. Now, I can start designing the character! I make a copy of the 3D model and rasterize it, and make some copies of the rasterized 3D model, as follows:

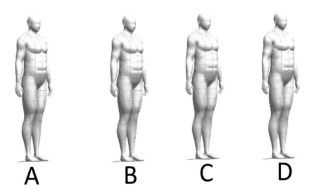

Figure 9.50 – Rasterized body type

Now, I will just make some quick sketches before going into detail. I just need to find some ideas at this point, not create the final character. I will not trace the body shape I've created; if I do that, I will probably create three characters that are all the same. You can see the output here:

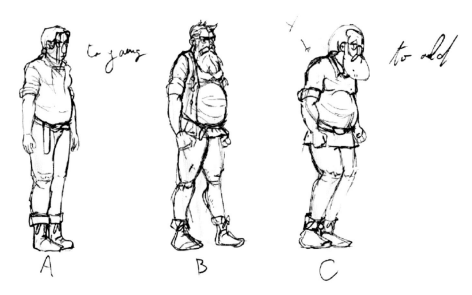

Figure 9.51 – Concept of the character

I decided to go with the base concept of **B**. He seems old, has some muscles, and gives off a *daddy* feel. Now, I just need to refine it, as I want it to be a little bit more imposing.

For creating faces, I use a little system in which I simplify the cranium into a sphere, pyramid, or cube, and I combine it with another sphere, pyramid, or cube for the jaw. I do more or less the same thing for the rest of the body. You can see an example of the system here:

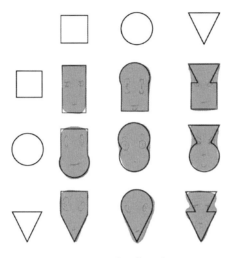

Figure 9.52 – Example of my face system

Now, I will start designing the head using this system. It's not perfect, but it's a useful guide. I start by refining the head I've just drawn so that I can see what I don't like about it a little bit better. You can see the output here:

Figure 9.53 – Refined base head

Now, on the fly, the shape of the head is a little bit too generic. A good example of an expressive shape of the head is in the movie *Klaus* by Sergio Pablos Studios. Every character has a distinct and expressive head shape. Another thing I'm not sure of is that the expression seems too angry, and the hair and the mustache shape don't fully convince me. So, I need to redo a lot of things. Don't worry about this—it's completely normal to not nail it the first time; it's part of the process. And strictly speaking, usually the first try is the most uninspired and bland thing.

> **Tip**
> When you're at this experimental stage, I recommend using a vector layer.
> In doing so, you can erase the lines you make more easily, giving you a lot of
> flexibility.

After some trial and error, the best ones were these two:

Figure 9.54 – The two finalists

I will go with **B**, because it has a more stern rather than an angry look. Now, I will refine the body, as follows:

Figure 9.55 – Finished character

Now, I need to choose a color palette for my character. For this, CSP can help us greatly. Do you remember the **Fill** layer? That layer will fill all the layers with precise color, but the most important part is that it is editable.

Now, we just need to select the ink layer as a **Reference layer** and use the **Auto select** tool to select what we want to color. As an example, I will color the jacket, as follows:

1.   I select the jacket, like this:

Figure 9.56 – Selection

2.   Go to **Layer | New layer | Fill(M)...**, as illustrated in the following screenshot:

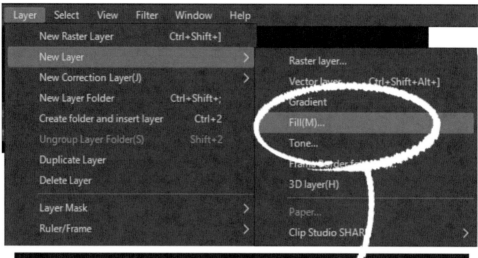

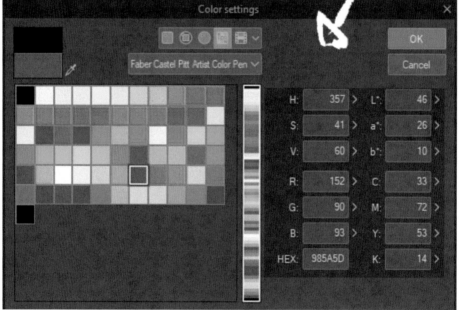

Figure 9.57 – New fill layer location and options

3.   I choose a color and click **OK**, as illustrated in the following screenshot:

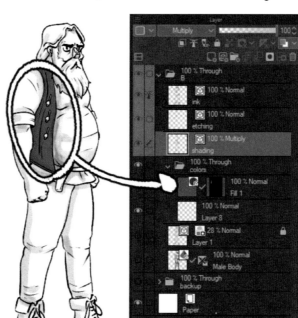

Figure 9.58 – Final results

4.   Now, if I want to change the color, I just need to double-click on the **Fill** layer and I can edit it without a problem, as follows:

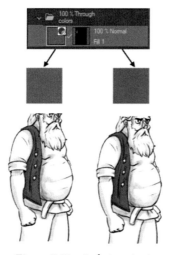

Figure 9.59 – Jacket variants

5. Now, I create a fill layer for every part, and I put them in folders with the name of the section, like this:

Figure 9.60 – Colored character

6. Now, I shade the character using a gradient layer. After this, I copy and paste all the character folders and put the copies somewhere on the canvas, and start experimenting.

> **Tip**
>
> When you select a color while on a fill layer, the color will be automatically changed. If you combine this with the **Object tool** with the **Selectable option** found in the **Sub Tool Detail** and uncheck everything except **fill layers**, you can easily change every color in a pretty short amount of time. Because you can select the fill layers directly, the object tool can let you select layers.

My color palette will use as a base the colors located in the **intermediate color** window. You can see the result here:

Figure 9.61 – Color variation of the character

I will go with **4** because it gives me the right feeling. Using these methods, I have completed a concept for a character in approximately 1 hour!

In this chapter, you have learned every way I know (for now) of how to make concept art in CSP.

Summary

With this chapter, you learned that concept art is not so much defined by the final rendering, but by the level of your ideas. It's practically a different kind of skill set from the one used by illustrators.

You learned, as is the norm in this manual, how to set up your workspace and how to use the material folder in the most effective way for the task at hand, which may be creating a background or creating a brush to help you with your concepts.

After this, you learned how to use CSP in a fast and reliable way to create prop concepts and background concepts, using the resources inside CSP and on the internet.

As a bonus, you learned how to make some decoration and texture brushes in detail, and how to make some happy little trees, and then use them inside a concept drawing.

As a finisher, you learned how to create a character quickly, by using a 3D model, vector layers, and fill layers.

In the next part, we will learn how to prepare a portfolio using CSP.

10
Creating Your Own Portfolio

This chapter will be brief—really brief, because 99% of the work will be done by you. I will only show you a couple of tools that will help you organize your work in a coherent way. In other words, you will create a portfolio.

Now, here we are at the end of our journey. You have learned about **Clip Studio Paint** (**CSP**) and Clip Studio Modeler, and how to use Blender to speed up your work.

You now know how to make cartoon illustrations, painterly illustrations, comics, and concept art. You've learned the condensed version of what I learned in 8 years of using CSP. I'm writing this chapter in 2021… so, it's now 8 years.

Obviously, if you want to learn about digital software and if you bought this book, you will want to have a job as an illustrator, a comic artist, or a concept artist. For that, you need a portfolio. My job here is to give you the tools for that.

In this chapter, we will learn about the following topics:

- Portfolio creation and introduction
- Building an illustration portfolio
- Creating your comic portfolio
- Making your concept art portfolio

So… let's start creating your portfolio.

Portfolio creation and introduction

A portfolio is your main weapon when you want to be hired. No jobs ask for your age or your study titles while applying; they only want a strong portfolio that shows you're a good fit for the project. This means that even if you didn't go to art school or university, you can still be hired. Bear in mind that I'm not saying that studying is useless, as studying art history and seeing how previous artists worked is a huge bonus in your education as an artist, but it's not essential to go to art school, so maybe an Atelier mentorship could be more useful on a practical level.

In this chapter, I will teach you how to use CSP to create a portfolio. Just bear in mind that if, for example, an editor at Marvel says that they want a portfolio in a precise way, their requests supersede whatever I say. In other words, my job here is not to teach you how to create a definitive portfolio that will get you hired; for that, you need to research what they want in the company you wish to be hired by. My job, as I said before, is to give you the tools to create a portfolio.

Every market requires a different skillset, as outlined here:

- Illustration requires good technical skills.
- Comics require good perseverance in their work. You will need to work for a long period of time.
- Concept artist jobs require you to have good ideas.

As a metaphorical example, creating a portfolio is like making an ice cream. You can have an ice cream in a cup, a cone, or a bucket—those formats cater to different needs. A cup is good if you don't want to dirty your hands; a cone is good if you want to take it on the go; a bucket is theoretically for when you have more people to serve, but we all know that sometimes it's for one single person… The taste of the ice cream is your style. If a company orders a chocolate-flavored ice cream and you arrive with a vanilla flavor, obviously they will reject your ice cream.

So, your job is to create the right format with the right taste for the company. In simple terms, a good portfolio shows your best works that are most relevant for the job and the company you're applying to.

My recommendation is to create a new portfolio every year, but I understand that if you're a university or art school student, sometimes you don't really have the time to do this. You may need to do work for your exams, and what you create for your exam is sometimes not what you want to make but is the work the teacher wants. My advice in this case is to have at least 10 focused, good pieces for the end of your university studies.

But there is an even worse scenario, in which your life problems—such as school or work—don't allow you the time to keep your skills up to date, so you create 10 good pieces but they are too different from each other, and you're not hirable. In this case, your priority is having a clear idea of where you want to go, or at least the field you want to work in. Having a good technical understanding of your craft requires 3-6 months of focused training, but understanding what you enjoy and where you want to be hired requires a lot more time, and that should be your main focus.

Regarding the time used to create a portfolio, there are no rules. You could spend 2 weeks putting it together, if you're really fast and you know your craft. It could also take up to a whole year. So, take your time—this is not something you want to improvise.

However, your portfolio is not only about your printed work, but also your online presence.

Talking about your work

When you talk about your work, you need to consider this: the more accessible your work is online, the better. You need to have a central hub that you can show to eventual clients. Fortunately for you, we are not in the early 2000s, at which time you needed to know a little bit of **HyperText Markup Language 5 (HTML5)**, **Cascading Style Sheets (CSS)**, and Java to create a website. Now, you can create a pretty decent website using only a block system that is more similar to digital art software than coding.

Before creating a website, you need to register a domain—this can be free or paid. In the latter case, you can choose a name without many restrictions. If you choose a free service, you will sometimes need to add a prefix or a suffix to your website. An example is *ArtStation*, in which you will need to add `.artstation` at the end of the name of your website.

When you register a domain, you do it using a **host**, a server in which your website will live. There are a lot of hosts, and the choice is all based on your preference and what you need. Some examples are given here:

- SiteGround

- Bluehost

- WordPress

But a good starting point is *ArtStation*. It gives you a simple website without much embellishment, but it will show your work in little folders and people can navigate through your work easily without problems. Less is more, in this case. A website doesn't need to contain your whole artistic life, only your best works.

ArtStation has another feature that is similar to a social network, so it's more probable people will see your work. It's also a place in which you can sell merchandise without worrying about taxes or product shipment. Trust me—it's a little bit of a headache because I own my personal store (www.lennybunny.com/en/store), so I know what I'm talking about.

I would advise that social networks aren't used as your central hub. Why? Because your central hub is somewhere where you put your prices, your resume, and your best works, so you need to keep it nice, simple, and clean. Social networks such as *Instagram*, *Facebook*, or *Twitter* won't allow you to have any of those three aforementioned things, but a social network has another function that a website can't give you: staying connected with people. Trust me when I say that it's important to stay connected with people on a larger base—I was contacted for this book because Packt Publishing had seen my account on Clip Studio Ask. Because I was a little bit shy and I didn't trust the effectiveness of social networks, I didn't post so much on social networks and I didn't involve myself too much in fandoms or chatting in a public space. But now I understand how damaging that was to my career. Bear in mind that I'm not saying that you need to be a famous artist with a ton of likes. If you post your drawings regularly (even the medium-quality ones), follow your favorite artists, find posts that intrigue you, and post comments, that is enough. In short, don't be a hermit. In the long run, a social media presence will be beneficial to your career.

The bottom line is: be a professional artist on your website, and do what you like on the social networks.

Before getting into the practical stuff, I need to tell you something important. If you send your printed portfolio, remember to include your contact information: an email address, your Instagram account, and your website with a written link or a **Quick Response** (**QR**) code, as it's very important that you can easily be contacted.

With that small introduction out of the way, let's start with the practical stuff.

Building an illustration portfolio

Creating an illustration portfolio is easy—you choose your 10 best works. My recommendation is to not go overboard and not print over A4 size. Why? Because you will need to take the prints to conventions, festivals, fairs, or whatever you have in your country. In those first periods of your career, you will be a door-to-door salesman, so you need to have all your work nicely packed in a container that is easy to open and shows the illustrations. You will probably need to show the illustrations while standing, so if your works are too big, this will create problems for you and your interviewer.

A little word of advice: what you're selling is your marketability, meaning that if they can put you in a category, it will be a little bit easier for a company to hire you or request an example of your work.

For example, my forte is cartoonish illustration, and that's something I can't change because I spent 10 years training in that. So, my portfolio reflects that: it's all cartoonish characters or illustrations. But I like to explore a little bit in a lot of other styles, such as a more painterly style, but the main weapon in my arsenal is still a cartoon style.

Now, creating this kind of portfolio doesn't require too much precision, but having a base layout can help. For the examples, I will use the images that I used on my website (`https://lennybunny.com/en/portfolio/`).

When creating a portfolio, it's better to have the EX version of CSP, but it's not necessary.

Creating a base layout is simple. We need to create shapes that snap to a grid. Follow these steps to learn how to do this:

1. If you have the PRO version of CSP, create a canvas of A4 size. If you have the EX version, you just need to use the comic settings to create your pages; just remember that the canvas needs to be no bigger than an A4 page.

2. Now, we need to go to **View | Grid**, as illustrated in the following screenshot. This will turn on a grid:

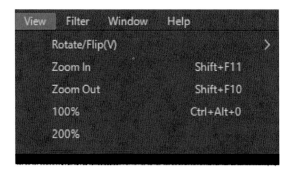

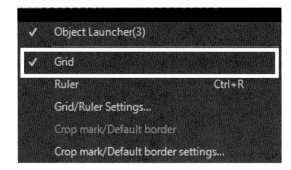

Figure 10.1 – Grid location and resulting grid

3. Now, we need to go to the **View | Grid/Ruler** settings.

4. To have a proper grid, we need to reduce the **Number of divisions** setting to 1, set the **Origin of grid/ruler** setting to **Center**, and put a gap at 1.41. In this way, we will have a more centered grid. This is because 1.41 is the ratio between the height and the width of an A4 page in European paper size. To know the ratio for your page size, just divide the longer side measurement by the shorter side measurement.

You can see an overview of the settings here:

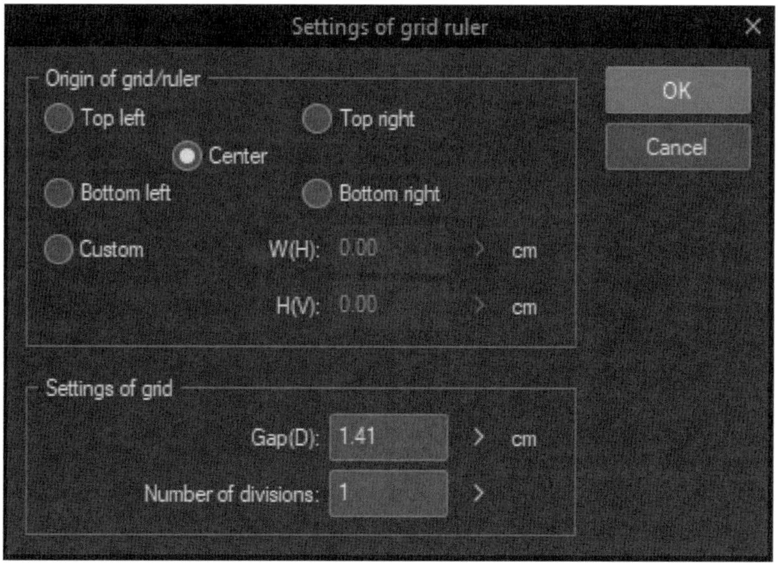

Figure 10.2 – Settings of grid ruler

5. Now, we go under **View** and see if **Snap to Grid** is checked.

6. Next, we create a new **Vector layer**.

7. Now, we take the **Rectangle** tool, which can be found under the **Direct draw** sub tool group.

8. We draw a rectangle, as follows:

Figure 10.3 – Resulting shape with the grid

Now that you have created a guideline, it will work as a safety margin. Now, save this wherever you want on your PC as *Portfolio guideline*. Now, let's start to see how to arrange our page. Let's start with the format of my images, which you can see in the following screenshot:

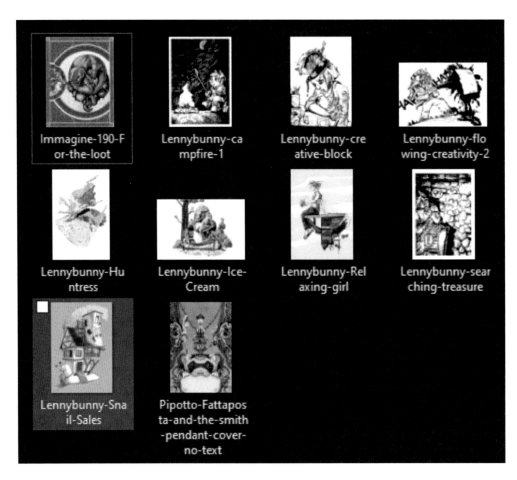

Figure 10.4 – Images from my portfolio

As you can see, I have two horizontal images, eight verticals, two highly detailed images, and four black-and-white images. So, I can place all images on their own page except for the horizontal ones, which will both be printed on the same page so that the interviewer can see them rapidly without rotating the page. The order will be like this:

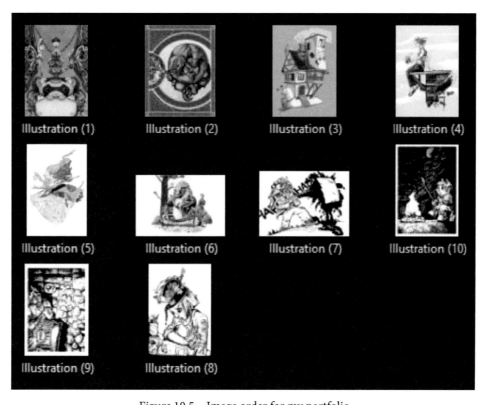

Figure 10.5 – Image order for my portfolio

Now, if you don't have the EX version of CSP, you just need to duplicate your *Portfolio guideline* file 10 times.

After doing so, you just need to import the images inside your guidelines. To do so, you just need to go to **File | Import | Image**. Place your image and align it with the guidelines. I've put as an example one of my illustrations:

Figure 10.6 – My second illustration inside the guidelines

Now, let's go to the page with two horizontal images. In here, I will create a guide on the top and a guide on the bottom, leaving one whole square of space in between the images. You can see the result here:

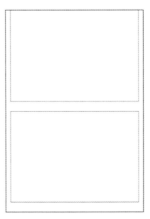

Figure 10.7 – Page with guidelines for horizontal illustrations

Now, I just add the illustrations, and I'm good to go. You can see the result here:

Figure 10.8 – Page with horizontal illustrations

It's customary (at least in my country) if you have created a piece using a real-life medium (as is the case with the two preceding illustrations) to write a little description of the piece and the techniques used. In my country, Italy, it's written along these lines: name of the work + size + techniques used. If your portfolio is dated, there's no need to specify the date. If it's a 2020 portfolio, in theory the work should have been done in 2020, right?

For example, I would detail the image shown in *Figure 10.9* like so:

"Eating ice cream", 35 x 25 cm, watercolor and Faber Castell artist pens.

Easy, right? My recommendation would be to use a sans-serif font of size something around 8-12, depending on whether the font is a light or a heavy one. **Google Fonts** is a good free gallery of fonts that you can use. If you have a **Creative Cloud** (**CC**) subscription, you can use **Adobe Fonts**. If you use **DaFont**, just be sure to check the copyright of the font.

Because my portfolio is a cartoon-style portfolio, I will use *Inkslinger LC BB* by Blambot. You can see the result here:

"Eating ice cream", 50x70cm, watercolor and faber castel artist pens

Figure 10.9 – Horizontal illustration with description

As you can see, creating an illustrator portfolio is not rocket science. There are no rigid rules, only your taste. Because of this, if the portfolio shows poor taste, it will mean that you as an artist have not developed your style enough to be hired.

Fortunately, designing a comic portfolio is a lot easier than designing an illustrator portfolio. Let's see how to create one in the next section.

Creating your comic portfolio

Ironically, a comic portfolio is the easiest to create. You export all your pages, and that's your portfolio. OK—we can move on to the next heading. Don't worry—I'm joking (more or less).

A comic artist needs to show that they can work well and can maintain consistent work for a long period of time.

There are two kinds of comic artist, as follows:

- A freelance comic artist, whereby they're paid when they submit an entire volume. These artists don't have contracts binding them to a single company.

- A contract comic artist, whereby they go to a company and are hired by them.

Those two types have different approaches and *modus operandi*. In the first case, you submit your work to a publishing house. The publishing house will have their own submission rules, so be sure to check them. For the contract type, you would send a bunch of pages (around 10-20) and wait to be contacted. Now, remember that if you send your work to Marvel or DC, you shouldn't send them simplified cartoon-style pages with Mickey Mouse; you send them well-crafted, inked superheroes pages. In the case of the Japanese market, it's a little bit different. You would submit a first chapter to a publishing company, such as Jump, and an editor will contact you if they want it to be serialized.

Now, I will show you how you can put an easy shareable link on your website or on Twitter or Facebook. Then, if a possible client wants to hire you, they can read a couple of pages of your work rather than just viewing a static image. I will assume that if you make comics, you have the EX version of CSP, because the steps I'm about to show you are only possible with the EX version. Let's get started. Proceed as follows:

1. The first step is to open **Clip Studio** and go to **Manage works**.

2. Now, right-click on the works you want to upload, and select **Send to Clip Studio SHARE(X)….** If you want to upload a webtoon, you need to click on **Send to Clip Studio SHARE (webtoon)(X)…**, as illustrated in the following screenshot:

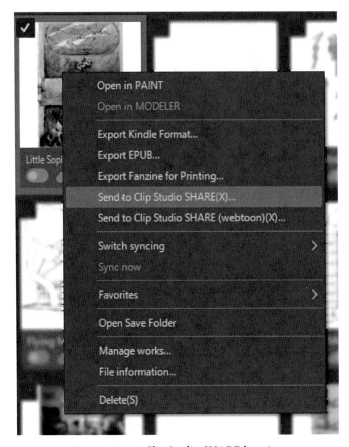

Figure 10.10 – Clip Studio SHARE location

3. This will prompt a window to appear in which CSP will ask if you want to export your work. You just need to click **OK**.

4. Wait a little bit. Make a cup of coffee or tea, because it will take time to export all of your work.

5. This will open a window in which you will need to add some information about your work, as illustrated in the following screenshot:

① Add title   ② Visibility

Title(required)

Little Sophia Escaping World

28 / 50

Thumbnail image

The thumbnail used when posting to related services and Web pages.

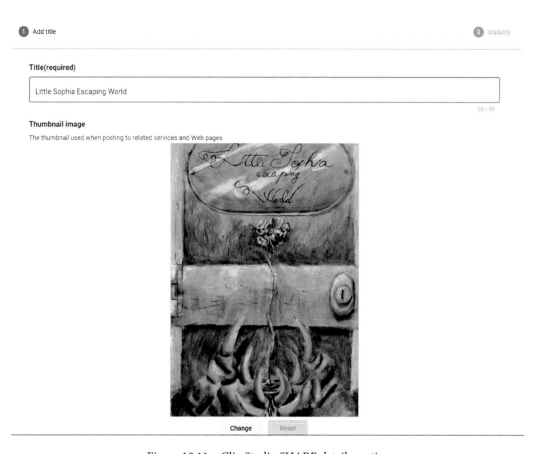

Change   Reset

Figure 10.11 – Clip Studio SHARE details section

6. You will need to insert a short synopsis of your work and a thumbnail that will show a preview of your work when you post it on social media.

7. Now you need to set up the booklet options.

    Because Clip Studio SHARE will create a **three-dimensional** (**3D**) preview of your work, you need to choose the final paper size, ranging in options from A4 to B5 to B6. You will also need to specify whether you want a flexible or rigid cover, and select the coating of the paper. **Coated paper** is glossy, **Gloss finish** is a little bit glossier still, and **No finish** means that you will have a rough surface. I prefer the last one. The last option to decide on is the page texture, in which you can select **Book paper** and **Coated paper**. For comics, I would recommend **Book paper**.

8. At the end of this process, you will find a **CREATE PREVIEW** option in the bottom-right corner, as illustrated in the following screenshot. If you click it, it will preview how your comic will be shown:

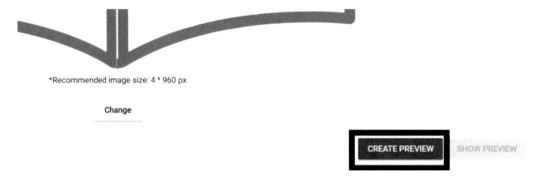

Figure 10.12 – CREATE PREVIEW

9. Based on whether you checked **Show in 3D viewer by default** or not, it will show either a 3D mockup or the pages in **two dimensions (2D)**, as illustrated in the following screenshot:

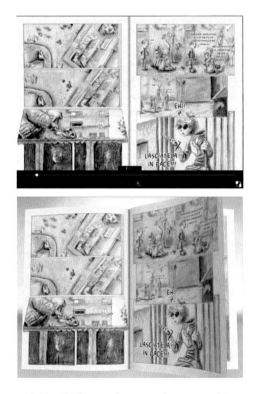

Figure 10.13 – Difference between the two reading modes

10. After deciding whether you prefer to use the 3D mockup or not, click on **Next**.

Now, CSP will ask you some **Visibility** questions, as illustrated in the following screenshot:

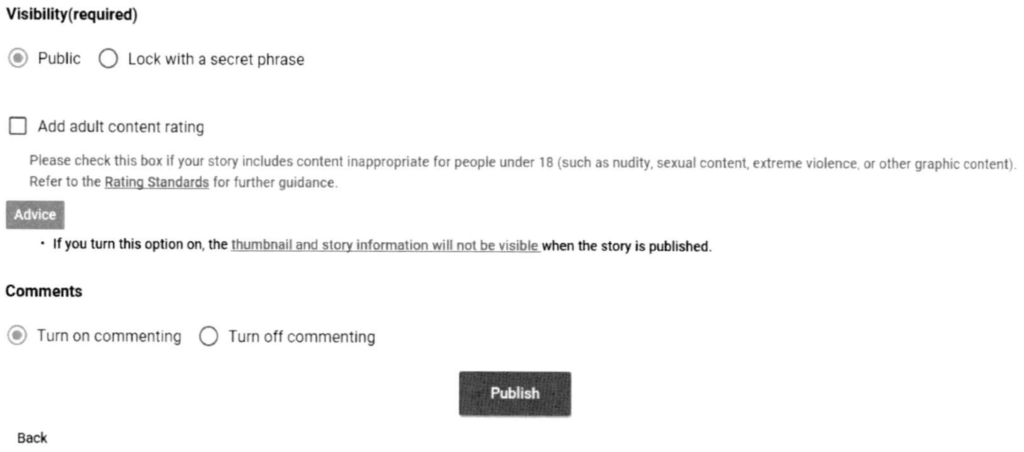

Visibility(required)

◉ Public   ○ Lock with a secret phrase

☐ Add adult content rating

Please check this box if your story includes content inappropriate for people under 18 (such as nudity, sexual content, extreme violence, or other graphic content). Refer to the Rating Standards for further guidance.

Advice

• If you turn this option on, the thumbnail and story information will not be visible when the story is published.

Comments

◉ Turn on commenting   ○ Turn off commenting

Publish

Back

Figure 10.14 – Visibility options for your comic

11. For the **Visibility** option, you need to check **Public**. Whether you need to check the **Add adult content rating** option is something that you need to decide on your own. This is also the case for whether you want to enable comments.

12. Now, just click **Publish**, and you're done.

This will prompt a window to appear in which CSP will give you a direct link, meaning that anyone who has the link can see the comic. CSP will also provide HTML embed code if you have a website and you know how to use it. This is illustrated in the following screenshot:

Your story has been posted successfully!

Why not add a link to a highlighted area of your choosing?

Add link

You can read your story at the following link.

https://share.clip-studio.com/en-us/contents/view?code=ba15b4a6-4d17-4e39-b92f-f1d16791ecb2&at=1610542822   **Copy URL**

HTML embed code

<iframe width='485' height='686' src='https://share.clip-studio.c

Go to My Stories

Figure 10.15 – Your comic link

If you're not into programming and you want something fast and reliable, a hosting service can usually give you the possibility to add a custom link that will open when you click on the image. My recommendation would be to create an image and add your comic direct link as a custom link.

If you close that tab in error or if something else goes wrong, you can find your uploaded stories on **Clip Studio Share** in the top-right corner in **My Stories**, as illustrated in the following screenshot:

Figure 10.16 – My Stories location

We have now finished the comic portfolio. Here's the last thing I will teach you for this book: the concept art portfolio. Let's dive into it.

Making your concept art portfolio

Making a concept art portfolio shows that you can be an idea furnace and that you can give all the information needed to the modeler or later on in the pipeline. So, creating a refined portfolio with the right font or the right distance between the images is a bonus, and not your main focus. It would be a good idea to have a business card showing that you can create a good paginated portfolio, but that's not your main concern.

Now, the first thing to do is to create a little template to apply to all your portfolio pages. In this template, you need to put your name, the year of the portfolio, and your contact information. This is mine:

Figure 10.17 – My portfolio template

Now, to record it as a template, which is really easy to do, we go—as always—to **Edit** | **Register Material**, but we now need to click on **Template** rather than **Image**.

This will prompt the same register material as always, but this time you can only choose only the **Search tag** and **Location to save material** options. We insert a location and we click **OK**, as illustrated in the following screenshot:

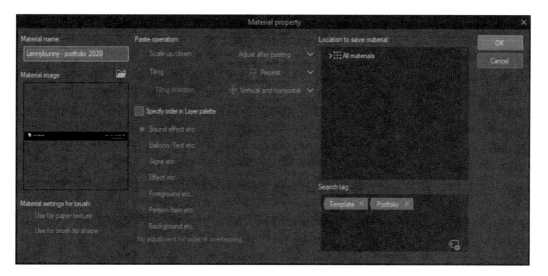

Figure 10.18 – Register Material: template options

Now, I will explain how to create a portfolio, working off the assumption that you have the PRO version of CSP. If you have the EX version, you just need to create a comic, go under **Multiple pages**, and check the **Combine into two-page spreads** option, as illustrated in the following screenshot. After that, the next steps will be the same if you have the PRO or the EX version of CSP:

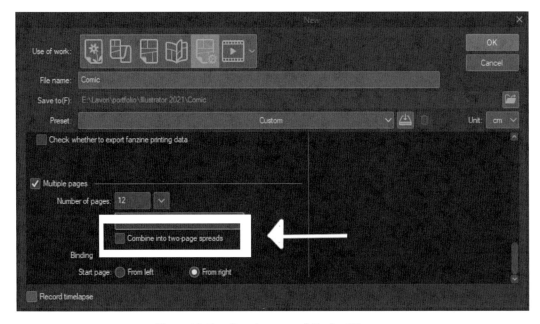

Figure 10.19 – Creating a portfolio for EX users

First, we must create a new canvas. Mine will be 2 cm less than an A3 format because it's less than the size of two pages of A4, meaning that it will not have problems during printing, because a printer always needs a little bit of margin to decently trim your book. Before going to print, ask the printer shop if they can make a print file using publisher software. You will pay extra, but if you don't have—or you don't know how to use—publishing software such as Affinity Publisher or Scribus, this is something that you can't avoid. If you have the EX version of CSP, you can create a print file by going to **File | Exporting multiple pages** .

During the creation of a new canvas, you need to check the **Template** option. This will prompt a little square on the right to appear; **Decoration Template** is what I selected. If you click on this square, a window for selecting a template will appear, as illustrated in the following screenshot:

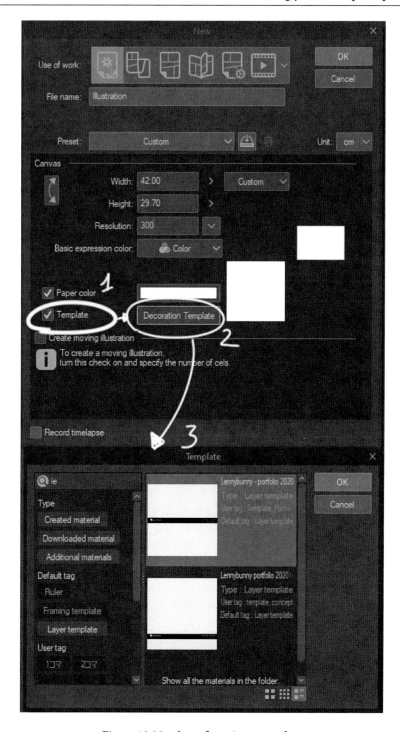

Figure 10.20 – Steps for using a template

Select a template for your work, click **OK**, and create your canvas. This is my result:

Figure 10.21 – My portfolio page with the template applied

I now have this set up, and I don't need to recreate anything every time I need to create a new page for my portfolio. I just need to slap this template on the page. Now, I will show you a page I've made for a Mudmancer of the Saint Order of the Golden Hazelnut, Berthold. He was cast out of the order because he ate the forbidden food—the Nutella:

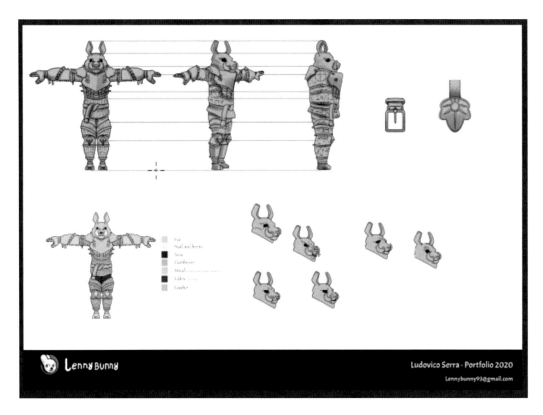

Figure 10.22 – Unrefined portfolio page

This page has all the information a modeler would need: a turnaround of the character, some belt details, expression studies, and material information.

> **Tip**
>
> It's preferable to create folders for every type of thing you want to show, such as `turnarounds`, `expression studies`, `material information`, and `armor details` folders. You don't need a folder for everything, but having it all organized is a huge help.

As you can see, everything is a little bit all over the place at the moment, so to organize it all, we will need to follow some of these simple steps:

1. Create a folder named `Backup`, and put a copy of all the layers into the folder, as illustrated in the following screenshot. We will lock this folder and hide it:

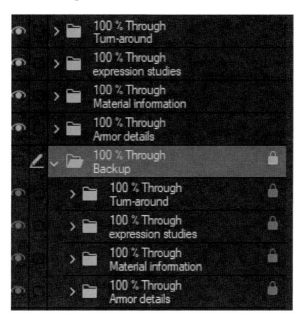

Figure 10.23 – Layer stack with backup for the portfolio

2. Now, start merging all the layers that can be merged—for example, for the expression studies, I merged the lines with the gray flats, creating a separate layer for expressions, as illustrated in the following screenshot:

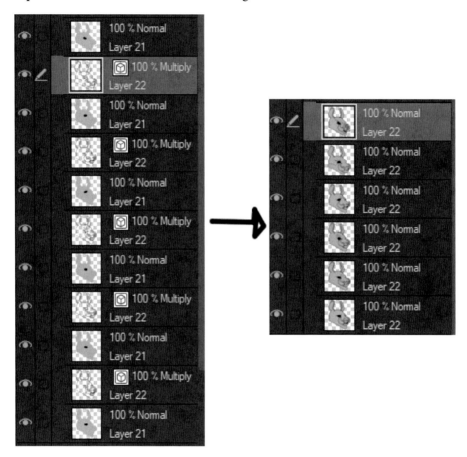

Figure 10.24 – Expression studies merged

3. Now, arrange the expressions until you are satisfied, like so:

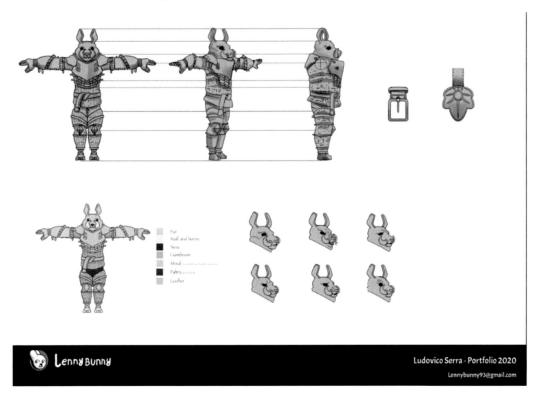

Figure 10.25 – Berthold concept page with arranged expression studies

4. Now, I add some descriptive text, writing which emotion it's showing.

5. Now, I will convert the whole `expression studies` folder into an **Image material layer**. To do so, just right-click on the folder and click on **Convert layer**. This will prompt the **Convert Layer** window to appear. In there, you change the type from **Raster layer** to **Image material layer**, as illustrated in the following screenshot:

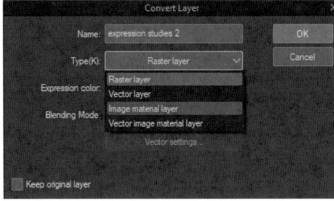

Figure 10.26 – Convert Layer process

6. This will merge all the layers inside the folder and automatically create an **Image material layer**, as illustrated in the following screenshot. This means that we can move the layer around the canvas with the **Object** tool, while maintaining the layer proportions:

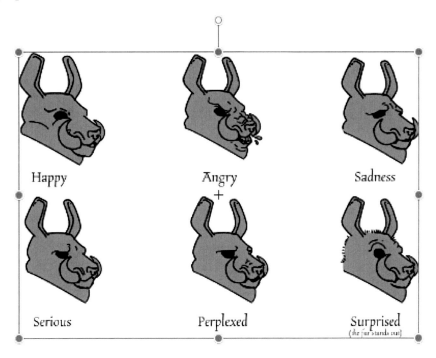

Figure 10.27 – Expression studies as image material

7. Now, I do the same with the belt details, the turnaround of the character, and the material information. I then activate the grid, go to **View | Grid**, and start experimenting a little bit until I'm satisfied with the results. You can see the final version here:

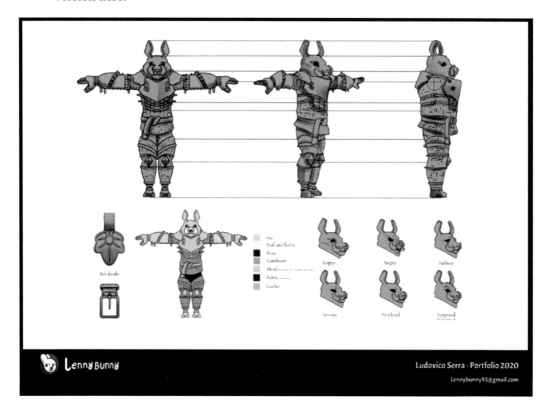

Figure 10.28 – Final Berthold: modeler information page

Now, remember your job as a concept artist is to put out ideas that can be used during the work pipeline, not to create a beautiful picture.

You have now learned how to create three different types of portfolio with CSP. Good work!

Summary

In this brief chapter, you learned some tricks to create a portfolio in CSP. First, you saw how to create a guideline using the **Grid** and the **Rectangle** tools. After that, you learned how to create an online comic portfolio that can be easily implemented on your website or social network. Finally, you learned how you can easily arrange various elements inside a page using the **Convert Layer** feature.

Now, as a final word, I really recommend that you use CSP for printing only when you don't have other options, or only use it for things that are not a comic or a single illustration. If you need to show a single image, this is not a problem. But CSP lacks some features that will help you during your portfolio creation, such as snapping to a grid, being able to align elements inside your canvas, master pages, some typography options, and so on. It's usable and you can produce some good results, but I don't recommend it for a fully professional portfolio. For that, I recommend using software such as Affinity Publisher, InDesign, or Scribus.

It's like walking on a wet surface with only socks on—you can do it, but it will not be a pleasurable experience.

I'm saying this because while I love this software with all my heart, I need to recognize its shortcomings to have a better relationship with it.

In the next chapter, you will find a guide to CSP terminology.

11
CSP Vocabulary

Hi, Reader

We have arrived at the end of our journey; I hope you learned a lot by reading this book.

In a way, I learned a lot while writing this book, because I needed to research outside of my comfort zone on how to use **Clip Studio Paint** (**CSP**) in ways that even a beginner can follow.

This chapter will be an easy-to-follow vocabulary for consultation in which I will list the options of CSP, so in case of any doubt, you can always take a look at this chapter and find an easy explanation of what you need.

When I said that the Concept Art portfolio would be the last thing I will teach, I was telling the truth. This chapter will be a long bullet-list form, a *Too Long; Didn't Read* version, in which I will list the options and I will explain what they mean—I will not teach anything new. This is simply a chapter aimed to give a quick reference, in case you have doubts about what something does.

In this chapter, you will learn about the following:

- Menu options
- Tool options

In short, this chapter will list the options you will find in CSP divided into menu options and tool options. Menu options are the options located in the menu at the top of your interface:

Figure 11.1 – Menu options

Tool options are the options you can find in the **Sub Tool Detail** window.

This vocabulary will be created with the May 2021 update as the most relevant version.

Every main setting, file, edit, story, and so on will be a subheading.

That being said, let's start this long bullet list!

Menu options

The menu options are your main source of interaction with CSP, and the button for creating a new layer (*Figure 11.2*) is just a visual shortcut for the **Layer | New Layer | New Raster Layer** process:

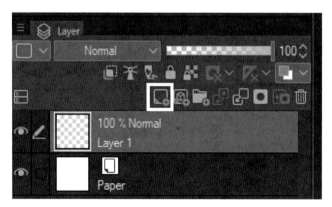

Figure 11.2 – New layer icon location

So, having a good understanding of what those options do is essential to knowing what you can do in CSP.

I will not touch the animation part of the menu, as animation is not covered in this book.

File

The following options come under the **File** menu:

- **Create New from Clipboard**: This will automatically create a canvas from a copied image.

- **Open**: This will prompt a window in which you can browse your computer to open a file.

- **Recent**: Hovering your mouse over this option will let you see your most recently used files.

- **Close**: This will close the window you're working on.

- **Save**: This will save your files automatically as a CSP file.

- **Save as**: This will give you the option to modify the extension of the file on which you're working. If I'm working on a `.psd` file and I saved it as a `.clip`, the file I'm working on will be the `.clip` one.

- **Save Duplicate**: This will let you create a duplicate of your file, without switching the file you're drawing. For example, if you're working on a `.jpg` and you save as a duplicate a `.png`, you will keep working on the `.jpg`.

- **Revert**: This will revert the canvas to a previously saved state.

- **Export (Single Layer)**: This will export your canvas, merging all the layers into a single layer. If you need to create a print file, you need to click on this option. You can export in the following file formats:

  a) `.Bmp`

  b) `.Jpg`

  c) `.Png`

  d) `.tif`

  e) `.Tga`

  f) `.psb`

  g) `.psd`

- **Export multiple pages**: This function is only for EX users. It will allow you to export multiple pages in a single format file. For all the options related to exporting multiple pages, go to *Chapter 8, Creating Your Own Comic*, to the *Exporting for Print* section.

- **Export animation**: This will let you export your animation.

- **Export webtoon**: Only for EX users, this is the same as **Export multiple pages** but it will remove the printing export options.

- **Export vectors**: If you have a vector layer, you can export the vector lines as a `.SVG` file. **Warning:** As of the 20th December 2020 update, pen pressure or brush tip information cannot be exported; you can only export brush strokes as a normal circle brush tip line.

- **Timelapse**: This will allow you to record and export a timelapse. It will be saved inside the canvas, and it will reset every time you open and close the canvas. The timelapse will be exported in `.mp4` format.

- **Import**: You can use this option to import various things, such as the following:

a) **Image**: It will import an image, easy as that.

b) **Pattern from Image**: It will import the image as a tiled image material layer.

c) **Create file object**: It will import an image as a file object.

d) **Movie**: It will import a video and it will be put into the timeline.

e) **3D Data**: It will import 3D files that are in the following file formats:

- Clip Studio character formats, `.cs3c`

- Clip Studio object formats, `.cs3o`

- Clip Studio background formats, `.cs3s`

- `.fbx`

- `.6kt`

- `.6kh`

- `.lwo`

- `.lws`

- `.obj`

Figure 11.3 – File formats

f) **Vector**: It will import SVG files as vector lines. You need to note that even in this case, brush tips and pen pressure options will not be imported.

g) **Audio**: This will import an audio file to your timeline.

h) **Batch import**: This is for EX users; you can import multiple images and they will be imported automatically onto your pages. It will import one image per page.

i) **Pose Scanner**: If you selected a 3D layer with a character in it, this import function will take the image of a person and apply the pose of the person to the 3D character.

j) **Scan**: CSP will connect to your scanner and you can directly import an image from your scanner.

k) **Continuous Scan**: EX users only; this is the same as **Batch Import**, but directly from your scanner.

l) **Select Scan Device**: This will let you select the scanning device.

m) **Exposure sheet**: This is a precise importing feature for animation. I don't know much about it, sorry!

- **Batch process**: EX users only; this will repeat the same action on all your pages or the selected pages. To see how it works in depth, go to *Chapter 8, Creating Your Own Comic*, to the *How to use the story editor* section.

- **Print Settings**: This will prompt a window in which you can set your print settings before printing. Here, you can determine things such as the print size and expression color.

- **Print**: This will send the file to your printer for printing.

- **Preferences**: This will prompt a window in which you can choose your preferences for CSP:

a) **Tool**: In this menu, you can edit tool-related preferences such as **Length of keypress to switch tool**, in which the tool will change permanently if you press it under the selected timeframe.

b) **Tablet**: This option is a little inside joke in Clip Studio Ask; 99% of problems relating to pen pressure and similar stuff come from this option. **Wintab** is for desktop computers with a tablet attached; **Tablet PC** is for tablets such as the Surface Pro. Probably, if you have problems with pen pressure or similar problems, it's because this option is set wrong.

c) **Touch gesture**: This option is for touch devices only. It will let you change the behavior of CSP while you pinch, rotate, tap, or swipe your finger.

d) **Command**: This controls the behavior of the **Transform** option, and how an SVG file is copied in your clipboard.

e) **Interface**: These are the preferences that control the interface of CSP, such as the interface color.

f) **Performance**: This will let you choose which disk to use for temporary actions, such as undos and redos, and how much memory to give. Plus, you can set how many undo levels you want to store.

g) **Cursor**: You can change the cursor's appearance.

h) **Cursor details**: If you have selected the **Brush shape** option from the **Cursor** menu for one of the cursor types, then you can change how the brush shape will be shown on the canvas using this menu.

h) **Layer/Frame**: In here, you can choose the naming behavior of CSP when creating a new layer and general layer settings. You can also choose the color of the masked area, and how the frame border gutter will behave.

i) **Light Table**: This will let you choose the behavior of the **Light Table** option. It's for animation.

j) **Camera path/Camera**: This lets you choose options on how the camera used for animation will behave.

k) **Ruler/Unit**: This menu will let you choose the colors of the various rulers in CSP and their opacity, and the unit of length to be used (mm/in or px) for brush sizes, grid sizes, and so on. You can also determine the text unit (Q or pt) that will be used by the software.

l) **Canvas**: This will control the behavior of the canvas, such as the percentage at which you zoom, the display resolution, and the degrees at which the canvas will rotate when you use the Rotate tool or you use *Shift + mouse scroll*.

m) **File**: In here, you can set the auto-save feature, something that I would recommend you activate. You can also find some page management options, such as **Auto save when switching page**.

n) **Color conversion**: In here, you can choose the color profiles used when exporting work by using the **Export single layer** option.

o) **Edit text**: In here, you can change the behavior of the text inside CSP. For example, you can choose the paragraph breaks and how the text will be inserted by default (vertical or horizontal).

p) **3D**: This option lets you choose which version of the 3D human model you want to use and whether you want to use multi-sampling or not.

q) **Privacy settings**: You can check or uncheck whether you want to send anonymous usage logs, which are used to fix issues such as bugs or sudden crashes.

• **Command Bar Settings**: This allows you to modify the command bar, by adding or removing options to it. The command bar works like the **Quick Access** window; the difference is that the command bar has a fixed position, the top of your workspace. A little hidden feature of the command bar is that you can group your options. You just need to click and drag an option over another icon and it will group together. If you can't do this by simply clicking and dragging, you just need to do it by pressing *Ctrl/Cmd*. On a personal note, I prefer the Quick Access window:

Figure 11.4 – Normal command bar (top) and command bar with grouped options (bottom)

• **Shortcut Settings**: You can change the binding of your shortcuts. You can only use letters for the tools, but you can use whatever combination you want for the other settings. For example, my **Undo** button is bound to *Ctrl + F12*.

• **Modifier Key Settings**: This allows you to modify the behavior of the modifiers, such as *Ctrl/Cmd*. The eraser part of your pen is called the **tail switch**.

• **Tab-Mate Controller**: This is an option for setting up the previous version of the Clip Studio Tabmate; if memory serves me right, it's not available in western countries.

• **CLIP STUDIO TABMATE**: If you hover your mouse here, you will have the following two options:

a) **CLIP STUDIO TABMATE settings**: You can use this to bind the keys of your Tabmate to CSP functions.

b) **Tool Rotation Settings**: One of the Tabmate features allows you to rotate between precise tools by pressing the same key. This option allows you to choose which tool will be rotated.

• **Pen Pressure Settings**: This will prompt a window in which you can adjust how CSP will analyze the pressure information sent by your tablet. After performing an analysis of this pressure data, CSP will apply the pen pressure settings set in **pen Dynamics**.

- **QMARION**: This is a doll used for posing a human model in CSP. It's pretty cool tech, but unfortunately, it's not available outside Japan.

- **Open CLIP STUDIO**: This one is easy; it will open Clip Studio.

- **Quit CLIP STUDIO PAINT**: This simply closes the software.

This concludes our list of the **File** options. We will move on to the next menu, that is, **Edit**.

Edit

You will find the following options under the **Edit** menu:

- **Undo**: This allows you to undo your last action.

- **Redo**: This will undo the action of the previous undo option, meaning that you will undo your undoing.

- **Cut**: This will cut the content of the layer and save it in your clipboard.

- **Copy**: This will store a copy of the layer in the clipboard.

- **Copy vectors as SVG**: This will copy a vector layer line as an SVG that you can copy into other software. It will be pasted as a stroke.

- **Paste**: This will paste the most recent clipboard item.

- **Paste to shown position**: By default, CSP will paste an item in the top-left corner. By using this option instead, the item will be pasted directly under the pen.

- **Delete**: This will delete the content of the layer or the selection.

- **Delete Outside Selection**: This is the same as **Delete**, but it will delete anything outside the selection.

- **Smart Smoothing**: This option reduces the pixel noise created by increasing the dpi of a canvas.

- **Remove tones**: With this, you can remove half-tones that you applied. You can decide to convert them in complete fill gray or remove them completely. It works pretty well with dot-type half-tones, but it's a little bit clunky with line-based half-tones.

- **Fill**: This will fill inside the selection or the entire canvas. If you need to fill something in with the selected color during an auto-action, you need to use this.

- **Advanced Fill**: This will let you fill inside the selected layer using more options, such as using a reference layer. This option is useful for creating silhouettes when you have a lineart.

- **Colorize**: This will automatically blur the color, while not going over the lineart of the reference layer. It creates a fake watercolor feeling.

- **Convert to drawing color**: This will convert the color of everything in the layer to the color you selected.

- **Outline Selection**: This will create a border on the edge of your selection.

- **Convert brightness to opacity**: Every white pixel will become transparent and every black pixel will have 100% opacity. If you have a 50% gray pixel, it will be translated to a 50% opacity black pixel.

- **Register Material**: I think that after this book, you know full well what this does. It allows you to register whatever is inside the layer as a material.

- **Tonal Correction**: This will apply a tonal correction to the layer; you can't edit it later.

- **Transform**: In here, you can transform everything you have selected, even between multiple layers. In here, there is **Mesh Transformation**, **Scale/Rotate**, and **Free Transform**—plus other transformation options such as **Perspective** transform.

- **Change Image Resolution**: This option will let you modify the dpi of your drawing.

- **Change Canvas Size**: This will let you change the size of your canvas—pretty self-explanatory.

- **Crop**: Using this option will crop your canvas based on your selection.

- **Rotate/Flip canvas**: This will let you flip your canvas horizontally or vertically, or rotate your canvas by 90° or 180°. Remember that those changes will be applied on your canvas, meaning that you will have them after exporting your image.

- **Canvas Properties**: This option will prompt a window that will let you change your canvas size, resolution, basic expression color, and paper color. Plus, if you are an EX user, you can add comic settings, such as safety margins.

- **Clear Memory**: This will delete the history of your canvas, meaning that you will not be able to undo anymore.

- **Pick screen color**: This will prompt a color picker that you can use to pick a color from your monitor, even outside of CSP.

- **Hide windows and pick screen color**: This does the same thing as **Obtain screen color**, but it will minimize your CSP window. It's useful if you're on a tablet or you have only one monitor.

That's all for the **Edit** menu! Next up is the **Story** menu.

Story

This menu is only for EX users and these are the options under it:

- **Open page with new tab**: This will open the page in a new tab without closing your already opened page.

- **First Page**: You will go directly to your first page.

- **Previous Page**: You go to the previous page.

- **Next Page**: You go to the next page.

- **Last Page**: You will go directly to your last page.

- **Specific Page**: You can select a specific page to open.

- **Add Page**: This will add a page based on your base work settings, in other terms, how you set up the canvas during the creation of the file.

- **Add Page (Advanced)**: This will prompt a new window in which you can decide the information of the new page.

- **Import Page**: You can import other `.clip` files as a page.

- **Replace page**: You can replace a page with another `.clip` file.

- **Duplicate Page**: This will duplicate the page.

- **Delete Page**: This will delete the selected page. Remember that if you have a spread page in your story, that spread can't be separated, meaning that if you delete a page, it will divide a spread in CSP and it will not let you delete the page.

- **Combine Pages**: This will combine a page to create a spread page.

- **Split Pages**: This will split the pages.

- **Change page settings**: This will change the settings only for the selected page.

- **Change project settings**: This will change the settings of all the work.

- **Sort page file names**: When you rearrange the pages inside **Page Manager**, the names of the files will not change; this option renames the files based on the new page position.

- **Page Manager**: This will open the page manager.

- **Page Manager Layout**: This will change where the page manager will appear.

- **Page Reordering**: This will let you decide the behavior for moving your pages, by clicking and dragging or *Ctrl + clicking* and dragging.

- **View**: This will allow you to choose whether you want a page-by-page view of your work or a webtoon view.

- **Webtoon reading direction**: This will change the reading order of your webtoon (whether it is from right to left or from left to right).

- **Binding process**: This is a list of settings more geared toward fanzine artists:

  a) **Show binding list**: This will prompt a window in which you can see the printing filename, the folio of the page, the basic expression, and the resolution of the page. Plus, you can add memos.

  b) **Settings of printing file name**: With this, you can choose how CSP names the files when exporting them to create the printing files.

  c) **Allow covers pages to be moved**: This will let you choose a new cover page within your pages.

- **Edit text**: In this menu, there are all the options related to the story editor. These are as follows:

  a) **Open story editor**: This will prompt the story editor.

  b) **New text**: This will create a new box of text.

  c) **Delete text**: This will delete the box of text.

  d) **Apply tool property to text**: This will apply the properties of the tool text to the selected text box.

  e) **Find and Replace**: This will find and replace words used in the text.

- **Group work**: In here, there are all the options related to group work data; they're explained in depth in *Chapter 8*, *Creating Your Own Comic*, in the *Group work* section.

And with this, we have finished with the **Story** options. We will now move on to the **Layer** menu.

Layer

If you right-click on a layer, it will prompt the same menu:

- **New Raster Layer**: This will create a new raster layer.

- **New Layer**: This submenu is for creating layers that are not raster layers, such as the following:

  a) **Raster layer**: This will create a vector layer.

b) **Vector layer**: This will create a vector layer.

c) **Gradient**: This creates an editable gradient.

d) **Fill**: This will create an editable color that will cover all the canvas.

e) **Tone**: This layer creates a half-tone layer that will be applied to the selected area.

f) **Frame Border folder**: This creates a frame folder, if you don't want to use the dedicated tool.

g) **3D layer**: This will create a layer in which you can put 3D material.

h) **Paper**: This will create a paper layer. A paper layer is the same as a fill layer, but it will always be created at the bottom of the layer stacks.

i) **Clip Studio SHARE**: In here, you can find the foil layer, which is a special layer in which everything inside will have a metallic effect applied when uploaded to Clip Studio Share, using the Clip Studio software.

- **New Correction Layer**: This will create an editable correction layer, such as a gradient map or a level correction layer.

- **New Layer Folder**: This will create a new folder inside your layer stack.

- **Create folder and insert layer**: This will automatically put the selected layer inside a folder.

- **Ungroup Layer Folder**: This will remove the layers from a folder and delete the folder.

- **Duplicate Layer**: This will duplicate the layer.

- **Delete Layer**: Guess what this does? It will delete the layer.

- **Layer Mask**: This submenu has all the options related to masking, such as masking outside or inside the selection.

- **Ruler/Frame**: In here, you can find all the options related to rulers:

a) **Selection from Ruler**: When you create a closed shape with the linear/curve/figure ruler and ruler pen tool, this option enables you to create a selection based on that closed shape.

b) **Draw along ruler**: When you create a line with the linear/curve/figure ruler and ruler pen tool, you can automatically create a lineart based on the ruler.

c) **Ruler from vector**: This will transform a vector line into a ruler.

d) **Delete ruler**: This will delete the selected ruler.

e) **Show ruler**: If you press *Shift* while clicking on the ruler icon in the layer stack, you will hide it. With this option, you can unhide it. But on another note, you just need to re-click on the ruler icon in the layer stack to show it again.

f) **Link ruler to layer**: This will link the ruler to the layer, meaning that whenever you transform something inside the layer, the ruler will move along with the transformed part.

g) **Create Perspective Ruler**: This will start the procedure to create a perspective ruler.

h) **Divide frame border equally**: If you've selected a frame folder, you can divide the frame folder equally, vertically or horizontally.

i) **Combine frames**: If you select two frame folders in the layer window, you can use this option to combine them.

j) **Show in All Layers**: The ruler will be applied in all the layers.

k) **Show in Same Folder**: The ruler will be applied only on the layers inside the same folder.

l) **Show Only When Editing Target**: The ruler will be applied only on a single layer.

m) **Link guide to ruler**: When you use the object tool, you can move things around. When you check this option, the ruler will move with the layer whenever you move things around with the object tool.

- **File object**: In here, there are all the options related to managing file objects.

- **Layer Settings**: Do you remember all the little icons above your layer stacks? Those icons are visual shortcuts for the options located in this submenu:

a) **Set as Reference Layer**: This will set every layer selected as a reference layer. If you select a folder, it will automatically select all the layers inside the folder.

b) **Set as Draft Layer**: This will set all the selected layers as draft layers. This type of layer can be automatically removed when you export your image.

c) **Clip to Layer Below**: When you check this option, you will paint only over whatever there is on the below layer. It's a type of mask that masks everything outside the below layer.

d) **Lock Layer**: This will prevent any kind of actions on this layer, from transforming to drawing.

e) **Lock transparent pixels**: This will prevent you from drawing outside of what you've drawn. Meaning that if I've drawn a box, I can't draw outside of the box. A little counterintuitive behavior regarding this option—when you activate **Lock transparent pixels** and you use a blur tool, or a paintbrush, you will not add transparency to your drawing. However, if this setting is off, you will introduce a certain degree of transparency with every stroke.

f) **Show Layer**: This will show/hide the layer.

g) **Change Layer Name**: This will change the name of the layer. If you need to change a layer name for an auto-action, you need to use this option and not rename it by double-clicking on the layer.

h) **Display palette colors in parent folder**: This will apply the layer color tag to the folder in which the layer is nested.

i) **Display palette colors on canvas**: This will display the color tag on the canvas as a color, with 50% transparency, that will fill the whole layer.

j) **Advanced Settings**: This will prompt a window that will let you modify fill/tone/gradient map layers.

- **Selection from Layer**: This submenu creates a selection based on the layer:

a) **Create Selection**: This will create a selection based on what's drawn on the layer. It's the same thing as clicking on the layer preview while pressing *Ctrl/Cmd*.

b) **Add Selection**: This will add what's drawn in the layer to your selection. It's the same thing as clicking on the layer preview while pressing *Ctrl/Cmd + Shift*.

c) **Delete Selection**: This will delete your selection based on what's drawn on the layer. It's the same as clicking on the layer preview with *Ctrl/Cmd + Alt* pressed.

d) **Select Overlapping Area**: This will select the overlapping area between your selection and what's drawn in the layer. If you press *Ctrl/Cmd + Shift + Alt*, it will have the same effect.

- **Rasterize**: This will transform a vector layer into a raster layer.

- **Convert Layer**: This will convert a layer to another type of layer.

- **Convert to lines and tones**: EX users only; this will create a line art based on a 3D model. It can auto-apply half-tones.

- **Transfer To Lower Layer**: This will transfer the content of the selected layer to the layer below, without deleting the selected layer.

- **Merge with layer below**: This will merge the selected layer with the layer below.

- **Merge selected layers**: This will merge all the layers you have selected into a single layer.

- **Merge visible layers**: This will merge all the layers in your layer stack except the hidden ones (ones without the little eye icon).

- **Merge visible to new layer**: This will merge all the visible layers into a new single layer, without deleting the layers.

- **Flatten image**: This will create a single layer from all the layers in your layer stack; there is no way to preserve a copy of the layers using this option.

- **Layer Order**: This will move a layer above or below in the layer stack. It will be recorded when you create an auto-action.

- **Change Selected Layer**: This will change your selected layer, moving from your selected layer to one above or below. It will be recorded when you create an auto-action.

Well done! We've finished covering the **Layer** menu. Let's see what comes under the **Select** menu next.

Select

There are the following options under this menu:

- **Select All**: This will select all the canvas.

- **Deselect**: This will deselect everything.

- **Reselect**: This will reselect the last selection you created. This is a new action meaning that you're not undoing your deselection, but you're reselecting your last selection.

- **Invert selected area**: This will invert the selected area.

- **Expand selected area**: This will expand the area based on the value you set.

- **Shrink selected area**: This will shrink the area based on the value you set.

- **Blur border**: This will blur the border of your selection on the outside of your selection; this works while using brushes or the fill tool.

- **Select Color Gamut**: This selection option will let you select a color in all the canvas. You can choose to use the reference layer for the selection.

- **Select Overlapping Vectors**: The wording is a little bit strange, but with this option, you can select the full length of the vector lines of all the vector lines that are inside the selection. So even if a single pixel of the line is inside the selection, it will select the whole line.

- **Select Vectors Within Area**: This will select only the vector lines that are fully inside the selection.

- **Quick Mask**: If you check this option, this will create a quick mask layer; everything you paint here can be converted into a selection after unchecking this option. Please note that the selection will be a perfect copy of what you've drawn in regards to transparency, texture, and so on. It can be used as an alternative for flat colors in comics, because just by double-clicking it, you can create a selection based on the quick mask.

- **Convert to Selection Layer**: This will create a new selection layer. It practically works the same as **Quick Mask**; I don't find any difference with it.

- **Convert Selection Layer to Selection**: This converts a selection layer back to a selection.

That is all for the **Select** menu. Next up, the **View** menu.

View

The following options fall under the **View** menu:

- **Rotate/Flip**: This option is similar to **Flip Canvas** found in **Edit | Rotate | Flip canvas,** but this change is not permanent, meaning that it will not affect your exported image.

- **Zoom In**: This will zoom in on the canvas.

- **Zoom Out**: This will zoom out of the canvas.

- **100%**: This will set the zoom as 100%, meaning that a pixel on the monitor will have the same size as a pixel on the canvas.

- **200%**: The zoom level will be set as 200%.

- **Fit to Screen**: This means that the canvas will be set on a level of zoom in which all the canvas will be shown.

- **Reset Display**: This will reset any kind of flip or rotation of the **View | Rotate/Flip** option.

- **Fit to Navigator**: This is the same as **Fit to screen** but the canvas will fit to the whole window.

- **Print size**: The zoom will be applied in a way that you will have a 1:1 ratio between what you see on the canvas and the print. It's based on the display resolution setting located in **File | Preferences | Canvas**.

- **Scroll Bar**: This will show a little scroll bar on the sides.

- **Selection Border**: This will toggle the selection border, meaning that if you select something, you can deactivate that little border and you can see what you've selected. This is useful when you need to work on some details, and you don't want distractions.

- **Selection Launcher**: This refers to that little bar under the selection you've created.

- **Selection Launcher Settings**: This will let you modify what appears in the selection launcher.

- **Transform launcher**: This refers to that little box under the selection that appears when you transform an object.

- **Text launcher**: This refers to the little bar you find under the text when you select it.

- **Object Launcher**: This refers to the bar under the 3D models.

- **Grid**: This will activate/ deactivate the grid.

- **Ruler Bar**: This will toggle a ruler bar that will appear at the top and on the left of your workspace.

- **Grid/Ruler Bar Settings**: This will let you choose the grid square length and their subdivisions.

- **Crop mark/Default border**: Only for EX users: this will show/hide the crop mark default border.

- **Crop mark/Default border settings**: Only for EX users: this will let you change the settings of the crop mark/default border.

- **Safety margin**: Only for EX users: this will let you hide/show the safety margins.

- **On-screen area (webtoon)**: This will activate a preview of what the viewer will see while using a cell phone.

- **On-screen area settings (webtoon)**: This will prompt a window in which you can select the ratio of the on-screen area. This means that width=1 and height=2 will have the same results as width=0.3 and height=0.6.

- **Story Information**: Only for EX users: this will hide/show the story information such as page number or author.

- **Paper**: This will hide/show the paper layer, which is useful for checking the level of transparency inside your work.

- **Show Tone Area**: The options in here will basically color all the tone/image material layer on the canvas, letting you see where you used tones or image materials.

- **Show vector paths**: The same thing as **Show Tone Area** but for vectors.

- **Show playback fps**: This will show/hide the framerate.

- **Snap to Ruler**: Checking this option as **On** will mean that while drawing, your line will be snapped to a linear/curve/figure ruler and pen ruler.

- **Snap to Special Ruler**: Checking this option as **On** will mean that while drawing, your line will be snapped to special rulers such as a concentric circle or perspective ruler.

- **Snap to Grid**: This is the same as **Snap to Ruler**, but with the grid.

- **Toggle special ruler snapping**: This will let you switch between different special rulers.

- **Color profile**: This requires a little bit of attention, because it will let you see a preview of what the color will look like when printed on a specific type of paper. If you want to see your colors in CMYK, you need to go here.

Great news, we have finished with the **View** menu options. We will move on to the **Filter** menu next.

Filter

Remember that filters are not editable once applied. These are the options that fall under the **Filter** menu:

- **Blur**: In here, you can find a wide array of filters that will blur your image.

- **Correct line**: You have the following two filters in here:

  a) **Adjust line width**: You can use this to increase or decrease the width of the line; it's like adding a border to your lines.

  b) **Remove dust**: This is applicable only to raster layers. Sometimes when you scan something, there are little black dots. With this filter, you can remove them.

- **Distort**: In here, you can find filters such as a whirlwind or fish-eye lens. They distort the image.

- **Effect**: In here, you can find the following three effects:

  a) **Artistic**: This will create a fake painterly effect.

  b) **Mosaic**: This will create a pixelated effect.

  c) **Remove jpeg noise**: Have you ever zoomed in on an image and you've seen that some pixels have strange colors near them? This filter removes those strange colors.

- **Render**: Within this option, there is only **Perlin noise**.

- **Sharpen**: In here, you can find a way to sharpen your image, meaning that the image will have more defined edges.

And with that we have finished with the **Filter** menu. There aren't many under this, but they get the job done. Let's see what comes under the **Window** menu in the next menu.

Window

OK, every tool you can use in CSP is here. You can find all your panels here. If you have closed one in error, you need to come here and check it again:

- **Canvas**: Here, you can switch between the canvas you've created and you can create a duplicate of your canvas by clicking on **New Window**. The duplicated canvas and your canvas are two separate instances of the same work. This means that every change you make will be reflected on the duplicated window. The only exception for this is **Color profile/Color preview**. If you set up the color preview in the duplicated canvas, you can work in the native color profile of CSP, while keeping tabs on how it will look in print.

- **Workspace**: This will let you organize your workspace, such as creating and deleting workspaces or changing the workspace you're using.

- **Command Bar**: This will show/hide the command bar, a small bar on the top of the screen that is like the quick access bar, but with a fixed position.

- **Quick Access**: In here, you can put all your most-used options, brushes, and windows. If you're on a tablet or a small screen, this is your best friend.

- **Tool**: This is practically the toolbar. Here, there are all the tools in CSP, maybe even a new album.

- **Sub Tool**: Here, you can find sub tools. For example, you have the **Pen** tool and the **Pen** and **Marker** sub tools.

- **Tool property**: Here, you can find the basic options of a sub tool, such as brush size or opacity.

- **Brush size**: Here, there are presets for your brush size.

- **Sub Tool Detail**: This window will let you see all the options related to the sub tool.

- **Color Wheel**: This window allows you to choose the color using a visual input; you can choose a square or a triangle as a visual input to choose the saturation and luminosity of the color.

- **Color Slider**: With this, you can choose the color using sliders. You have the RGB, HSV, and CMYK color profiles to choose from.

- **Color Set**: Here, you can find your color palettes. You can record various colors.

- **Intermediate Color**: Here, you can choose four colors and have the in-between colors. You can find a more in-depth analysis in *Chapter 7*, *Making Your Own Illustration*, in the *Setting up the workspace* section.

- **Approximate Color**: Here, you can create variations of the selected color, based on hue/saturation/luminosity/luminance and the RGB color profile. A more in-depth analysis can be found in *Chapter 7*, *Making Your Own Illustration*, in the *Setting up the workspace* section.

- **Color History**: Here, you can find the colors you have used.

- **Layer**: Here, you can find your layer stack, and above the layer stack you can find your layer options. I will explain the options from left to right:

Figure 11.5 – Layer window options

1 in the preceding figure contains the following options:

- **Change palette color**: This will set a color tag that will be shown on the left of your canvas.

- **Blending mode**: This will set how the layer reacts to the layers below. As an example, multiply blending mode means that it will darken your drawing, moving the colors toward black.

- **Layer opacity**: This will change the opacity of the whole layer.

2 in the preceding figure has the following options:

- **Clip to Layer Below**: When you check this option, you will paint only over whatever there is on the below layer. It's a type of mask that masks everything outside the below layer.

- **Set as Reference Layer**: This will set every layer selected as a reference layer. If you select a folder, it will automatically select all the layers inside the folder.

- **Set as a Draft Layer**: This will set all the selected layers as draft layers. This type of layer can be automatically removed when you export your image.

- **Lock layer**: This will prevent any kind of actions on this layer, from transforming to drawing.

- **Lock transparent pixels**: This will prevent you from drawing outside of what you've drawn. This means that if I've drawn a box, I can't draw outside of the box. A little counterintuitive behavior regarding this option: when you activate **Lock transparent pixels** and you use a blur tool, or a paintbrush, you will not add transparency to your drawing. However, if this setting is off, you will introduce a certain degree of transparency with every stroke.

- **Enable Mask**: This will let you see your mask options.

- **Set showing area of the ruler**: This little submenu lets you see all the ruler options.

- **Change layer color**: This will activate an option in which, by default, all the black pixels will transform into a cyan color and every white pixel will remain white. To change the colors, go to the layer property.

3 in the preceding figure has the following options:

- **New Raster Layer**: This will create a new raster layer.

- **New vector layer**: This will create a new vector layer.

- **New Layer Folder**: This will create a new folder. If you click and drag layers over this icon, they will be inserted into a folder automatically.

- **Transfer to lower layer**: This will transfer the contents of the selected layer to the layer below, without deleting the selected layer.

- **Combine to layer below**: This will merge with the layer below the one selected.

- **Create layer mask**: This will create a mask based on the selection. If you didn't select anything, the mask will not cover anything. To cover something, you need to select the mask and use the transparent color. For the other way around, you just need to use whatever color you want.

- **Apply Mask to Layer**: This will apply your mask to the layer.

- **Delete Layer**: This will delete the layer.

4 in the preceding figure has one option:

- **Show layer in 2 panes**: This will divide your layer stack into two panels that show two different points in your layer stack. This is useful if you have a lot of layers.

And that's it for the **Layer** options. Let's continue with the rest of the **Window** options:

- **Search Layer**: Here you can filter your layers by type, color profile, whether they are hidden or not, and other parameters.

- **Layer Property**: Here you can find the properties of your layer. I will explain the layer properties from left to right:

Figure 11.6 – Layer Property window

a) **Effect**:

- **Border effect**: This will add a border.

- **Extract line**: Only for EX users: this will create a line art based on the 3D model.

- **Tone**: This will convert what you've drawn into a half-tone.

- **Layer color**: This will activate an option in which, by default, all the black pixels will transform into a cyan color and every white pixel will remain white. To change the colors, go to layer property.

Figure 11.7 – Effect options

b) **Expression color**: This will change your basic expression color from color, gray, and monochrome. With the last two expression colors, you can choose to show only black or white pixels.

- **All sides view**: This is a window that will let you see your 3D model in a 3D space, in which you can move the camera and your model.

- **Navigator**: This window will let you see your canvas in its entirety. There will be a little red square that will show what you're seeing on your canvas.

- **Sub View**: This will let you see reference images, and you can pick colors from those images.

- **History**: This records every action you make; you can scroll through the actions you have made to return to a previous state of your drawing.

- **Auto Action**: This window will let you record a set of actions that you can play again, without needing to repeat the same steps all the time.

- **Information**: This window shows your RAM usage, where your cursor is in an x, y coordinates system, and the height/width of your selection.

- **Item bank**: With this window, you can save your most used materials. If you find that in your comics you use a lot of the same textures, you can save them in the item bank, so that you just need to click and drag them onto the canvas using the item bank.

- **Material**: Here you can find all your saved assets. To find your downloaded content, you just need to go to the **download** menu.

- **Hide/Show All Palettes**: This will hide/show all the windows except the menu.

- **Hide Menu Bar**: This will hide the title and the menu; to return them you just need to press *Shift + Tab*.

- **Always Show Tab in Canvas**: This will always show the name of your canvas in a little box above your canvas.

- **Palette dock**: This option lets you choose whether you want your windows to be a popup, meaning that if you click on the window icon, only that window will appear, or as a tab, in which the windows will be hidden and shown at the same time.

And with this, we have finished the **Window** list… Moving on!

Help

There are the following options under this menu:

- **Training and Tutorials**: This will open the Clip Studio Tips website.

- **Getting Started**: This will prompt a short introduction to CSP.

- **Instruction Manual**: This will open the official CSP manual, in which they explain all the options to you. It does not tell you how to use them, only what you can do with them.

- **Support**: This will open Clip Studio Ask on your internet browser.

- **Get license**: If you downloaded a demo or something similar, this will let you buy a license for CSP.

- **Review/Change License**: This will let you upgrade from Pro to EX. Or, it will show you what your current license is.

- **File Associations**: If you have multiple versions of CSP installed on your computer, it will connect the `.clip` file to the version you've opened, meaning that if you've installed CSP 1.8 and 1.9, and the computer automatically opens version 1.8, you just need to open 1.9 and use this option to tell the computer to automatically open 1.9.

- **About CLIP STUDIO PAINT**: This will show a simple information window of CSP and its creator, CELSYS.

- **Version information**: This will show you your version number.

And with this, we have finished with all the options in the CSP menu at the top of your workspace. Next, we're moving on to the tool options!

Tool options

I will start with a brief list of all the tools and sub tool groups in your arsenal. CSP has lots of tools that can help you with your illustrations and comics, but it can be a little bit daunting the first time you open the software to know which one you need. In this section, I will show you the main categories of this huge array of tools.

Tool list

There are 255 tools (give or take) in total in your arsenal in CSP as of the 20 December 2020 update. It's impossible to explain all the tools in CSP, but showing at least all the tools and sub tool groups is a little bit more feasible. I will show the tools using the following figure as a reference, and I will explain them from left to right:

Figure 11.8 – Tool window

Let's get started:

- **Zoom**: Here you can find tools that let you zoom in and zoom out.

- **Move**: Here you can find the hand tool and rotate tool.

- **Operation**: Here you can find operation tools such as the object tool and select layer.

- **Move layer**: Here you can find tools that let you move the entire layer or a specific type of layer.

- **Selection area**: This sub tool group lets you choose between a wide array of selection tools based on drawing input.

- **Auto select**: Here you can find an array of selection tools based on your click input.

- **Eyedropper**: Here you can find color selection tools that let you obtain colors from your screen.

- **Pen**: In this sub tool group, you can find inking tools based on the pen format:

  a) **Pen**

  b) **Marker**

- **Pencil**: Here you can find the pencil tools:

  a) **Pencil**

  b) **Pastel**

- **Brush**: Here you can find a wide array of brush type tools, generally with color mixing activated, such as oil paint brush and opaque watercolor:

  a) **Watercolor**

  b) **Realistic watercolor**

  c) **Thick paint**

  d) **India ink**

- **Airbrush**: Here you can find airbrush tools.

- **Decoration**: Here you can find a huge array of textures and decoration tools. In a way, it's what made CSP famous back when it was Manga Studio:

  a) **Effect**

  b) **Hatching and sand pattern**

  c) **Clothing**

  d) **Pattern**

  e) **Flower**

  f) **Vegetation**

  g) **Artificial scene**

  h) **Natural scene**

  i) **Ruled line**

- **Eraser**: Here you can find the raster eraser and vector eraser.

- **Blend**: Here you can find the blend tools and the copy stamp tool.

- **Fill**: Here you can find all you need for filling something with color, such as **Refer other layers** and **Enclose and fill**.

- **Gradient**: Here you can find gradient tools such as the following:

  a) **Gradient**.

  b) **Freeform gradient**:. This is a tool that is unique to CSP. You just need to draw two lines of color and using this tool you can create a gradient automatically.

- **Figure**: Here you can find a huge array of tools that let you draw figures, ranging from something simple such as a rectangle to something a little bit more complex such as a scattered stream line:

a) **Direct draw**

b) **Stream line**

c) **Saturated line**

- **Frame border**: Here you can find all the tools related to creating frame borders and how to manage them:

a) **Create frame**

b) **Cut frame Border**

- **Ruler**: Here you can find the true one ring to rule them all. Just kidding. Here you can find a huge array of rulers for technical and non-technical drawing. Examples include the perspective ruler tool or the symmetrical ruler tool.

- **Text**: Here you can find the text tool.

- **Balloon**: Here you can find all the balloon, effect balloon, and balloon tail options and tools:

a) **Balloon**

b) **Flash**

- **Correct line**: Here you can find tools to change and edit the vector lines, except for the **Remove dust** sub tool group, which can be used even on a raster layer:

a) **Correct line**

b) **Remove dust**

We have now finished the brief list of the tools and sub tool groups at your disposal. In the next section, I will show you the sub tool details of the most used tools in CSP.

Sub tool details

In this section, I will create a list of the options for the brush/eraser/blend tool, fill/selection tool, and figure tool. This can't be a comprehensive guide to all the options for the 255 tools of CSP for two simple reasons:

- A lot of options just repeat themselves.

- Just doing quick math of the pages needed, I would go over 50 pages (give or take).

So, I will just list the most used sub tool details of the most used tool types.

Brush sub tool detail

I think that the most used tool is absolutely the brush tool, and here, you can find a *Too Long; Didn't Read* version of the options of the brush tool. The options are the same with all the brush drawing-related tools, so the brush, eraser, and blend tools all have the same options—they just have different settings:

- **Brush Size**: Here you can find options related to the brush size. You can connect pen dynamics settings to it using this option.

- **Ink**: Here you can find all the options related to the opacity and color mixing of your brush:

   a) **Opacity**: Here you can change the opacity of your brush and link it to pen dynamics.

   b) **Blending mode**: Here you can set the blending mode of your brush. The blending mode will affect the colors in the same layer. The only difference between an eraser and a normal brush is that an eraser has an **Erase blending** mode.

   c) **Color mixing**: If this option is checked as **On**, it allows you to mix the colors while you paint. The only difference between a blur brush and a normal brush is that on blur brushes, this option is checked. The main difference between a blended and running color is that the first one mixes the pixels, and the other moves the pixels and adds transparency based on how much you move the pixels.

- **Color Jitter**: This option lets you change the hue/saturation/color you selected based on pen dynamics. You can find a more in-depth analysis of this option in *Chapter 7, Making Your Own Illustration*, in the *Making an "idea" brush* section.

- **Anti-aliasing**: Here you can decide how much you want to blur the border of your brush tips.

- **Brush shape**: Here you can record and apply your brush shapes, in other terms, the brush tips used:

   a) **Brush tip**: Here you can decide how your brush tip will behave:

- o **Tip shape**: This option lets you decide whether you want a circle or materials as your brush tip.

- o **Hardness**: This option is only active with circle brush tips. It will let you decide how much of a blurred border you want for your brush. It's an extreme version of anti-aliasing.

- o **Thickness**: This will let you elongate your brush tip based on pen dynamics:

    - ▪ **Direction**: This will let you decide the direction to apply an elongating effect.

- o **Angle**: This will let you decide the angle of your brush tips; it can be linked to pen dynamics.

- o **Flip horizontal**: This will let you decide whether you want to flip your brush tip horizontally; you can add a random value to it.

- o **Flip vertical**: This will let you decide whether you want to flip your brush tip vertically; you can add a random value to it.

- o **Brush density**: This will let you decide the brush density of your brush. It's like the starting opacity point of your brush. This will not create the marker effect (the effect where, when you overlap your lines, the color will be darker).

- o **Adjust brush density by gap**: This will adjust the brush density based on the gap of the brush tips.

Figure 11.9 – Brush tip options

b) **Spraying effect**: If checked, the brush will behave like an airbrush. To find a more in-depth analysis, go to *Chapter 9*, *Building Your Own Concept Art*, in the *Creating concept art of your environment*, *Spraying effect brush* section.

c) **Stroke**: Here you can find options to decide the gap of your brush tips and how your brush tips will repeat themselves.

d) **Texture**: Here you can add and change the behavior of the texture applied.

e) **2 - Brush shape**: Here you can toggle the **Dual Brush** feature and modify how it's applied to your main brush.

f) **2 - Brush tip**: Here you can modify the brush tip of your dual brush.

g) **2 - Spraying effect**: Here you can modify the spraying effect of your dual brush.

h) **2 - Stroke**: Here you can modify the stroke of your dual brush.

i) **2 - Texture**: Here you can modify the texture of your dual brush.

- **Watercolor edge**: With this option, you can add a fake watercolor edge to your brush. These are the same options as found in **Layer properties window | Border effect | Watercolor**:

  a) **Opacity**: This lets you modify the opacity of the edge.

  b) **Darkness**: How black your edge will be.

  c) **Process after brush stroke**: Because the watercolor edge is a RAM process, sometimes this can slow down your workflow. So, with this option checked, the watercolor edge will be applied after your brush stroke.

  d) **Blurring width**: How much the edge will be blurred.

- **Erase**: If you set the brush blending mode to erase, you will have this option. This will let you choose whether you want a vector or raster eraser.

- **Correction**: Here you can find options that help correct your brush strokes:

  a) **Sharp angles**: If this option is checked after the brush stroke, your angles will be sharper, which is useful for technical drawing.

  b) **Stabilization**: This option was what sold me to CSP 8 years ago. This will automatically stabilize your line; at value 0 you don't have any kind of stabilization, and at 100 you have full stabilization. The line will be a little bit slower, but you don't need to worry about jagged line. **Adjust by speed** option will increase or decrease the stabilization based on your speed.

  c) **Post correction**: In short, this will apply a stabilization after your brush stroke.

  d) **Taper**: This option will move your brush tip a little bit after you remove your pen from your monitor.

- **Starting and ending**: In this menu, you can configure options for changing the starting and ending of your brush stroke after you've finished your stroke.

- **Anti-overflow**: This is useful if you have a clean line art, or a line art with a lot of closed figures. Here you can set it up so that the brush stroke will not go over the vector path. This is useful when you're coloring your illustration or comic page.

We have now finished with the brush options, so the next options to look at will be the fill tool type.

Fill and selections tools

Fill and selection tools share the same type of settings between them aside from some small differences:

- **Selection area**: This is for selection-based tools. It will let you decide whether you want to add or remove a selection. The same results can be obtained with *Shift* + *Click* to add a selection, and *Alt* + *Click* to remove a selection.

- **Fill**: This option will let you change the base properties of your fill tool:

  a) **Apply to connected pixels only**: This is a little bit of a mind-blowing option, if we're being honest here. If you check this option, the selection or the fill area will cover only the connected pixels, but if you uncheck it, it will use your whole layer for your selection or fill:

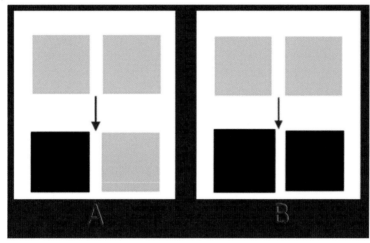

Figure 11.10 – Apply to connected pixels on (A) and off (B)

  b) **Close gap**: If there is a space between two lines, it will automatically close the gap between those lines when you're selecting or filling something.

  c) **Fill narrow area**: This will fill a little bit over the gap.

  d) **Tolerance**: This will set the tolerance of your tool to recognize the difference between two colors. At value 0, it will always take only the same color, even if the difference is just a 1 point value in the saturation. At 100, it will select everything.

  e) **Area scaling**: This will automatically scale the area of the selection inward or outward.

f) **Scaling mode**: This lets you choose which type of scaling you want.

g) **Snap to symmetry ruler**: This lets you decide whether you want your selection or fill to be mirrored.

- **Closed area fill**: This option replaces the fill option for the enclosed and fill brush. The main difference is that it will add the **Target color** option, which will let you choose how the autofill works.

- **Reference**: Here you can find the options that will let you refer to other layers:

    a) **Refer multiple**: This will let you refer to multiple layers for your selection. You can decide whether it will refer to all the layers, the reference layer, the selected layer, or a layer in the same folder.

    b) **Exclude**: This will let you decide whether you want to exclude the draft layers, the text layers, the current layer, the paper layer, or blocked layers from reference.

    c) **Refer to image border**: This is referring to the frames tools; it will consider the border line as a line that needs to be considered while using the fill or selection tool.

    d) **Refer overflow frame**: This refers to the border of your animation files.

    e) **Fill up to vector path**: If this option is checked, the fill tool will automatically cover to the middle of the vector line. It doesn't matter whether you used a texture or the brush tips have a slight texture.

    f) **Include vector path**: This will include the whole width of the vector line.

    g) **Do not start filling for this color**: If you check this option, the color selected will not be filled or selected.

That's all for the fill/selection type of tools.

Figure tools

Figure tools consists of direct drawing tools and line drawing tools; line drawing tools will create a series of lines based on your input. The frame tools share the same type of options as the direct drawing tools. The figure tool, without a fill option, can be drawn on a vector layer, so you can edit them later:

1) **Direct draw**: These tools are the rectangle, ellipse, or straight-line tool (or similar types of tools).

    a) **Figure**: This a type of option that you can have only with the closed type of direct drawing tools, such as the rectangle. These are the options under this:

- o **Figure**: Here you can decide whether you want to create a rectangle, a circle, or a polygon.

- o **Number of corners**: You can select how many corners your polygon will have, from 3 to 32.

- o **Roundness of corner**: Here you can decide how much your corner will be rounded.

- o **How to specify**: Here you can decide whether your figure will have a precise measurement:

  - **Specified ratio**: The measurement will be based on the ratio. If you set up W=1 and H=1, you will have a perfect square.

  - **Specify length**: The size will be based on a precise measurement, so if you set W=1 and H=1, you will have a 1 mm/in square every time you click.

Figure 11.11 – Figure options

b) **Shape operation**: Here you have the basic shape operations:

- o **Start from center**: By default, CSP will create a shape using the top-left corner as a point of creation. By checking this option, it will be the center as the point of creation.

- o **Adjust angle after fixed**: After you have clicked to create the shape, if this option is checked, you can adjust the angle before creating the shape.

- o **Step of angle**: Normally, if you press *Shift*, your line will snap to the interval set here. If you check this option, it will always snap to those angles.

Figure 11.12 – Shape operation options

c) **Continuous curve**: This option is for the non-polygonal direct drawing tool; a polygonal type is the ellipse tool:

   o **Line/fill**: Using this, you can decide whether you want a pure fill, a pure line or fill, or a line polygon as a result. If you choose a pure line, it will not automatically create a polygon. The line width is editable in **brush size**.

   o **Line color**: Here you can decide whether the color of your line will be your main color, sub color, or a user-chosen precise color.

   o **Fill color**: Here you can decide whether the color of your fill will be your main color, sub color, or a user-chosen precise color.

   o **Curve**: This decides how you will draw your curve: you can choose between straight line, spline, quadratic Bezier, or cubic Bezier.

   o **Close line**: This will activate if you've chosen either a pure line or line and fill in the **line/fill** option. It will close your line by double-clicking.

   o **Show line preview**: This will show a preview of your line. This will be active only if you've selected a Bezier type of curve.

   o **Step of angle**: Normally, if you press *Shift*, your line will snap to the interval set here. If you check this option, it will always snap to those angles.

   o **Add/delete control points while drawing**: If you check this option, you can add/delete control points while drawing your lines.

Figure 11.13 – Continuous curve options

2) Line type tools: These kinds of tools are the **Stream line** and **Saturated line** tools or similar types of tools. Other than the **Continuous curve** option, you will have the following:

   • **Speed lines**: Here you can find all your basic options for creating a line layer:

   a) **Destination layer**: Here you can decide whether you want to create a completely new layer, draw on a pre-existent line layer, or create the stream line or saturated line on the selected layer, meaning that you can't edit it later.

b) **Use radial/parallel line ruler for angle**: If you have a radial line or a parallel ruler, you can find them both under the **special ruler** tool, they will snap the angle of the lines to the ruler.

c) **Toning**: If this is checked, the stream/saturated line layer will have **layer properties>tone** checked upon creation.

d) **Make curve**: This will add a new control in which you can curve the lines. It's a pretty funny thing to see.

e) **Angle** Only for stream lines: you can control the angle of the lines you will create.

f) **Fill center** Only for saturated lines: with this option, you can fill the inside of your saturated line.

- **Drawing interval**: This set of options lets you choose the interval between the lines:

a) **Gap of line (angle)**: This is only for saturated line tools. This will create a distance between lines based on an angle.

b) **Gap of line (distance)**: This is the default distance of both line tools. It bases the distance of the lines using mm/in. Under this, the **Disarray** option will read disarray as a random value.

c) **Grouping**: This will group the lines based on the distance set. Under this, the **Gap** option refers to the gap between the grouped lines.

d) **Maximum number of lines**: This is only for stream line tools: here you can set the maximum number of lines created by the tool.

- **Drawing position**: Here you can find all the settings related to the position and length of your lines:

a) **Length**: This will specify the length of the lines.

b) **Extend lines**: This will extend the lines over their set length; if it's a stream line, it will cover the whole canvas, practically speaking. If it's a saturated line, this option will be available only with **reference position inner side**.

c) **Reference position**: If you've checked the extend line option, this setting is useless. It will let you decide whether the starting point will be the starting/middle/ending point of your reference line:

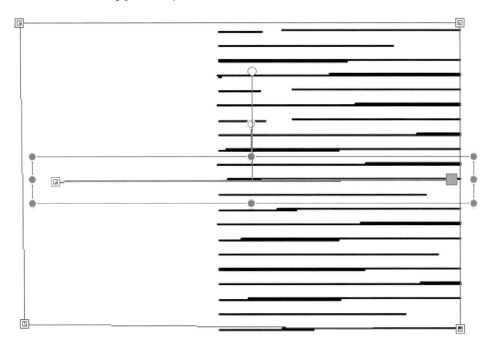

Figure 11.14 – The stream line tool with a reference line (red)

d) **Gap from reference position**: This will give a little random gap between the reference position and the start of the line.

e) **Uneven reference position**: This can only be used with saturated line tools. It will make the inside fill a little bit jagged. We have two options under this, that is, **Number**, this value is how prickly the line you create will be and **Height**, this value is how long the jags will be.

With this, we have finished with the figure tools.

Other tools

Now we just need to talk about a couple of tools that don't strictly follow the format of the other categories:

a) **Gradient tool**: The gradient tool has gradient options, in which you can choose how you want to create a gradient:

- **Specify color of the gradient**: With this setting, you can choose which color to add to your gradient; you just need to select a color and click on those little squares on the top:

Figure 11.115 – Specifying the color of the gradient appearance

- **Advanced settings**: This will prompt a window in which you can add more steps to your gradient, invert your gradient, and change the opacity of your gradient.

- **Shape**: You can decide the shape of your gradient: whether you want a straight line, a circle, or an ellipse.

- **Edge process**: This lets you decide how the gradient will extend over the designated area. You can extend it without repetition meaning that if your gradient starts with white, it will start again with white when it repeats, with a repeat of the gradient, with a flipped repetition, or no repetition.

- **Dithering**: In simple terms, when this is checked, it creates a better locking gradient.

- **Start from center**: This will be shown only for circle gradients and ellipses: it will use the center of the gradient as a creation point.

b) **Object tool**: The object tool is a little wildcard, because it will let you modify everything that is not a raster layer. As an example, in a vector layer, it will let you change the color of the lines. It has only two native options:

- **Operation**:

    1) **Operation of transparent part**: When you're clicking and dragging the object tool on an empty part, usually outside of your canvas, it will activate a selection rectangle. With this option, you can choose how it will behave.

    2) **Selectable object**: This will decide what the object tool can select or not. If you deactivate raster, it will consider a raster layer as an empty part.

c) Other tools: The other tools I didn't cover are tools with so few options that all the options are located directly inside the tool properties. This means that you don't need to go in the **Sub Tool Details** window. For example, the **Remove dust** tool has only **Dust size** and **Mode**. In simple terms, it's what we'd consider dust options.

And with this, we have finished the CSP vocabulary!

Summary

Hi, Reader!

This is the end of the book, and I don't have anything else to say. I hope it was a good journey and that you did learn a lot.

Now, I want to extend a little thanks to Packt, who published this book.

I'd also like to add another little thanks to Sofi Rogers, who helped with the grammar of this book, because I'm not a native English speaker, and Mrudgandha Kulkarni and Rakhi Patel, who both checked whether all I've said was comprehensible (and not the babbling of a madman) and that my bad humor wouldn't offend anyone.

Now, if you will excuse a little bit of self-promotion! If you want to be taught a little bit more by me, I offer one-to-one lessons, and you can find all the details on my website: lennybunny.com. Or, if you want to buy my brush packs, you can find them there too. If you want to commission me for work, just send an e-mail to lennybunny93@gmail. com.

And with this, I bid you goodbye with all my love, and I hope that this was the book you needed.

Other Books You May Enjoy

If you enjoyed this book, you may be interested in these other books by Packt:

Blender 3D By Example - Second Edition

Oscar Baechler , Xury Greer

ISBN: 978-1-78961-256-1

- Explore core 3D modeling tools in Blender such as extrude, bevel, and loop cut
- Understand Blender's Outliner hierarchy, collections, and modifiers
- Find solutions to common problems in modeling 3D characters and designs
- Implement lighting and probes to liven up an architectural scene using EEVEE
- Produce a final rendered image complete with lighting and post-processing effects

Mastering Adobe Photoshop Elements 2021 - Third Edition

Robin Nichols

ISBN: 978-1-80056-699-6

- Identify the five parts of Elements and set up your computer, camera, and monitor
- Import, organize, and keep track of your imported media library
- Develop advanced image retouching skills
- Discover how to add text and graphics to photographs
- Cultivate your understanding of multi-image, multi-layered editing techniques
- Develop illustrative skills with the many drawing tools available in Elements 2021

Packt is searching for authors like you

If you're interested in becoming an author for Packt, please visit `authors.packtpub.com` and apply today. We have worked with thousands of developers and tech professionals, just like you, to help them share their insight with the global tech community. You can make a general application, apply for a specific hot topic that we are recruiting an author for, or submit your own idea.

Hi!

I am Ludovico Serra, author of *Clip Studio Paint by Example*. I really hope you enjoyed reading this book and found it useful for increasing your productivity and efficiency in Clip Studio Paint.

It would really help me (and other potential readers!) if you could leave a review on Amazon sharing your thoughts on *Clip Studio Paint by Example*.

Go to the link below or scan the QR code to leave your review:

`https://packt.link/r/1800202725`

Your review will help me to understand what's worked well in this book, and what could be improved upon for future editions, so it really is appreciated.

Best Wishes,

Ludovico Serra

Index

Made in the USA
Las Vegas, NV
20 July 2021